BEYOND HORATIO'S
PHILOSOPHY

Borgo Press Books by DAVID STEVENS

Beyond Horatio's Philosophy: The Fantasy of Peter S. Beagle
J. R. R. Tolkien: The Art of the Myth-Maker (with Carol D. Stevens)

BEYOND HORATIO'S PHILOSOPHY

THE FANTASY OF PETER S. BEAGLE

DAVID STEVENS

THE BORGO PRESS

MMXII

The Milford Series
Popular Writers of Today
ISSN 0169-2463
Volume Seventy-Six

BEYOND HORATIO'S PHILOSOPHY

FIRST EDITION

Published by Wildside Press LLC

www.wildsidebooks.com

BEYOND HORATIO'S PHILOSOPHY

THE FANTASY OF PETER S. BEAGLE

DAVID STEVENS

THE BORGO PRESS
MMXII

The Milford Series
Popular Writers of Today
ISSN 0169-2463
Volume Seventy-Six

BEYOND HORATIO'S PHILOSOPHY

FIRST EDITION

Published by Wildside Press LLC

www.wildsidebooks.com

DEDICATION

Dedicated to the memory of Professor Thomas L. Wymer, teacher and scholar, who taught so many of us what science fiction and fantasy criticism is all about.

Special thanks to Professor Kate Spencer, who first inspired me to write about Beagle for a Popular Culture Association panel in 1978 and whose kind review of the early stages of the manuscript helped improve this book.

And as always, for my colleague, collaborator, friend, and spouse, Professor Carol D. Stevens, who puts up with my serial monomania, and without whom this book would not have been possible.

C O N T E N T S

INTRODUCTION

"There are more things in heaven and earth, Horatio,
Than are dreamt of in your philosophy."
                                    —*Hamlet*, I, v, 166-67.

I.

Peter S. Beagle burst upon the literary scene in 1960 with the publication of his first novel, *A Fine and Private Place*, written before he was twenty years old. After that auspicious beginning he slowed down a bit but still produced a significant and well-received body of work, including "Come Lady Death," 1963, a novella; *I See By My Outfit,* 1979, a memoir of a cross-coutry motorscooter trip; *The Last Unicorn*, 1968, his comic masterpiece and best-known novel; "Lila the Werewolf," 1971, another novella; *The Folk of the Air*, 1986, a return to the incursion of the fantastic into the modern world; *The Innkeeper's Song*, 1993, a hard-edged pure fantasy containing both the best fight scene and the best sex scene in modern fantasy; *The Unicorn Sonata*, 1996, a young adult novel where the borders of the mundane and fantastic worlds merge mysteriously; *Tamsin*, 1999, another young adult novel again returning to his favorite device of the fantastic impacting the modern world, and revisiting the impact of ghosts on reality as he had in his first published work; and "A Dance for Emilia," 2000, a novella also dealing with ghosts in the modern world, involving the possession of a cat by the spirit of a man unwilling or unable to leave this earth without saying goodbye to his friends. His early works, including *A Fine and Private Place*; *The Last Unicorn*; and the two novellas "Lila the Werewolf" and "Come Lady Death," were republished in *The Fantasy Worlds of Peter S. Beagle*, 1978; and his shorter fiction has been collected in *Giant Bones*, 1997, in which he revisits the world of *The Innkeeper's Song*, also published as *The Magician of Karakosk and Other Stories* in 1999; *The Rhinoceros Who Quoted Nietzsche and Other Odd Acquaintances*, 1997, 2003, a retrospective collection of stories and essays dating back to 1957; *The Line Between*, 2006, containing ten new stories including four fables, a children's story, a Sherlock Holmes pastiche, an old tar's tale, a sequel to one novel and a prequel to another, and the germ of a prospective witch novel; and *We Never Talk About My Brother*, containing one previously uncollected story from 1981 but concentrating on new fiction from 2007-2009, including three pieces published in 2008 in a limited edition called *Strange Roads*. *Mirror Kingdoms: The Best of Peter S. Beagle*, a retrospective collection of short fiction, came out in February, 2010. His novella extending the story of *The Innkeeper's Song*, called "Return," was released in September, 2010. A new collection of short stories, *Sleight of Hand*, including a new Schmendrick story, was published in March, 2011.

Beagle has announced a magical realist retelling of the Persephone myth, to be called *Summerlong* (formerly titled *For All We Know*), supposedly to be published in 2012. He has announced a complete revision and expansion of *The Folk of the Air*, to be called *Avicenna*, and a radically expanded and altered four-volume rewrite of *The Unicorn Sonata*. His children's fantasy novel, *I'm Afraid You've Got Dragons*, may also be published in 2011 or 2012. He is working on a young adult novel extending his story "El Regalo," to be called *My Stupid Brother Marvyn, the Witch*. More important to his many fans, however, Beagle has also announced a sequel to *The Last Unicorn*, and published *The Last Unicorn: The Lost Version* in 2006. A new collection entitled *The First Last Unicorn and*

Other Beginnings has been announced for April, 2012. Included will be a novella-length adventure of the last unicorn, in which she bands together with a duo of ambivalent demons to seek out her lost brethren, apparently either from or adapted from *The Lost Version*. Additional chapters from *A Fine & Private Place*, from the unpublished novel *Mirror Kingdoms*, and even snippets from Beagle's childhood and teenaged years will included. Correspondence, running commentary, and interviews should give insight into Beagle's creative process. Additionally, he has sold but not yet published *Green-Eyed Boy: Three Schmendrick Stories*, which is scheduled for publication in 2011 or 2012. Several other collections are also in the works, including *Three Faces of The Lady,* 2011 or 2012 (collection centered on "Come Lady Death"); *Three Unicorns,* 2011 or 2012 (story collection with additional essay); *Four Years, Five Seasons,* 2011 or 2012 (story collection released as an audiobook in 2010); and *Sweet Lightning,* 2011 or 2012 (1950s baseball fantasy novel). It remains to be seen how many of these promised works will see the light of day, given that his seventieth birthday is behind him, but Beagle continues to turn out short stories at a prolific rate.

The first thing that impacts a reader is the variety Beagle brings to the writing of fantasy. While the writer's almost overwhelming sense of humor pervades all of his work (most noticeable in *The Last Unicorn* and least noticeable in *The Innkeeper's Song*), the worlds of most of the other novels, novellas, and even short stories are separate and distinct, with the specific exceptions of the stories of *Giant Bones*, which was purposefully set in the world of *The Innkeeper's Song*, and the other stories set in the universe of *The Innkeeper's Song*, and his continuing return to Joe Farrell as the reader's guide to the fantastic intruding into our cozy world. This may be explained at least in part by Beagle's explicit declaration in his Foreword to *Giant Bones* that, "From the first, *A Fine and Private Place*, I wanted my novels to be as different from one another as I could make them, within the limitations of my skill and imagination." In his headnote to "Two Hearts," a brief sequel to *The Last Unicorn* which appears in *The Line Between*, he puts it differently: "I always had a real horror of repeating myself." That he has succeeded so well is a testament both to his skill as a writer and to his imagination, or perhaps to his acquiescence to horror in his life.

II.

Peter Soyer Beagle was born in New York City on April 20, 1939, to Simon Beagle, a history teacher, and Rebecca Soyer Beagle, also a teacher, and he was raised in the Bronx within sight of the Woodlawn Cemetery, which inspired his first novel. He proudly carries his mother's birth name as his middle name, a constant reminder that his grandfather, Abraham Soyer, was a writer. Abraham was born in Russia and emigrated to the United States with his family in 1912. He wrote articles for the Jewish press in Hebrew and Yiddish, and one of his collections of fables, *The Adventures of Yemima and Other Stories*, first published in Hebrew in Tel Aviv, has been translated into English by his daughter Rebecca and his daughter-in-law Rebecca L. Soyer and published in 1979. His son Raphael Soyer, a well-known artist, contributed the illustrations, and Peter contributed a brief foreword. Raphael's two brothers, Moses and Isaac Soyer, were also artists. Another of Abraham's books, *Forgotten Worlds*, was similarly translated by Rebecca Beagle and Rebecca Soyer and published in 1991. Abraham lived with the Beagles in the Bronx until his death in 1940 when Peter was ten months old, and was reportedly the only one who could quiet Peter when he cried as a baby.

Peter broke into what might be called the family business by entering a contest in *Seventeen* when he was only 15 years old and a student at the Bronx High School of Science, and he came to the notice of Bryna Ivens, who was Louis Untermeyer's spouse. In 1955 a poem he entered in the Scholastic Writing Awards Contest won him a scholarship, and he went off to college at the University of Pittsburg. During his sophomore year a story of his won the *Seventeen* contest, and he graduated with a B.A. in creative writing and a minor in Spanish in 1959, having just turned twenty, and having submitted *A Fine and Private Place* for publication. He followed the old tradition of the Grand Tour, spending close to the next year in Europe.

Marshall Best of Viking Press was his editor, improving the book by suggesting elimination of a mystery subplot and suggesting the title ultimately used in place of Beagle's proffered *The Dark City*. Beagle recalls him as "a great editor," who showed "loving attention and focused literary concern."

A Fine and Private Place earned Beagle critical acclaim and a Wallace Stegner Creative Writing Fellowship for study at Stanford University when he returned to the United States. While there he worked on an unpublished novel begun in Europe entitled *The Mirror Kingdom* while fellow students Ken Kesey and Christopher Koch worked on *One Flew Over the Cuckoo's Nest* and *The Year of Living Dangerously*. Another of his fellow students was Larry McMurtry, who was working on *Leaving Cheyenne*. *The Mirror Kingdom* was not fantasy; it was about "a young American musician's romantic adventures in Paris," written when Beagle himself had just been a young American writer having romantic adventures in Paris, as he tells us in the Introduction to *The Line Between*.

Beagle's second book, *I See By My Outfit*, was also published by Viking in 1966, edited by Aaron Asher. A memoir of his cross-country motorscooter trip from New York with his friend Phil Sigunick to his new home in California, it was first published in two parts in *Holiday* under the title "A Long Way to Go" and was also very well received. In 1964 Beagle had married Enid Nordeen, whom he had met at Stanford, and adopted her three children, Vicki, Kalisa, and Danny. He dedicated *I See By My Outfit* to them and the other "people in the house," Phil and Tom. Phil was Phil Sigunick, his closest childhood friend who later became a successful artist, with whom he made the cross-country motorscooter trip that was memorialized in the book; it is not clear who Tom was. His well-received novella "Come

Lady Death" was published in *Atlantic* in 1963, and he later adapted it into the libretto for an opera entitled *The Midnight Angel*. David Carlson wrote the music.

In 1968, at the ripe old age of twenty-nine, Beagle achieved literary immortality of a sort with the publication of *The Last Unicorn*. This fairy tale for adults garnered great critical attention, but Beagle may have found it difficult to top since his next novel did not see the light of day until 1986. In the interim he supported himself as a freelance writer, publishing his widely-loved novella "Lila the Werewolf" in an Ace Books collection in 1971. Beagle and Enid divorced in 1980.

During the 1970s Beagle increasingly wrote screenplays, including the animated version of *The Last Unicorn* produced by Rankin-Bass, which was released in 1982, and Ralph Bakshi's animated *The Lord of the Rings* in 1978. He later wrote one of the best episodes of *Star Trek: The Next Generation*: "Sarek," Episode 71, which aired in 1990. He had been involved in a contract dispute with London-based Granada Media over royalties for *The Last Unicorn* film; the matter was settled out of court in the summer of 2011. Beagle harbors some hopes of a live-action film at some point in the future, given the successes of the Tolkien and C. S. Lewis fantasy films. During the 1970s he also indulged his avocation as a folk singer, appearing every weekend at L'Oustalou, a club in Santa Cruz, California, from 1973 to 1985. He sings in English, Yiddish, French, and German, and has released an album, *Acoustics: The Lost '62 Tape*. In 1988 he married writer and artist Padma Hejmadi. *The Innkeeper's Song* was dedicated to her.

Beagle says *The Folk of the Air*, published in 1986, was the first time he ever wrote about Berkeley, with which he fell in love in about 1960. Place is always important in his fiction, and he has said with regard to his forthcoming novel *Summerlong* that he couldn't have written about Seattle while he was living there (he spent one year in a condominium on Queen Anne Hill and five more on Bainbridge Island, both of which appear in *Summerlong*). *The Innkeeper's Song*, however, is his favorite work; he thinks of it as his first grown-up novel. It is neither a ghost story nor a fairy tale, but an attempt to deal with very real people in an imaginary world. He doesn't classify it as a grown-up novel simply because it contains what he calls his first group sex scene, but because he thinks it contains a depth of emotion that marks the beginning of a mature period. Beagle believes he was able to access certain things, such as what love means, more fully than he had been able to do before.

Unfortunately, by 2001, in Beagle's words he "was 62 years old and living in Davis, California, then, second marriage a shipwreck, nice house where I'd once been happy now in foreclosure and scheduled for auction, work not happening, outlook so numbed by disaster that I couldn't really absorb how bad things had become." It was at that time that he began a literary relationship with Connor Cochran, and reinvented himself as a writer of short fiction. The rest, as they say, is history.

Beagle's story "Two-Hearts" won the Hugo Award in 2006 and the Nebula Award in 2007. He won the Inkpot Award for Outstanding Achievement in Science Fiction and Fantasy in 2006. Beagle won the inaugural WSFA Small Press Award for "El Regalo," published in *The Line Between*, and he was given the World Fantasy Award for Lifetime Achievement in 2011.

III.

British critic C. N. Manlove, in his influential 1975 book *Modern Fantasy: Five Studies*, defines a fantasy as:

> "A fiction evoking wonder and containing a substantial and irreducible element of supernatural or impossible worlds, beings or objects with which the reader or the characters within the story become on at least partly familiar terms."

He further discusses what he meant by "a fiction"; "evoking

wonder"; "supernatural or impossible worlds, beings or objects"; "a substantial and irreducible element"; and "with which the mortal characters in the story or the readers become on at least partly familiar terms." Manlove distinguishes between what he calls "comic" or "escapist" fantasy and "imaginative" fantasy, and provides his analysis of the failings of the attempts of Charles Kingsley; George MacDonald; C. S. Lewis; J. R. R. Tolkien; and Mervyn Peake, whom he characterizes as "among the best known of modern writers of fantasy," in avoiding "escapist" failings. He concludes that not one of them succeeds in sustaining his original vision, and suggests that "[t]he basic problem seems to be one of *distance*, distance between the 'real' and fantastic worlds, or between nature and supernature." According to Manlove, "the gap between the worlds has grown too wide for more than an occasional vision (MacDonald, Peake) of its healing." There are very real obstacles to writing modern fantasy, but even considering that Manlove would not claim great things for any of the writers he has considered. He ultimately dismisses the genre as "lacking in the full character of reality" despite any compensatory strengths. He leaves it to "the cultists."

In his later *The Impulse of Fantasy Literature*, Manlove examines George MacDonald, Charles Williams, E. Nesbit, Ursula K. Le Guin, T. H. White, and Mervyn Peake, finding there to be some merit to the genre. He specifically dismisses William Morris, Lord Dunsany, E. R. Eddison, and Beagle, however, as writing "anemic" fantasy.

Despite Manlove's early scorn for the writing of all modern fantasy, and his dismissal of Beagle in particular, his definition is useful. Although some of Beagle's work aspires to nothing more than fantastic escape (*A Fine and Private Place*; *The Last Unicorn*; *A Dance for Emilia*) some of it (*The Folk of the Air*; *The Innkeeper's Song*; *Tamsin*) is as fully imaginative as the works Manlove examines and approves.

Kathleen L. Spencer put forward a useful definition and discussion of what she calls "The Urban Gothic" in her "Purity and Danger: *Dracula*, The Urban Gothic, and the Late Victorian Degeneracy Crisis," in 1992, and in her 1987 doctoral dissertation, "The Urban Gothic in British Fantastic Fiction, 1860-1930." While concentrating on what is essentially a subgenre of fantasy, she discusses various theoretical constructs of the fantastic, including those of Tzvetan Todorov (*The Fantastic: A Structural Approach to a Literary Genre*, 1975); Tobin Siebers (*The Romantic Fantastic*, 1984); Rosemary Jackson (*Fantasy: The Literature of Subversion*, 1981); Eric Rabkin (*The Fantastic in Literature*, 1976), and Andrzej Zgorzelski ("Is Science Fiction a Genre of Fantastic Literature", 1979; "Understanding Fantasy", 1972). She sees terror as an important element of the Urban Gothic, as well as an explicitly modern urban setting. The term may be applicable to some of Beagle's fantasy, and Spencer's meticulous theoretical underpinning certainly is applicable to all of it.

Spencer essentially adopts Zgorzelski's definition of the fantastic, which he asserts "consists in the breaching of the internal laws which are initially assumed in the text to govern the fictional world." All texts contain meta-textual information about genre, generally in the opening paragraphs. In the case of the fantastic, this is a fictive world based upon objective reality, or what Zgorzelski calls "a mimetic world model." The intrusion of a fantastic element breaches the model and changes it into a different world which follows different laws. Fantastic texts "build their fictional world as a textual confrontation of two models of reality" (emphasis deleted).

Ursula K. Le Guin, in addition to being an award-winning fantasy writer, has also disseminated a body of criticism that is useful in discussing not only her fantasy but that of other writers such as Beagle. In "From Elfland to Poughkeepsie," her best-known critical essay, first published in 1979, she discusses the fantasy writer's use of language, preferring the "high style" of J. R. R. Tolkien and Evangeline Walton. More recently, in "Some Assumptions About Fantasy" and "The Critics, the Monsters, and the Fantasists," she argues for both the usefulness and the delightfulness of fantasy. "The tendency to explain fantasy by extracting the fantastic from it and replacing it with the comprehensible," she asserts, "reduces the radically unreal to the secondhand commonplace." She sounds like a latter-day Tolkien, arguing for the value of a sense of wonder, or a more comprehensible Darko Suvin, speaking of the "arresting strangeness" of fantastic literature. Despite Suvin's jargon, Tolkien's Catholic apology, and Le Guin's Taoist roots, all three are essentially talking about the same thing, and no single writer exemplifies it better than Peter S. Beagle.

IV.

Previous examinations of Beagle's fiction have been limited. For example, as early as 1975 David Van Becker examined "Time, Space and Consciousness in the Fantasy of Peter S. Beagle." In 1977 D. P. Norford published "Reality and Illusion in Peter Beagle's *The Last Unicorn*." In "Incongruity in a World of Illusion: Patterns of Humor in Peter Beagle's *The Last Unicorn*," I briefly reviewed Beagle's use of comic technique in his second novel in 1979; this article forms the basis for Chapter Two below, and further served as an inspiration for this book. The next year A. H. Olsen in "Anti-Consolatio: Boethius and *The Last Unicorn*" examined a different aspect of that work, as did R. E. Foust in "Fabulous Pardigm: Fantasy, Metafantasy, and Peter S. Beagle's *The Last Unicorn*."

In 1986 Jean Tobin published both "Myth, Memory, a Will-o'-the Wish: Peter Beagle's Funny Fantasy" and "Werewolves and Unicorns: Fabulous Beasts in Peter Beagle's Fiction." Don Riggs in 1988 examined "Fantastic Tropes in *The Folk of the Air*, and he republished it in 1997. Richard C. West has also published his study of Beagle twice, as "Humanity and Reality: Illusion and Self-Deception in Peter S. Beagle's Fiction" in 1988, and "Humanity Cannot Bear Very Much Reality: Illusion and Self-Deception in the Fiction of Peter S. Beagle" in 1997. In *Peter*

Beagle, Kenneth Zahorski attempted a comprehensive evaluation of Beagle's fiction in 1988 but was limited by the restrictions of the series in which the work appeared and by the fact that much of Beagle's best work was yet to come. In "Alchemy of Love in *A Fine and Private Place*," Joel N. Feimer in 1988 examined Beagle's first novel. George Aichele, Jr., compared Beagle and Philip K. Dick in "Two Forms of Metafantasy" in 1988.

David M. Miller examined *The Last Unicorn* in 1990 in "Mommy Fortuna's Ontological Plenum: The Fantasy of Plenitude," while Dave M. Roberts offered a different perspective on the first novel in "Love in the Graveyard: Peter S. Beagle's *A Fine and Private Place*" in 1999. Also in 1999 Maureen K. Speller published her "Unicorns, Werewolves, Ghosts and Rhinoceroses: The Worlds of Peter S. Beagle." In 2005 Sue Matheson discussed "Psychic Transformation and the Regeneration of Language in Peter S. Beagle's *The Last Unicorn*."

Many of these often excellent studies were first presented as papers at various academic conferences, most often the annual International Conference on the Fantastic in the Arts, and so first saw the light of day as roughly twenty-minute presentations. Note that almost all follow the tongue-in-cheek academic tradition of an ironic or comic title with a serious subtitle; I have done the same with this book. None of the previous treatments of Beagle can claim to be comprehensive, and all but one is limited to less than fifteen pages. Additionally, there have been several interviews with Beagle published; other articles in what are essentially fanzines such as *Mythlore* have appeared; theses and dissertations have been churned out; and various works for hire such as those published by Salem Press have treated Beagle.

V.

    In this book I intend to examine the longer fiction of Peter S. Beagle using the helpful definitions provided by Manlove and Spencer. For each novel and novella I will attempt to discern the "substantial and irreducible element of the supernatural" or the "impossible worlds, beings or objects" with which the reader becomes familiar, with an eye toward establishing Beagle's effectiveness as a writer of fantasy. Ultimately the question in each case will come down to another of Manlove's questions: to what extent does the text "evoke wonder" in the reader? Where appropriate I will utilize Spencer's idea of The Urban Gothic; Le Guin's statements on the value of fantasy; Tolkien's ideas of fantasy, recovery, escape, and consolation; and even Suvin's concept of arresting strangeness. My primary critical mode, however, will be what is called "reader-response" criticism. Reader-response criticism focuses on the reader, or audience, and his or her experience of a literary work, rather than focusing primarily on the author or the content and form of the work. That is, I will examine each work from the point of view of an intelligent reader, making connections and responding to the text as appropriate. This approach has proven valuable in the analysis of popular fiction such as fantasy, science fiction, horror fiction, the western, the thriller, and the mystery.

    In each of the following chapters I will discuss one of Beagle's novels, along with any associated shorter fiction, with a final chapter for the major shorter fiction. Unfortunately my space is too limited for a comprehensive analysis of all the short fiction; there has simply been too much of it in the past ten years or so. My ultimate goal shall be to assess how well Peter S. Beagle conforms to the classic purposes of art: to teach and to please. How does he please us, and how does he teach us? The answers to these questions will provide us with sufficient insight to come to an understanding of Beagle's effectiveness as a writer of modern fantasy.

In each chapter save one I shall proceed along two levels of analysis simultaneously: the fictional level and the functional level. The fictional level deals primarily with what Aristotle called *mythos*, or plot; the arrangement of the incidents. It is necessary first of all in understanding a work of fantasy, as any fiction, to understand who does what to whom. I perhaps err on the side of overinclusion in this analysis; but it is my assumption that most readers of this book will not be familiar with most of the works treated. The functional level deals with author-reader communication. After a reader understands what is going on in a work of fiction, it is then necessary to understand how the writer manipulates character, thought, and diction, Aristotle's *ethos*, *dianoia*, and *lexis*, to communicate with a reader. My functional level analysis in all but one of the chapters that follow is interspersed with the fictional level analysis, and it leads to some specific conclusions in each chapter as well as a general conclusion to this book.

The one exception to this scheme is Chapter Two, in which I deal with *The Last Unicorn*. In this chapter my method is reversed: I deal with the functional level primarily, with discussion of the fictional level interspersed throughout as needed. The reason for this change in methodology is that I assume many if not most readers of this book will already be familiar with *The Last Unicorn*, either from the book itself, the animated film, the graphic novel, or perhaps the audio edition, and thus much less fictional level analysis is required. When in Chapter Two, however, I deal with lesser-known works (*The Last Unicorn: The Lost Version*; "Two Hearts"), I revert to my more usual mode.

CHAPTER ONE: *A FINE AND PRIVATE PLACE*

Beagle takes his epigram for *A Fine and Private Place* from Andrew Marvel's "To His Coy Mistress": "The grave's a fine and private place,/ But none, I think, do there embrace." He turns this thought upon its head, showing us a grave where the dead do in fact embrace, and where certain living mortals communicate with them while they do so. The novel is peopled (ghosted?) with a sprightly cast of characters including mortals Jonathan Rebeck and Gertrude Klapper and ghosts Michael Morgan and Laura Durand. Michael and Laura, although dead, fall in love and remain together to face an uncertain eternity, while Rebeck and Mrs. Klapper also fall in love and embark on their own journey towards an unknown future. Love redeems Rebeck, and might be said to redeem Michael as well, although Michael's redemption is perhaps not as significant as Rebeck's.

Beagle dedicates the novel to his mother and father, Simon and Rebecca, among others, and this is not the last of his fiction to be so dedicated. *Tamsin*, for example, is dedicated: "To the memory of Simon Beagle, my father. I can still hear you singing, Pop, quietly, to yourself, shaving." He dedicated one of his collections of short stories, *The Rhinoceros Who Quoted Nietzsche and Other Odd Acquaintances*: "for my mother, Rebecca Soyer Beagle, who told me stories, and never thought I was weird." One can imagine the teen-aged writer basing his main characters, Rebeck and Gertrude Klapper, on idealized versions of his parents, although of course such a conjecture cannot be verified. Beagle has said, however, that the idea for the novel came about when he and his mother took a walk through a New York cemetery more than 40 years ago. Some of the mausoleums were so large, his mother remarked, that you could practically live in them. By the time they walked out of the cemetery, according to Beagle he had the complete plot for his first book.

There is also a talking raven who plays a significant role in the novel, a wise-cracking, Jewish-sounding bird who would be right at home in the comic world of *The Last Unicorn*. His function on one level is to bring Rebeck food; he has been doing so for the nineteen years Rebeck has confined himself to the grounds of a New York cemetery because he could no longer stand the things that happened outside. The nameless raven does it because it is his nature, and ravens have always brought people food since Elijah. As he explains, "We're closer to people than any other bird, and we're bound to them all our lives, but we don't have to like them. You think we brought Elijah food because we liked him? He was an old man with a dirty beard." But on another level the raven functions to keep the audience from taking Rebeck too seriously. It would be far too easy for the character to slip the bonds of sanity, and decline into despair. In another novel perhaps he would. But not here. Beagle has another fate in mind for Rebeck.

Enter the ghost, stage left. One of Rebeck's distinguishing characteristics is that he sees, hears, and talks to ghosts. He doesn't know why, and we never find out why. After Beagle sets up Rebeck and the raven in Chapter One, he immediately introduces Michael in Chapter Two. There can be no doubt that Michael is dead; his ghost rises through his coffin and watches his own funeral and his weeping widow. No one can see him or hear him—except Rebeck, whom he sees sitting before a mausoleum. Rebeck explains that he enjoys helping the dead adjust to their new state. He speaks to them, plays chess with them, does whatever they need or want until finally "they drift away, and where they go I cannot follow. They don't need me then; they don't need anyone, and this pleases me because most of them spent their lives trying not to need."

In Rebeck's world, "the body dies quickly, but the soul hangs on to life as long as it can because living is all it knows." Or perhaps "memory" is a better word than "soul": "Living is a big thing, and it's pretty hard to forget."

> "You find yourself becoming greedy of people; whenever they come to visit here you watch every movement they make, trying to remember the way you used to do that. And when they leave you follow them all the way to the entrance, and you stop there because you can't go farther.... They had it all backwards, you see, those old ghost stories about the dead haunting the living. It's not that way at all."

The dead, in *A Fine and Private Place*, are confined forever to the cemetery where their bodies are interred. Heaven and hell are for the living, not the dead. Eventually the dead forget things, because they no longer wish to remember. But Rebeck makes Michael this promise:

> "As long as you cling to being alive, as long as you care to be a man, I'll be here. We'll be two men to- gether in this place. I'll like it, because I get lonesome here and I like company; and you'll like it, too, until it becomes a game, a pointless ritual. Then you'll leave."

But the leaving is metaphorical, not physical; at some point, in *A Fine and Private Place* ghosts merely lie down and wrap themselves in the earth. They remain in the cemetery for eter- nity, only pretending to sleep. Being dead is "Like nothing at all. It is like nothing at all." So says one who should know, at the climax of the novel.

Enter a second ghost, stage right. After introducing Mrs. Klapper for Rebeck in Chapter Three, Beagle rounds out his cast with Laura for Michael in Chapter Four. Laura, too, is dead, and comes into the cemetery with her funeral party. She and Michael meet and discuss their situation; while Michael was not ready for death, and continues to fight against it, Laura was more than ready and is prepared to embrace it. But she discovers that the dead can't sleep, as the living can, and when she lies down and closes her eyes it's as if she still had them open. Rebeck tells her, "Each man's death is his own concern, and whether he sleeps or doesn't sleep is of less importance than how he accepts it—or how he rationalizes it."

The primary conflict in the novel arises from Rebeck's fear of life outside the cemetery. Both Rebeck and Michael are in denial. Rebeck fears that he cannot cope with the modern world, and Michael has fantasized that his wife murdered him, which prevents him from admitting that he killed himself. The main problem to be resolved is how Rebeck will be reintegrated into society, and the secondary problem is how Michael and Laura can remain together when Michael's body is moved to another cemetery because of his suicide.

Rebeck, of course, being alive, does not belong in the cemetery. Michael, being a suicide, does not belong there either. Both must be removed for the world to return to its natural state. Mrs. Klapper, who came to the cemetery to visit her dead husband's mausoleum (enter the third ghost, through a trap), returns to see Rebeck and eventually falls in love with him. She gives him the courage he needs to walk away and reenter the world. Laura, who did not love in life, learns to love in death, and gives Michael the courage to face his deepest fears. When Michael's body is exhumed and taken to a more appropriate final resting place, Rebeck arranges for Laura's body to be moved surreptitiously to the same location. That way they can be together for whatever time is left them before one or both finally forgets what it is to be alive. Rebeck thinks being loved is one way to become real, but the ghost of Morris Klapper, Mrs. Klapper's dead husband, corrects him: "I think the only way to become real is to be real to yourself and to someone else. Love has nothing to do with it." Ultimately *A Fine and Private Place* is about how a man learns to be real to himself and to someone else. Love has everything to do with it.

As was the case with *The Last Unicorn* (*see* Chapter Two, below), IDW is scheduled to bring out a comic book and graphic novel version of *A Fine and Private Place*.

CHAPTER TWO:
THE LAST UNICORN

While humor is peripheral to much fantasy, it is central to Peter Beagle's *The Last Unicorn.* Beagle creates a quasimedieval universe with built-in anachronisms to serve as the setting for his fairy tale that is at once high romance and self-parody. He presents a serious theme, that we are what people think us and we become what we pretend to be, with a comic technique, and much of the success of the novel can be traced to its humor.

Beagle leaves no doubt about his comic intentions very early in the novel. Before any of the important mortal characters are introduced, the unicorn meets a butterfly. While some important exposition is presented, the main purpose of the encounter is humorous. In Beagle's world butterflies can talk, but all they can do is repeat what they have heard. This butterfly has apparently heard a lot of popular songs, a lot of television commercials, and a lot of Shakespeare and other medieval and Renaissance English poetry. Its speech is a combination of these elements, and the juxtaposition of the ridiculous and the sublime is very funny:

> "Death takes what man would keep," said the butterfly, "and leaves what man would lose. Blow, wind, and crack your cheeks. I warm my hands before the fire of life and get four-way relief."

The other speeches from this brief section are just as incongruous. Responding to the unicorn's question, "Do you know who I am?" the butterfly cheerfully pulls a few appropriate lines from its memory: "Excellent well, you're a fishmonger. You're my everything, you are my sunshine, you are old and gray and full of sleep, you're my pickle-face, consumptive Mary Jane." In response to nothing at all, but merely to pass the time, the butterfly leaps into the following soliloquy:

> "One, two, three o'lairy.... Not, I'll not, carrion comfort, look down that lonesome road. For, oh, what damned minutes tells he o'er who dotes, yet doubts. Hasten, Mirth, and bring with thee a host of furious fancies whereof I am commander, which will be on sale for three days only at bargain summer prices. I love you, oh, the horror, the horror, and aroint thee, witch, aroint thee, indeed and truly you've chosen a bad place to be lame in, willow, willow, willow."

It almost seems natural that, preparing to leave, the butterfly says: "I must take the A train."

Incidentally, Beagle has recently said that the butterfly is as close to a self-portrait as he has ever written. A complete guide to the butterfly's allusions will be contained in *The First Last Unicorn and Other Beginnings*, due from Conlan Press in 2012.

If the incongruities in the speech of the butterfly are rather obvious, they are only the beginnings of Beagle's skillful use of incongruity for comic effect. We first learn the main character's name, for example, in the following manner: "'I am called Schmendrick the Magician,' he answered." "Schmendrick," of course, is a Yiddish word, meaning roughly "bungler," from the same general group as "schlemiel." Beagle says it means "someone who is out of his depth or his league, the boy sent to do a man's job." Schmendrick's first words are in themselves funny, but the magician says the opposite of what we expect when he adds, "You won't have heard of me." Nor does it take a great leap of imagination to see "Schmendrick the Magician" as a play on words for "Mandrake the Magician." Beagle has recently said that the idea for the character came from stories he used to tell his daughters about the world's worst magician.

Incidentally, there is a delicious irony in Beagle's use of the name "Amalthea" for the last unicorn in human shape. The mythology surrounding the young Zeus includes stories of the goat Amalthea who fostered him, one of whose horns the young god broke off and turned into the cornucopia, or horn of plenty. Amalthea in the myth thus became the first unicorn.

Beagle's general use of incongruity is well illustrated in the following expository passage, where everything that is mentioned is twisted into the opposite of what is expected:

> "He made an entire sow out of a sow's ear; turned a sermon into a stone, a glass of water into a handful of water, a five of spades into a twelve of spades, and a rabbit into a goldfish that drowned. Each time he conjured up confusion, he glanced at the unicorn with eyes that said, 'Oh, but *you* know what I really did.' Once he changed a dead rose into a seed. The unicorn liked, that, even though it did turn out to be a radish seed."

In most cases the incongruity involves an item that lowers the high, heroic tone that has been established: the incongruity deflates the puffed-up prose. In one instance, however, during the sequence in the camp of Captain Cully, a self-appointed Robin Hood, the incongruity serves to inflate the level. Jack Jingly, a member of the band of "merry" outlaws, says of the other men: "Cooped up in the greenwood all day, they need a little relaxing, a little catharsis, like." It is also in the camp of Captain Cully that Schmendrick, to flatter his host, reels off a series of romantic escapades that he has heard of in connection with the Captain and then reveals to us that he "had never heard of Captain Cully before that very evening, but he had a good grounding in Anglo-Saxon folklore and knew the type."

Beagle uses songs with incongruous elements throughout the novel, perhaps not surprising when we recall that he is an accomplished folk singer, at one time appearing at a local club in Santa Cruz, California, every weekend for 12 years. It is partly through these songs that the theme is revealed. Captain Cully is so concerned with songs about himself that he has written thirty-one of his own, and is constantly on the look-out for Mr. Child, in order to be properly classified and annotated. Cully has one of them sung to Schmendrick, whom he half-believes to be Mr. Child, and stanzas two and three (of the twenty-five!) show us Beagle's technique:

> "'What news, what news, my pretty young man?
> What ails ye, that ye sigh so deep?
> Is it for the loss of your lady fair?
> Or are ye but scabbit in your greep?'
>
> 'I am nae scabbit, whatever that means,
> And my greep is as well as greep may be,
> But I do sigh for my lady fair
> Whom my three brothers ha' riven from me.'"

The two songs with incongruous elements that most clearly reveal Beagle's theme are Prince Lír's song to the Lady Amalthea, and Schmendrick and Molly's song as they go away together at the end of the novel. Both deserve citing at length.

> "When I was a young man, and very well thought of,
> I couldn't ask aught that the ladies denied.
> I nibbled their hearts like a handful of raisins,
> And I never spoke love but I knew that I lied.
>
> And I said to myself, 'Ah, none of them know
> The secret I shelter and savor and save.

I wait for the one who will see through my seeming,
And I'll know when I love by the way I behave.'

The years drifted over like clouds in the heavens;
The ladies went by me like snow on the wind.
I charmed and I cheated, deceived and dissembled,
And I sinned, and I sinned, and I sinned, and I sinned.

But I said to myself, 'Ah, they none of them see
There's a part of me pure as the whisk of a wave.
My lady is late, but she'll find I've been faithful,
And I'll know when I love by the way I behave.'

At last came a lady both knowing and tender,
Saying, 'You're not at all what they take you to be.'
I betrayed her before she had quite finished speaking,
And she swallowed cold poison and jumped in the sea.

And I say to myself, when there's time for a word,
As I gracefully grow more debauched and depraved,
'Ah, love may be strong, but a habit is stronger,
And I knew when I loved by the way I behaved.'"

The point is reinforced in Schmendrick and Molly's song,
which is the last thing that we read in the novel:

"'I am no king, and I am no lord,
And I am no soldier at arms,' said he.
'I'm none but a harper, and a very poor harper,
That am come hither to wed with ye.'

'If you were a lord, you should be my lord,
And the same if you were a thief,' said she.
'And if you are a harper, you shall be my harper,
For it makes no matter to me, to me,

For it makes no matter to me.'

'But what if it prove that I am no harper?
That I lied for your love most monstrously?'
'Why, then I'll teach you to play and sing,
For I dearly love a good harp,' said she."

The theme is clearly stated by Schmendrick earlier in the novel, using a technique that is elsewhere used for comic effect: verse as prose. Schmendrick is speaking to the unicorn:

> "'It's a rare man who is taken for what he truly is,'
> he said. 'There is much misjudgment in the world.
> Now I knew you for a unicorn when I first saw you,
> and I know that I am your friend. Yet you take me for a
> clown, or a clod, or a betrayer, and so I must be if you
> see me so. The magic on you is only magic and will
> vanish as soon as you are free, but the enchantment of
> error that you put on me I must wear forever in your
> eyes. We are not always what we seem, and hardly
> ever what we dream. Still I have read, or heard it sung,
> that un[i]corns when time was young, could tell the
> difference 'twixt the two—the false shining and the
> true, the lips' laugh and the heart's rue.'"

The running gag is a favorite comic device, and Beagle makes good use of it. Speaking disparagingly about the power of Mommy Fortuna's magic, Schmendrick says: "She can't turn cream into butter." A few pages later, Rukh tells Schmendrick: "You can't turn cream into butter." When Schmendrick later meets Molly Grue, she cheerfully deflates his ego by asserting the same thing: "You can't turn cream into butter." And finally, King Haggard, speaking to the Lady Amalthea about Schmendrick, quite independently comes to the not-so-surprising conclusion: "I don't think he could turn cream into butter." The running gag has run its course, each iteration delighting the reader more than the last.

By far the most important mode of humor used in the novel is anticlimax—a sudden drop from the dignified or important in thought or expression to the commonplace or trivial. Beagle uses this technique literally dozens of times, beginning on the first page with the description of the unicorn: "and the long horn above her eyes shown and shivered with its own seashell light even in the deepest midnight. She had killed dragons with it, and healed a king whose poisoned wound would not close, and knocked down ripe chestnuts for bear cubs." While perhaps not the most hilarious example that could be chosen, it certainly indicates that this will be a novel that does not take itself too seriously.

Schmendrick is responsible for many of the anticlimactic lines, which seems perfectly appropriate since the character resembles an out-of-work stand-up comic down on his luck. For example, when he introduces himself to the unicorn, he says: "...For I too am real. I am Schmendrick, the magician, the last of the red-hot swamis, and I am older than I look." Speaking of their destination, Schmendrick explains its origins like this:

> "Haggard's fortress...Haggard's dire keep. A witch built it for him, they say, but he wouldn't pay her for her work, so she put a curse on the castle. She swore that one day it would sink into the sea with Haggard, when his greed caused the sea to overflow. Then she gave a fearful shriek, the way they do, and vanished in a sulphurous puff. Haggard moved in right away. He said no tyrant's castle was complete without a curse."

Approaching Hagsgate, Schmendrick seems surprised: "It must be Hagsgate, and yet there's no smell of sorcery, no air of black magic. But why the legends, then, why the fables and fairy tales? Very confusing, especially when you've had half a turnip for dinner."

We can always count on Schmendrick to break the mood. Having had too much to drink, he sounds as if he could be on The Tonight Show:

"'You don't know what a real curse is. Let me tell you *my* troubles.' Easy tears suddenly glittered in his eyes. 'To begin with, my mother never liked me. She pretended, but I knew—'"

Later, when the questing group is followed out of Hagsgate, Schmendrick tries to figure out why: "Perhaps Drinn has started to feel guilty about underpaying his poisoner.... Perhaps his conscience is keeping him awake. Anything is possible. Perhaps I have feathers." Finally, at what could be a tender moment, Schmendrick advises the Lady Amalthea: "You are truly human now. You can love, and fear, and forbid things to be what they are, and overact."

But anticlimax is not limited to Schmendrick's speech. Molly, too, can change the mood with a word or two. After Schmendrick has turned the unicorn into the Lady Amalthea, he is explaining how he carries the true magic: "I am a bearer.... I am a dwelling, I am a messenger." Without missing a beat Molly says: "You are an idiot." Speaking about the need for wine to fulfill the riddle that will finally lead them to the Red Bull, Molly says to Schmendrick: "I thought if you had some water to start with...Well, it's been done. It's not as though you'd have to make up something new. I'd never ask that of you."

The Lady Amalthea even gets into the act, as unlike that sweet and beautiful lady as that may sound. Trying to mislead King Haggard she says: "The Red Bull. But why do you think I have come to steal the Bull? I have no kingdom to keep, and no wish for conquest. What would I do with him? How much does he eat?" In a rare moment of candor, Prince Lír, too, uses anticlimax with the Lady Amalthea: "I became a hero to serve you, and all that is like you. Also to find some way of starting a conversation."

Minor characters as well use this comic device to good effect. Captain Cully, for example, wants to pump Schmendrick for news about Cully's reputation in the wide world. He phrases his dinner invitation this way: "Come to the fire and tell us your tale. How do they speak of me in your country? What have you heard of dashing Captain Cully and his band of freemen? Have a taco." The cat who tells Molly how to get to the Red Bull seems very mysterious—until the last line:

> "'When the wine drinks itself,' he said, 'when the skull speaks, when the clock strikes the right time— only then will you find the tunnel that leads to the Red Bull's lair.' He tucked his paws under his chest and added, 'There's trick to it, of course.'"

Naturally, the skull the cat spoke of speaks, and just as naturally it uses anticlimax. When speaking to Schmendrick, the skull remarks: "Matter can neither be created nor destroyed.... Not by most magicians anyway." And while sounding the alarm for King Haggard, the skull shrieks: "Help ho, the king! Guards, to me! Here are burglars, bandits, moss-troopers, kidnapers, housebreakers, murderers, character assassins, plagiarists! King Haggard! Ho, King Haggard!"

It seems clear that this comic device is not being used for character delineation but simply for humorous effect. This belief is confirmed by the number of uses of anticlimax in narrative and expository passages where there is no dialogue. For example, the confrontation between the followers from Hagsgate and Schmendrick and company goes like this: "The magician stood erect, menacing the attackers with demons, metamorphoses, paralyzing ailments, and secret judo holds. Molly picked up a rock."

A typical evening in King Haggard's castle is described as follows: "And in the evenings, before she went to bed, she usually read over Prince Lír's new poems to the Lady Amalthea, and praised them, and corrected the spelling." Finally, Molly's typical day is described:

> "Molly Grue cooked and laundered, scrubbed stone, mended armor and sharpened swords; she chopped wood, milled flour, groomed horses and cleaned their stalls, melted down stolen gold and silver for the king's coffers, and made bricks without straw."

All of these uses of humor have a common effect: they break the empathic bond that the reader might form with the characters by drawing attention to themselves as devices of the author. There is no subtlety here, but a purposive and carefully planned exaggeration. The mechanics of the form are being laid bare, and the writer's technique revealed. The basic critical question must by *why*, and the answer can be found in one final pattern of incongruity existing in the text: a consistent pattern of self-parody. *The Last Unicorn* is cast in the form of a fairy tale, and throughout the novel the various characters (but especially Schmendrick) make observations about the form and how their story fits it.

For example, in Hagsgate Drinn describes Prince Lír's birth like this:

> "'I stood by the strange cradle for a long time, pondering while the snow fell and the cats purred prophecy.' He stopped, and Molly Grue said eagerly, 'You took the child home with you, of course, and raised it as your own.' Drinn laid his hands palm up on the table. 'I chased the cats away,' he said, 'and went home alone.... I know the birth of a hero when I see it,' he said, 'Omens and portents, snakes in the nursery. Had it not been for the cats, I might have chanced the child, but they made it so obvious, so mythological.'"

Molly, talking to Schmendrick about the apparent cruelty of leaving the child to die in the snow, says: "They deserve their

fate, they deserve worse. To leave a child out in the snow—"
Schmendrick, of course, knows better, and replies: "Well, if
they hadn't, he couldn't have grown up to be a prince. Haven't
you ever been in a fairy tale before?" And on the next page he
says: "It's a great relief to find out about Prince Lír. I've been
waiting for this tale to turn up a leading man."

Another reference to the story within the story occurs shortly
after Schmendrick turns the unicorn into a human being:

> "You're in the story with the rest of us now, and you
> must go with it, whether you will or no. If you want
> to find your people, if you want to become a unicorn
> again, then you must follow the fairy tale to King Hag-
> gard's castle, and wherever else it chooses to take you.
> The story cannot end without the princess."

The exaggeration that we saw in Beagle's description of
Molly's typical day is enlarged upon in Prince Lír's discussion
with Molly about his deeds:

> "I have swum four rivers, each in full flood and none
> less than a mile wide. I have climbed seven mountains
> never before climbed, slept three nights in the Marsh
> of the Hanged Men, and walked alive out of that forest
> where the flowers burn your eyes and the nightingales
> sing poison. I have ended my betrothal to the princess
> I had agreed to marry—and if you don't think that was
> a heroic deed, you don't know her mother. I have van-
> quished exactly fifteen black knights waiting by fif-
> teen fords in their black pavilions, challenging all who
> came to cross. And I've long since lost count of the
> witches in the thorny woods, the giants, the demons
> disguised as damsels; the glass hills, fatal riddles, and
> terrible tasks; the magic apples, rings, lamps, potions,
> swords, cloaks, boots, neckties, and nightcaps. Not to

mention the winged horses, the basilisks and sea serpents, and all the rest of the livestock."

Any one of these deeds, of course, would be sufficient to win the hand of the fair lady in the average fairy tale—but this is far from the average fairy tale. Prince Lír knows the way things are, and he tells the Lady Amalthea:

> "My lady.... I am a hero. It is a trade, no more, like weaving or brewing, and like them it has its own tricks and knacks and small arts. There are ways of perceiving witches, and of knowing poison streams; there are certain weak spots that all dragons have, and certain riddles that hooded strangers tend to set you. But the true secret of being a hero lies in knowing the order of things. The swineherd cannot already be wed to the princess when he embarks on his adventures, nor can the boy knock on the witch's door when she is away on vacation. The wicked uncle cannot be found out and foiled before he does something wicked. Things must happen when it is time for them to happen. Quests may not simply be abandoned; prophesies may not be left to rot like unpicked fruit; unicorns may go unrescued for a long time, but not forever. The happy ending cannot come in the middle of the story."

After he becomes King, Lír says to Schmendrick: "A hero is entitled to his happy ending, when it comes at last." But since Lír cannot have the Lady Amalthea, a substitute must arrive, and Beagle obliges. Just before Schmendrick and Molly ride off into the sunset, "out of this story and into another," a damsel in distress (apparently out of another story, but certainly in need of a hero) rides up, saying:

> "A rescue! a rescue, *au secours*! An ye be a man of mettle and sympathy, aid me now. I hight the Princess

Alison Jocelyn, daughter to good King Giles, and him foully murdered by his brother, the bloody Duke Wulf, who hath ta'en my three brothers, the Princes Corin, Colin, and Calvin, and cast them into a fell prison as hostages that I will wed with his fat son, the Lord Dudley, but I bribed the sentinel and sopped the dogs—"

Shmendrick replies, apparently keeping a straight face: "Fair princess, the man you want just went that way."

This continued reference to the story within the story has been called "metafantasy", or more broadly "metafiction." It is one of the hallmarks of postmodernism, and it is perhaps somewhat surprising to see it as the centerpiece of Beagle's communication with his audience. It certainly indicates that Beagle was not writing for children, or at least not for children only, in *The Last Unicorn*. Such a sophisticated technique can be used in a variety of ways, and we will see it again in Beagle's later work.

Schmendrick and Molly and the others refuse to take themselves seriously in *The Last Unicorn*, and so the reader doesn't take them seriously either. Beagle has carefully and lovingly created a work that satirizes and glorifies its form, much in the same way that the music of P.D.Q. Bach satirizes and pays homage to baroque music. Various forms of incongruity play a major role in the success of the enterprise.

Beagle published *The Last Unicorn: The Lost Version*, containing the text of his first start at *The Last Unicorn* from 1962, in 2006. He says in his Introduction that he began the book "with absolutely no plan for anything except a light, Nathanesque fable of modern society, and equipped only with a hazy vision of a unicorn journeying *somewhere* with *some* sort of companion." He abandoned it after about eighty pages.

In *The Lost Version* the unicorn's traveling companions were Azazel and Webster, the two heads and personalities of a demon exiled from hell. Beagle says the "snarky" dialogue between them "is clearly modeled after the conversations, private jokes, and role-playing games that Phil and I entertained ourselves with in those days, during long late-night waits for the D train, and in the cabin, and during our arduous scooter trip across America." "Phil" was Phil Sigunick, Beagle's closest childhood friend, with whom he rented a cabin in Massachusetts during the summer of 1962 and with whom he went on the trip memorialized in *I See by My Outfit*.

There are other significant differences from the published version as well. The butterfly was the one original character beyond the unicorn who survived, but its dialogue was wider-ranging. There was a dragon which was a major character which disappeared completely, and the time was most definitely the twentieth century instead of once-upon-a-time. Beagle in his Afterword says of both of these things that in order "to recast the story as a fairy-tale, the dragon had to go, along with the entire twentieth century."

There are two encounters that stand out in *The Lost Version*, one with a beautiful female demon sent to pursue Azazel and Webster and who fools Azazel into giving her all of his jewelry, and the other with a modern city. The first is a source of mirth, as the demon is beaten at her own game, while the second appears merely to provide an excuse for Beagle's lamentation on life in the modern world. Neither episode survived into the published version, although a fat man who tries to capture the unicorn while seeing her as only a horse appears with his wife in *The Lost Version*, and there is a encounter with a virgin that also survives.

Very little need be said here about *The Lost Version*. It is interesting only as a curiosity to committed fans, with little of the charm or metafictional elements which stand out in the published version. Beagle, however, has also published a short story sequel to *The Last Unicorn* that is worthy of examination. "Two Hearts," winner of the Hugo and Nebula Awards for Best Fantasy Novelette, first appeared in the October/November 2005 issue of *The Magazine of Fantasy & Science Fiction* and was reprinted in *The Line Between* in 2006. It is especially interesting that Beagle eventually wrote a sequel to *The Last Unicorn*, since in his Foreword to *Giant Bones* he asserted emphatically that "never for a moment did I feel the least interest...in what became of Molly Grue and Schmendrick the Magician...." His fans apparently did, however, and Beagle obliged with "Two Hearts."

The narrator of "Two Hearts" is a nine-year-old girl named Sooz, but the more interesting characters are Schmendrick, Molly, and King Lír. The story picks up the characters many years later, and shows us how life goes on for them.

Sooz tells us she will be ten next month, on the anniversary of the day the griffin came. It stayed in the Midnight Wood, and ate sheep and goats until the last year, when it began eating children. The men tried to organize some sort of patrol, so they could see when the griffin, with its lion's body and eagle's wing, with its great front claws like teeth and a monstrous beak, was coming. They sent messages to the king, who sent first a single knight and then five knights together. They rode into the woods, and all but one were never seen again, and that one died before he could tell them what happened. The third time an entire squadron came, and after that they didn't send to the king any more. Then the griffin took Felicitas, Sooz's best friend even though she couldn't talk. That was the night she set off to see the king herself.

She thought the king must live somewhere near Hagsgate, which was the only town she had ever seen. So she sneaked out of the house in the middle of the night and hid under some sheepskins in her Uncle Ambrose's cart, knowing that he would leave for Hagsgate early in the morning. When they turned into the King's Highway, she jumped out of the cart without being seen and watched it roll away down the road. She had never been so far from home before, or so lonely.

Sooz had no idea which way to go, and she didn't even know the king's name. She turned to the left, for no reason than that she wore a ring on her left hand that her mother had given her. She found a stream and drank until she couldn't hold any more. She looked up only when she heard horses nearby, playing with the water. They were ordinary livery-stable horses, one brownish, one grayish. The gray one's rider was out of the saddle, peering at the horse's left forefoot. Both riders had on plain cloaks, dark green, and trews so worn you could hardly make out the color. She didn't know one was a woman until she heard her voice. The other voice was lighter and younger-sounding, and Sooz already knew he was a man because he was so tall. The man started to get off of his brown horse to look at the other horse's forefoot, but before he did so he placed two hands on his horse's head and mumbled a few words that Sooz did not hear. Amazingly enough, the horse answered him.

The man looked at the hoof and discovered a stone splinter. He stood over it, as Sooz had seen the blacksmith do, but he had no blacksmith's tools. Instead he sang to it, for a long time, until all at once he stopped singing and straightened up, holding something that glinted in the sun. He showed it to the horse, then threw it away.

He told the woman they ought to camp there; the horses were weary, and his back hurt. At that she laughed and said, "The greatest wizard wallking the world, and your back hurts? Heal it as you healed mine, the time the tree fell on me." He touched her hair, which was thick and pretty, even though it was mostly gray. "You know how I am about that. I still like being mortal too much to use magic on myself. It spoils it somehow—it dulls the feeling. I've told you before."

The woman sounded irritable for a moment, but then told him in a softer voice that she sometimes wished with all her heart that they could both live forever, and she thought he was a great fool to give it up. Then she remembered things she'd rather not remember, and she thought perhaps not. The tall man put his arms around her, and for a moment she rested her head upon his chest. Sooz didn't hear what she said after that.

Although Sooz didn't think she had made any noise, the man looked directly at her and said that they had food. She moved toward them, and they stood very still, waiting for her. Close to, the woman looked younger than her voice, and the tall man looked older. She wasn't young at all, but the gray hair made her face look younger, and she held herself really straight. The woman's face was not beautiful, but it was a face you'd want to snuggle up to on a cold night. The man first looked younger than her father, then older than anybody she ever saw. His eyes were the greenest green she had ever seen; greener than grass, greener than emeralds, maybe as green as the ocean, although she had never seen the ocean. If you go deep enough into the woods, sooner or later you will always come to a place where even the shadows are green. That was how green his eyes were. She was afraid of his eyes at first.

She told them, when they asked, that she was not lost, her name was Sooz, and she had to see the king. They looked at each other for a long time and the woman said that the king did not live nearby, but he did not live very far away, either, and they were going to visit him themselves. Sooz was immediately relieved, and said she would go along with them, but the woman was troubled. She said that they didn't know how things were. The king was a good man, and a good friend, but people change, kings more than ordinary people.

The man replied that the two of them had once asked to be taken along on a quest; that he himself had begged, in fact. The woman, however, wouldn't let up, insisting that they could be taking the girl into grave peril. They could not take the chance; it wasn't right.

Sooz, though, interrupted. She was *coming* from great peril; there was a griffin nested in the wood, and he was eating children. She burst into tears. The woman comforted her, but she only stopped crying when the man pulled a big red handkerchief out of his pocket, twisted and knotted it into a bird-shape, and made it fly away.

The man's name was Schmendrick, and the woman's was Molly Grue. Molly told her the king's name was Lír, and that they had known him when he was a young man, before he became king. He was a true hero, a dragonslayer, a giantkiller, a rescuer of maidens, a solver of impossible riddles. He may be the greatest hero of all, because he is a good man. They aren't always. But Molly was worried that he may have changed; he may no longer be the man he was. Schmendrick, though, took a notion that Lír needed them, so there they were. You couldn't argue with him when he got like that.

Sooz replied that her mother said thay you just wait until he goes out, or is asleep, then do whatever you want. Molly told her Schmendrick and she were not married, just together, and they had been together quite a long while. To Sooz they looked married, sort of.

Sooz wondered if it would take them long to reach the king. Molly wanted to know what she expected when she met the king; what did she have in mind when she set off to find him? Sooz didn't even have to think about it; she wanted the king to come and take care of the griffin himself. He's the king; it's his job.

They started off the next morning, Schmendrick singing a lot as they rode along, sometimes in languages she couldn't make out a word of, sometimes making up silly songs to make her laugh, like this one:

> *"Soozli, Soozli,*
> *speaking loozli,*
> *you disturb my oozli-goozli.*
> *Soozli, Soozli,*
> *would you choozli*
> *to become my squoozli-squoozli?"*

He never did any magic, except once when he seemed to call a hawk to chase off a crow that kept diving at the horses. At least she guessed that was magic.

They passed through pretty country, which Schmendrick told her had all been barren desert where nothing grew before Lír. It was said the land was under a curse, but Lír changed everything. Except poor Hagsgate.

Schmendrick was sure that as soon as she told him her

troubles he would snatch up his great sword and spear, whisk
her up to his saddlebow, and be off after her griffin with the
road smoking behind him. Young or old, that's always been his
way. Molly overworries; that's her way. We are who we are.
Schmendrick then sang another verse:

> "Soozli, Soozli,
> you amuse me,
> right down to my solesli-shoesli.
> Soozli, Soozli,
> I bring newsli—
> we could wed next stewsli-Tuesli."

Sooz learned that the king had lived in a castle on a cliff
by the sea when he was young, less than a day's journey from
Hagsgate, but it fell down—he would not say how—so he built
a new one somewhere else. She was sorry about that, because
she had never seen the sea, and she had always wanted to. But
she had never seen a castle, either, so there was that.

It took them three full days to reach King Lír. Sooz was
disappointed; the castle was pretty, but she wanted a fortress.
The moment she saw that nice, friendly castle, with its one blue
banner with a picture of a white unicorn on it, she was afraid the
king would not help her, hero or not. They did not go to the top,
either; Schmendrick led them through the great hall and on past
the kitchens and the scullery and the laundry, to a room under a
staircase. The king was in there, all by himself.

He was sitting in an ordinary chair, not a throne, and it was a
really small room. Sooz was ready for him to have a long beard,
spreading out all across his chest, but he only had a short one,
like her father, except white. He wore a red and gold mantle, and
there was a real golden crown upon his white head. He had a
kind face, with a big old nose, and big blue eyes like a little boy.
But his eyes were so tired and empty Sooz didn't know how he
kept them open. He peered at the three of them as if he knew
them, but not why. He tried to smile.

Schmendrick very gently told him that it was Schmendrick and Molly Grue. Molly added that it was Molly with the cat—he remembered the cat, didn't he? Schmendrick told Molly that *she* would often forget herself like that, and then Molly would always have to remind him that *she* was a unicorn.

At the word the king changed. All at once his eyes were clear and shining with feeling, like Molly's eyes. He recognized them, and stood to embrace his friends. Sooz saw then that he had been a hero, that he was still a hero, and that maybe everything was going to be all right after all. She told him about the griffin eating children, and when she told him the name of her village he surprised her by saying he knew it, and he had been there. Now he would have the pleasure of returning.

They were interrupted by a small, dark woman who introduced herself as Lisene, the king's secretary, translator, and protector. Schmendrick had never known him to need any of those things, especially a protector, but she told him: "Time sets its claw in us all, my lord, sooner or later. We are none of us that which we were." The king sat down obediently in his chair and closed his eyes.

Schmendrick was angry, and growing angrier, but did not show it. Sooz knew it because that is how her father gets angry. He told Lisene that the king had agreed to return to the girl's village with her to rid her people of a marauding griffin. They would leave the next day.

Lisene, however, would not hear of it. The king was in no fit condition for such a journey, let alone such a deed. They came seeking the peerless warrior they remembered, but found instead a spent, senile old man.

Schmendrick cut her off, eyes flashing. He pointed his finger at the woman, and Sooz expected her to catch fire. He said, "Hear me now, I am Schmendrick the magician, and I see my old friend Lír, as I have always seen him, wise and powerful and good, beloved of a unicorn."

And with that word, a second time, the king woke up, blinked, and grasped the arms of the chair. He looked at Lisene, and told her he would go with them. It was his task and his gift; she would see to it that he was ready. When she begged him to reconsider, he reached out tenderly and took her head between his big hands; Sooz saw there was love between them. He said, "It is what I am for. You know that as well as *he* does. See to it, Lisene, and keep all well for me while I am gone."

Lisene looked so sad, and so lost, that Sooz didn't know what to think, about her, about the king, about anything. Lisene told the king that she would see to it. As she left the room, she turned and said to Schmendrick, "His death be on your head, magician." Sooz thought she was crying, only not in the way that grownups do.

Schmendrick replied, with a voice so cold Sooz wouldn't have recognized it if she hadn't known it was him speaking, "He had died before. Better that death—better this, better *any* death—than the one he was dying in that chair. If the griffin kills him, it will yet have saved his life." Sooz heard the door shut as Lisene left the room.

Sooz asked Molly what Schmendrick meant about the king having died before, but rather than answer Molly knelt at the king's feet, took one of his hands between hers, and begged him to remember. The old man was swaying on his feet, but he placed his other hand on Molly's head and assured Sooz that he would come to her village.

> "The griffin was never hatched that dares harm King Lír's people. But you must remind me, little one. When I...when I lose myself...when I lose *her*...you must remind me that I am still searching, still waiting...that I have never forgotten her, never turned from all she taught me. I sit in this place...I *sit*...because a king has to sit, you see...but in my mind, in my poor mind, I am always with *her*...."

Sooz had no idea what he was talking about then. Later, when she told the story, she did.

Lír fell asleep again, then, holding Molly's hand. Sooz tried to write a letter home, but she fell asleep, too, and slept the rest of the day and all night, too. When she awoke Schmendrick was at her bedside, urging her to rise. They would start by noon, anyway, if he could get Lisene and the others to realize they were not coming along. When he said he might have to turn the lot of them to stone Sooz thought he was joking, but with Schmendrick you never knew. He told her King Lír was not mad, or senile; he was Lír still. She noticed the change in him when Schmendrick spoke of one unicorn who loved him. He had not seen her since he became king, Schmendrick told Sooz, but he is what he is because of her. When they spoke of her, or said her name, which they had not yet done, then he was recalled to himself, as they often had to do for her, so long ago. Sooz did not know that unicorns had names, or that they loved people, and Schmendrick explained that they did not, except this one. Her name was Amalthea.

When Sooz next saw the king he was so changed that she froze in the doorway and held her breath. Three men were bustling around him like tailors, dressing him with his armor. He looked like a giant. When he saw her he smiled, and it was a warm, happy smile but it was a little frightening, too. It was a hero's smile; she had never seen one before. He asked her to come and buckle his sword. She managed to do so, and he swore to her that the next time that blade was drawn it would be to save her village.

When Schmendrick complained that it was four days' ride, and that there was no need for armor until he faced the griffin, the king reminded him that he went forth as he intended to return; it was his way. Molly, seeing him in his armor, could only exclaim how grand and beautiful he was. Molly wished *she* could see him. The three of them stood there for a long time, then the king looked at Sooz and said, "The child is waiting." And that was how they started off for Sooz's home, the king, Schmendrick, Molly, and Sooz.

Sooz rode with the king most of the time. Lír assured her that his skittery black mare would be at her best when the griffin swooped down on her; it was only peaceful times that made her nervous. Sooz still didn't like the mare much, but she did like the king. He didn't sing to her, but he told her stories, real, true stories about things that happened to him. She knew she would never hear such stories again.

Lír told her many things, but when she asked him why the castle fell down, he wouldn't exactly say. His voice became very quiet and faraway. "I forget things, little one.... I try to hold on, but I do forget." She could never get him to say a word about the unicorn.

Lír's mind kept moving in and out. Frequently at night he would wander away, and often Schmendrick or Sooz would bring his mind back in focus by mentioning the unicorn. One day he charged at a rutting stag that was pursuing them, and that night he sang an entire long song about the adventures of an outlaw named Captain Cully. Sooz had never heard of him, but it was a really good song. Lír apologized for putting her in danger; he had forgotten she was with him. Then he smiled that hero's smile of his, and said, "But oh, little one, the remembering!"

They reached the village on the fourteenth day, and Schmendrick told Sooz it would be better to tell the people that this was just the king's greatest knight, and not the king himself. She had to trust him; he always knew what he was doing. That was his trouble.

Sooz did as she was told, but her father was not happy about it. Just another knight would be dessert for the griffin; you could be sure the king would never come there himself. He might have cared once, but now he was an old man, and old kings only care about who is to be king after them.

The next morning when Sooz came to the camp, Molly was helping the king put on his armor and Schmendrick was burying the remains of the last night's dinner. Sooz ran up to Lír and threw her arms around him, like Lisene, begging him not to go. The king kept trying to pet her with one hand and push her aside with the other. He said,

"No, no little one, you don't understand. There are some monsters only a king can kill. I have always known that—I should never, never have sent those poor men to die in my place. No one else in all the land can do this for you, and for your village. Most truly now, it is my job."

And he kissed her hand, just like he had kissed the hand of so many queens.

Molly came to her then and took her from him, telling her that there was no turning back for him now, or for her either. It was her fate to bring this last cause to him, and his fate to take it up. Neither of them could have done differently, being who they were. She must be as brave as he is, and see it all play out. Or rather she must learn about how it all plays out, because certainly she was not coming into the forest to see for herself.

They all of course had to say goodbye. Molly said she knew they would see each other again, and Schmendrick told her she had the makings of a real warrior queen, only he was certain that she was too smart to be one. King Lír said to her very quietly, so no one else could hear: "Little one, if I had married and had a daughter, I would have asked no more than that she should be as brave and kind and loyal as you. Remember that, as I will remember you to my last days."

And then the three of them rode into the wood, only Molly looking back to make sure Sooz was not following. And perhaps she would not have followed, had it not been for her dog, Malka. Malka should have been with the sheep, of course; that was her job, just as being king and going to meet the griffin was Lír's job. But to Malka Sooz was a sheep, too, the most stupid, aggravating sheep she had ever had to guard, forever wandering into some kind of danger. What Malka did was jump up on Sooz until she knocked her down, and then take the hem of her smock in her jaws and start tugging her in the direction the dog thought she should go. This time, though, after knocking Sooz down Malka stared past her at the wood with all the white showing in her eyes and making a sound Sooz didn't think she could make. The next moment Malka was racing into the wood with foam flying from her mouth and her big ragged ears flat back. Sooz had no choice but to follow. Lír, Schmendrick, and Molly all had a choice, going after the griffin, but Malka did not know what she was facing, and Sooz could not let her face it alone.

Sooz ran and walked and ran again, following the hoofprints and the dog tracks, when all of a sudden the forest exploded a little way ahead of her. Malka was howling, and Schmendrick or the king or somebody was shouting, although she couldn't make out the words. Underneath it all was something that wasn't loud at all, a sound somewhere between a growl and that terribly soft call, like a child. Then just as she broke into the clearing she heard the rattle and scrape of knives, as the griffin shot straight up with the sun on its wings. Its cold golden eyes bit into hers, and its beak was open so wide you could see down and down into the blazing red gullet. It filled the sky.

And King Lír, astride his black mare, filled the clearing. He was as huge as the griffin, and his sword was the size of a boar spear. He shook it at the griffin, daring it to light down and fight him on the ground. But the griffin stayed out of range, circling overhead to get a good look at these strange new people. Malka screamed and hurled herself into the air again and again, snapping at the lion's feet and eagle claws, but coming down each time without so much as an iron feather between her teeth. The last time she leaped the griffin swooped and caught her full on her side with one huge wing, so hard she couldn't get a sound out. She flew all the way across the clearing, slammed into a tree, fell to the ground, and after that she did not move.

Molly told Sooz later that that was when King Lír struck for the griffin's lion heart. Sooz did not see it; she was flying across the clearing herself, throwing herself over Malka in case the griffin came after her again. She did hear the griffin's roar when it happened, and when she could turn her head she saw the blood splashing along its side. Lír threw his sword into the air, caught it, and charged in for the kill, ignoring Schmendrick who was standing by yelling, "Two hearts, two hearts!" until his voice split with it. Sooz didn't know what happened right then; all she was seeing and thinking about was Malka, feeling her heart not beating under her own. Malka, who guarded her cradle when she was born; Malka, on whose ear she had cut her teeth.

King Lír wasn't seeing or hearing any of them. There was nothing in the world for him but the griffin. When it flopped and struggled lopsidedly in the clearing, he got down from his black mare and went up to it, and spoke to it, lowering his sword until its point was on the ground: "You were a noble and terrible adversary—surely the last such I will ever confront. We have accomplished what we were born to do, the two of us. I thank you for your death."

And on that last word, the griffin had him. It was the eagle, lunging up at him, dragging the dead lion half along. King Lír stepped back, swinging the sword fast enough to take off the griffin's head, but the griffin was faster. The dreadful beak caught him at the waist, shearing through his armor the way an axe would smash through pie crust. There was blood, and worse; she could not have said if the king were dead or alive. Sooz thought the griffin was going to bite him in two.

Schmendrick could do nothing, since he had promised Lír that he would not intervene by magic. Sooz was not a magician, though, and she had not promised anyone anything. The griffin did not see her coming. She had a big rock in her left hand and a dead branch in her right, and the griffin looked up fast when the rock hit it on the side of the neck. It didn't like that, but it was too busy with King Lír to bother with her. She threw the branch as far as she could, and as soon as the griffin looked away she made a big sprawling dive for the hilt of the king's sword. She knew she could lift it because she had buckled it on him, but she couldn't get it free; he was lying on it and was too heavy. She kept pulling on the sword, while Molly kept pulling on her, and the griffin lifted her up and threw her on top of the king, his cold armor so cold against her cheek it was as if his armor had died with him.

Griffins do not speak, as dragons can (but only to heros, Lír had told her). But as the griffin looked into her eyes, it was as if it was telling her that although it would die, it had killed them all, and it would pick their bones before the ravens had his. The people would remember it, and what it did, when there was no one left who would remember her name. So it had won. And there was nothing but that beak and that burning gullet opening over her.

And then there was. Sooz thought it was a white cloud, only traveling so low and so fast that it smashed the griffin off King Lír and and away from Sooz and sent her tumbling into Molly's arms at the same time. Molly held her tight, and it wasn't until she wriggled her head free that she saw what had come to them.

They didn't look *anything* like horses; Sooz didn't know how people got that idea. Schmendrick was on his knees, with his eyes closed and his lips moving, as though he was singing. Molly kept whispering, "Amalthea...Amalthea...," not to Sooz, not to anybody. The unicorn was facing the griffin across the king's body, dancing with its front hooves, and with its head up. Then it put its head down.

Dying or not, the griffin put up a furious fight. It wasn't a bit fair, though, and Sooz did not feel sorry for the griffin. With its last strength the griffin flung itself on the unicorn, trying to rake its back and bite down on its neck as it had with the king, but the unicorn reared up, flung the griffin to the ground, whirled and drove its horn straight into the eagle heart.

Schmendrick and Molly raced to King Lír. He was still alive, barely. He did not know them, but he knew Sooz. As he looked past her he saw the unicorn, and his face was suddenly young and happy and wonderful. All you could see in the unicorn's dark eyes was King Lír. Sooz moved aside so she could get to him, but when she turned back he was gone. She was nine, almost ten; she knew when people were gone.

The unicorn stood over King Lír's body for a long time. Sooz went off the sit beside Malka, and Molly went with her. Schmendrick stayed by the body of the king, quietly talking to the unicorn. Sooz couldn't hear what he was saying, but she could tell he was asking for something, a favor. Unicorns can't talk, either, but after a while it turned its head and looked at him. Schmendrick walked away.

Sooz and Molly talked about Malka, each trying to comfort the other. Sooz did not notice the unicorn until the horn came slanting over her shoulder. The horn touched Malka, just where Sooz had been stroking her, and Malka opened her eyes. It took her a while to understand she was alive, and it took Sooz longer. She only started crying when Malka licked her face.

When Malka saw the unicorn she did a funny thing. She stared at it for a moment, then made a bow or curtsy, in a dog way. The unicorn nosed at her, very gently. It looked at Sooz for the first time; or maybe Sooz looked at it for the first time. What the unicorn's eyes did was to free her from the griffin's eyes. The unicorn had all the world in her eyes, all the world that Sooz was never going to see, and it didn't matter any more because she had seen it and it was beautiful.

None of them saw the unicorn go. Sooz heard Schmendrick tell Molly: "A dog. I nearly killed myself singing her to Lír, calling her as no other has *ever* called a unicorn—and she brings back, not him, but the dog. And here I'd always thought she had no sense of humor."

But Molly told him it was because she loved him, too. That was why she let him go.

Sooz worried that she would never see them again, any more than she would see the king. But again Molly had an answer. She gave Sooz a tune to whistle on her seventeenth birthday, and assured her that someone would come to her. Maybe it would be the greatest magician in the world, or maybe just an old lady with a soft spot for impudent children. Maybe even a unicorn. Because beautiful things will always want to see her again, and will be listening for her. Someone will come.

They took her home, on their way to taking the king to his long home, and Molly reminded her to wait until she is seventeen. Sooz practices the music in her head every day, and even dreams it some nights, but she never whistles it aloud. She talks to Malka about their adventure, because she has to talk to someone. Promises her that on that special day in the special place she has already picked out, Malka will be there with her.

Sooz hopes it is them. A unicorn is very nice, but they are her friends. She wants to feel Molly holding her again, and hear the stories Molly didn't have time to tell her. She wants to hear Schmendrick singing the old song again:

> "*Soozli, Soozli,*
> *speaking loozli,*
> *you disturb my oozli-goozli.*
> *Soozli, Soozli,*
> *would you choozli*
> *to become my squoozli-squoozli?*"

She could wait.

In "Two Hearts" Beagle gives his readers what they want, more about Schmendrick and Molly and Lír, and especially more about the unicorn. He also gives them a reiteration of some of his most important themes from the earlier work. But the writer of "Two Hearts" is almost forty years older than the writer of *The Last Unicorn*, and it would be strange indeed if he still saw the world the same way. Indeed, we see that Schmendrick and Molly no longer epitomize what they stated explicitly in *The Last Unicorn*: that we are what people think us, and we become what we pretend to be. There is no more need for pretense. In "Two Hearts" people do what they must, being who they are. The difference is significant.

It is also significant that the two hearts of the title is a pun in Beagle's inimitable style. On one level, the two hearts are those of the griffin, the heart of a lion and the heart of an eagle. But to the reader the two hearts are those of Schmendrick and Molly

Grue, beating together over the years.

Beagle's sense of humor is not so overpowering in "Two Hearts." There is the occasional pun, the occasional snide look back to the earlier text, and the iterated ironic song. But the main purpose here is nostalgia; the reader wants to know whatever happened to Schmendrick and Molly and Lír and the unicorn. And a secondary purpose is looking forward; Beagle sets up his sequel. On her seventeenth birthday, Sooz will whistle Molly's tune, and someone will come. No doubt the ensuing adventure will include Schmendrick and Molly, and probably the successor to King Lír. The unicorn will figure into the climax, as she did in "Two Hearts." And I wouldn't bet against Sooz turning out to be the warrior queen at the center of it all.

For not only did Beagle write a short story sequel for *The Last Unicorn*, he has gone on record in the foreword to it in *The Line Between* promising a novel-length sequel. When or whether it will see the light of day remains to be seen.

A multi-issue comic book adaptation of *The Last Unicorn*, published by I.D.W., appeared in 2010. Adapted by Peter B. Gillis and with art by Renae De Liz, the first issue takes the unicorn through the confrontation with the butterfly while the second continues through Mommy Fortuna and her meeting with Schmendrick. The first issue contains a new Introduction by Beagle and the first part of "A Conversation With Peter S. Beagle," originally posted on the internet. The second part appeared, naturally enough, in the second issue, and was concluded in the third. All six parts were combined in a graphic novel, published in February, 2011.

The illustrations are handsome, inspired by the animated film, perhaps, but ultimately a complete visual reimagining. They are printed with a mauve or lavender cast, which gives the art an appropriately sad nostalgia. The adaptation is straightforward, but as you might expect from the format opts for the simple rather than the complex, and thus the wonderful comic irony of the original is mostly lost. This is virtually inevitable in any adaptation, which by definition must be briefer than the original; the screenplay for the animated film suffered from the same defect, and Beagle wrote that adaptation himself. The released version of the film cut even more or Beagle's script, as he makes clear in his narration on the Blu-Ray version released in 2011.

The animated film version, comic books, and the graphic novel are interesting in themselves, if less so than the work upon which they were based, and have served and will serve as an introduction to one of the great modern fantasy novels for a new generation of readers.

CHAPTER THREE:
THE FOLK OF THE AIR

The main character of *The Folk of the Air* is, not by coincidence, Joe Farrell, whom Beagle first introduced some fifteen years earlier in his novella "Lila the Werewolf" (*see* Chapter Seven, below), and who also has been the main character in two short stories, "Spook" (2008) and "Julie's Unicorn" (1997). He has thus, as the narrator tells us at the climax of the novel, "in his life seen more shape-changing than most people." Farrell is a musician, as is Beagle, although Farrell plays the lute and Beagle the guitar. Beagle admits that he would like to be a really good guitarist, or at least good enough to work out proper arrangements behind his own singing. Farrell is both a really good lutist and an excellent arranger. On at least one level, then, Farrell is a personification of Beagle himself, or perhaps Beagle as he would like to be.

The novel is set in Avicenna (reminiscent of Abyssinia, slang for "I'll be seeing ya"), California, but there is no question that it is suggested by Berkeley. Aside from the fact that Beagle explicitly states that Avicenna is as much Berkeley as he wants it to be, the reader discovers from internal evidence that it is the home of a major university, across the bay from San Francisco, and distinguished by its bell tower. Additionally, Beagle uses the terms "berserk" and "berserker" throughout the novel, and residents of Berkeley often refer to their city as "Berserkeley." To Farrell, Avicenna is the "Museum of my twisted youth, vault of my dearest and most disgusting memories." He had graduated one day when he just got careless. "People hang on in Avicenna. This town is a La Brea tar pit for academic types," Ben tells Farrell, who replies, "I'm hip. They come out to do graduate work and wind up shoplifting. Dealing. All the cabdrivers came out on the G.I. Bill in 1961 and flunked their orals." Beagle himself came to Stanford in 1960, and knows the type, as the narrator remarked of Schmendrick in *The Last Unicorn*.

The first few chapters establish the major characters and the location, and then elements of the fantastic begin to intrude into the mundane world. Farrell is clearly an entirely human character, as is his oldest friend Ben Kassoy, whom Beagle also introduced in "Lila the Werewolf," now an assistant professor of Icelandic literature (an academic specialty he shares with J. R. R. Tolkien, perhaps by coincidence) at the university about to be promoted and tenured. Farrell returns to Avicenna after an absence of ten years, in an attempt to find himself, and hooks up with his once and future girlfriend Julie Tanakawa, who rides motorcycles that Farrell thinks of as "her familiar demons, a cross between hippogriffs and pit bulls." Ben is married to an unattractive older woman named Sia (short for Athanasia Sioris, born on the Greek island of Syros), whom Farrell sometimes recalls "being instantly certain that he had just met either an old friend or a very patient, important enemy." He feels strange trying to imagine not knowing who she is.

Ben had told Farrell that Sia's house is a cave, with every-thing smelling "of chicken blood and skins drying." To Farrell, however, it seems more like a green tree, with the rooms as the branches, "high and light and murmurous with the sounds that wood makes in the sun." Farrell discovers to his surprise that the house has more windows at night that during the day, and Ben informs him that the doors move around a little bit as well. Certain small rooms upstairs also seem to come and go as they please, and the closets never stay quite the same. Ben accepts it all, but to Farrell it is unsettling.

The other resident of the house is Briseis, an Alsatian wolf-hound. At their first meeting Farrell sees an image of Sia and

Briseis reflected in the glass of the window as he looks outside, but he sees a single figure which has "the vast stone body of a woman, and a dog's grinning head." This "vision," as the omniscient narrator tells us, "endured for less time than it took his eyes to translate, or his mind to sidestep, promising to write." Nonetheless, for a brief moment Farrell sees Sia as she truly is, and the reader is prepared for the revelations to come by Beagle's subtle foreshadowing. Farrell takes over the chore of walking Briseis in the evenings, and the dog responds by sleeping nowhere else but across his feet.

At their first meeting Sia asks Farrell to play his lute for her and he obliges, playing some Dowland, some Rosseter, and a Narvaez pavane that he is inordinantly proud of having transcribed for the lute. She draws from him the story of his life, which so far, unlike that of Odysseus, is composed of having the same adventure over and over again. Wherever he wakes up and finds himself, he takes some stupid job, makes a few colorful acquaintances, and sometimes finds a woman for a brief time. Then he wakes up somewhere else and it starts all over again. He believes it suits him, and that the best part of his life is his music, but Sia knows that he allows himself only the crust of his experiences, only the shadows, and that he always leaves the good part.

Sia is a counselor who sees clients in the house. Calling them "patients" is the one sure way to make her angry. The clients range from lawyers to parking-lot attendants to a dance instructor to a paramedic to a retired policeman. They come at all hours, although Sia keeps office hours of a sort. One of the clients, Suzy McManus, who is married to a surfing thug named Dave who believes cancer is contagious, pays her by doing housework. Others pay her in other ways.

Farrell's first stupid job in Avicenna is at Thumper's, a fast-food restaurant specializing in fried rabbit trucked in from Fullerton until "Disney sues the whole wretched outfit right into Backruptcyland." He has been a fry cook, and he has been a chef. "I don't mind giving," he tells Sia, "but I like to know exactly what I'm expected to give. Otherwise it gets confusing, and I have to think about it, and it troubles the music." For some reason this angers her, and she storms out of the room, returning placated when he plays the lute. Farrell plays brilliantly, but cannot answer when Sia asks him what he has chosen to give up to play like that. She diagnoses the problem with his music: it has no place where it belongs, just like him.

Farrell and Julie, his college girlfriend, are in the habit of meeting one another in strange places. She is strong and quite as tall as he is, and she is riding a motorcycle when he chances into her in Avicenna. She is wearing her black hair below her shoulders again, as she had in college. Although Farrell has not even known where she has been for the past three years, she comes into his arms as though she had never left them. Farrell has thought often in the past ten years, although never when he was with her, that these reunions with Julie after a long separation are about the best times, considering that when they are together they cannot stand each other longer than three days.

Julie, whom Farrell calls Jewel, has been in Avicenna for two years, having decided not to marry Alain, a paleontologist from Geneva. She and Farrell immediately fall back into the same comfortable sexual relationship they had had in Evreux and Paris, in Minorca and Pittsburg and Zagreb, in Nantucket and Lima, not to mention in Avicenna ten years before.

Julie does medical and scientific illustrating at the university. She had tried painting five years ago when she went back to school at Oberlin, but gave up what she could not do for what she could, drawing. Farrell tells her she can do anything, but she insists that he stop imagining her—it is time for that, too. Worried that he may never see her again, Farrell agrees to meet her for dinner at a Moroccan restaurant.

Farrell's second stupid job in Avicenna is at the zoo, driving an electric train in the shape of an alligator and lecturing to his passengers about the animals they are seeing. Upon returning to Sia and Ben's house from his successful interview, he comes upon drunken Dave McManus, with a gun under his jacket, who demands to see Suzy. When Suzy refuses to return with him for more abuse, Dave attempts to shoot her. Suzy calls on Sia for assistance, shouting, "*Mother, help me!*" Sia appears on the stairs, wearing a long flowered dress, barefoot, and carrying a plastic comb. McManus has shot himself in the leg, and over Suzy's objections Sia commands him to stand up and go away. "Never come near this house again. Never come near her again. She is under my protection, and if you trouble her, you will die. She is one of mine. Go now." When McManus insults her and lurches towards her menacingly, he crashes to the floor when his good leg buckles under him, although Farrell sees nothing that could have made him slip.

> "This was nothing like the reflected image he had seen of the huge woman with the dog's head. Sia herself was hardly there at all; she seemed to thin and dwindle almost to transparency, even in Farrell's mind. But for one truly unbearable moment—one instant in which names for things had not yet been invented—he was more aware of her presence than he had ever been of his own. He felt her breathing in the stairs and in the old floor under his feet; she surrounded him with her walls and her rooms, moving in the stones of the fireplace, looking at him from the pieces of the broken lamp, speaking in the sunlight's scrawl across the living room rug. Beyond the house, there was only more of her, no least refuge inside himself, for she was that place, too, laughing in his bones, teasing his atoms to make them rattle in the dark like dice. However he turned, he fell toward her, content."

Farrell has had his first glimpse of Sia's true nature.

Farrell immediately tells Julie everything he knows and suspects, including the fact that the gun moved in McManus's hand. He didn't drop it, and he wasn't holding it carelessly; the gun wriggled and pointed at him and shot him. Julie wants to know if Sia attracts him, and leaving her and Ben and everything else out of it, would he go to bed with her. Julie senses more than Farrell knows.

Ben and Julie are participants in activities of the League for Archaic Pleasures. Just as Avicenna is a thinly disguised Berkeley, the League is a thinly disguised Society for Creative Anachronism, an actual organization whose members take medieval names, dress in medieval garb, compete in tournaments, and hold regular events in the community. The League attracts outcasts of various kinds, including a smart-aleck fifteen-year-old girl named Rosanna Berry whose League persona is a witch named Aiffe of Scotland.

Farrell first comes across indications of the League as he drives into Avicenna, although he does not know it, narrowly avoiding an accident with a car driven by a large black man waving a sword. After his first night with Julie, he awakes next to a suit of chain mail which she had placed there as a joke. He asks what it is, and she replies, "Well, this is a hauberk and this is the camail, to guard your throat, and these are for your legs, the chauses. It's a complete suit, except for the gauntlets and the arming coat, the padding. And the surcoat. Most people generally wear some kind of surcoat over their mail." The helmet is not part of the suit she made; she just threw it in for effect. She had cut springs apart and interwoven them in a four-to-one pattern, and a friend whose house she had decorated had taught her to weld.

Julie makes clothing for people to wear to League events. She finds suitable gear for Farrell and takes him to his first event with him driving her bike while she sits sidesaddle and recites Robert Herrick's 1648 poem about a witch in his ear:

> "The hag is astride,
> This night for to ride—
> The devil and she together...."

En route Farrell encounters Rodney Micah Willows, an improbably tall apparently homeless black man who entreats him to "tell Aiffe of Scotland to remember Prester John." Farrell had heard of Aiffe previously, from a friend of Ben's at the university, who had named her as a girl of whom he was afraid.

At the event, officially the King's Birthday Revels of the League of Archaic Pleasures, Farrell first meets Darrell Sloat, who in the mundane world teaches remedial reading at a junior high school but who in the League is the Lord Seneschal Garth de Montfaucon. He then sees forty or fifty beautifully costumed people dancing a pavane. *"The folk of the air,"* he thinks, mistakenly. *"These are surely the folk of the air."* Later he notices that although most are his age or younger, most are surprisingly fat. Julie points out the King, Bohemond of Huy Braseal, an ethnomusicologist who won his crown in armed combat (albeit with wicker swords) at the Twelfth Night Tourney a couple of months previously. The King, while humming to himself what sounds like "Your Cheatin' Heart," dubs Farrell "Sir Pooh de Bear, most faithful of all my knights." Ben's friend Crof Grant wanders by, reciting part of Jane Elliot's "A Lament for Flodden." When Julie tells the King that Farrell is a musician, he is prevailed upon to play the lute for the company. Farrell plays and sings a French medieval prelude, which is very well received by all. He then plays "L'Entrade," a rowdy estampie to which everyone dances.

When Farrell sees Ben, the narrator tells us that:

> "He wore a blue, full-sleeved tunic under a black mantle lined with white, and a helmet with a wild boar's muzzle for a crest. Bronze ornaments glinted at his throat, a short axe in his wide copper belt. As Farrell stared, taking another step, Ben turned his scarred shield of a face and saw him, and did not know him."

Ben has his own confrontations with the fantastic, although not of his own choosing. Ben is channeled by a Viking named

Egil Eyvindsson, whose local lord Ben had studied for his doctoral dissertation. According to Julie, he is the best with a weapon she has ever seen, be it broadsword, greatsword, or maul. He has no control of his actions while possessed, and is frequently injured while running berserk. He tells Farrell he has had seizures since after college, but has kept it secret to protect his prospects for tenure.

One day while at work at the zoo Farrell is led to Ben by Sia's dog Briseis, and Ben is entirely possessed. He very nearly kills Farrell, until the latter calls him out of his trance with the childhood nickname "Rubberlips." Ben admits that his problem is not having seizures, and explains that Briseis is Sia's familiar. "In the house," says Ben of Briseis, "she's just a hassock with fleas—outside, she's Sia's eyes and legs, more than that sometimes. Old Briseis. I belong to Sia, like her, and she has to help me, but she is scared absolutely shitless of Egil. Makes things hard for her, poor old bunny."

Speaking of Egil, Ben tells Farrell: "He's real. That's the main thing. Egil is a real person, right now." Ben knows all about him, even that he's beginning to lose his hair; he sees that in the mirror from time to time. Neither he nor Egil can control the possessions. "I love him, Joe," Ben admits. "Whatever happens between us is an exchange, like love. He's alive in his world, exactly as I am in mine. We found a way to trade times, for ten seconds, five minutes, half a day, two days. It's just gotten out of hand, that's all. Like love." The League gives them a place to meet, where nobody thinks he is crazy. The seizures open the way, but Ben never had the seizures before Sia. "They come from living in her house, sharing her bed, being in her thoughts. People aren't supposed to do that, Joe. The gift is too great, we can't contain it, we *tear*. But it's a gift, a blessing, how can you say no to a blessing, even when it wasn't meant for you?"

Aiffe, it turns out, really is a witch, or at least has certain powers of witchcraft; she can make things move. In her attempt to conjure a demon she has raised an actual spirit. He goes by the name of Nicholas Bonner, and Farrell first sees him, naked as he has just emerged from her pentagram, immediately after Aiffe has conjured him. Farrell discovers that Bonner was banished to limbo five centuries earlier by Master Giacopo Salvini as Salvini died at the stake for witchcraft in Augsburg. All that Aiffe wants is "to mess with people.... I just want to get even, that's all."

"Names are magic, names are all the magic there is, every culture knows that. Got any sense, you don't even let the gods know your right name. " So says a Saracen bard named Hamid ibn Shanfara, who is in reality a black man with a classical education, to Farrell. Julie had earlier warned him, "Names mean something here." Farrell has so far declined to give anyone his name, citing a geas or prohibition that keeps him from revealing himself to anyone other than a king's daughter who is a maiden and with whom he has danced a galliard. As for Aiffe, Hamid tells Farrell that "[s]he shows off, that's all. She's fifteen years old." Farrell has his doubts; he recalls that he never wanted power as much as he did when he was fifteen. He worries that Aiffe has called into being a power she cannot control, but dances with her when she asks him to. After the dance Aiffe reveals that she is a king's daughter who is a maiden, and since they have danced a galliard together she demands to know his name. He cannot refuse, and tells her in a rush, "It's Joseph Malachi Lope de Vega Farrell, Rosanna, you want to make something of it?" When she insists on his true name, Farrell tells her privately that he is the Knight of Ghosts and Shadows, from *Don Quixote*. She is satisfied for the moment.

Ben does not come home after the event, and Sia convinces Farrell not to call the police. He is delivered to the door by Aiffe, who found him in the park where the event had been, climbing on playground equipment and yelling. When Farrell demands to know what she did to him, she replies angrily:

> "You can't talk to me like that anymore. Nobody can.... I'm Aiffe, and I can say whatever I want because I can do whatever I want. And you can't, so you

don't talk to me like I'm nothing, a baby, a nothing. You just watch your tone, and you just try really hard to make friends with me. Because it makes a difference if I'm your friend or not."

Sia senses Bonner hiding nearby, and speaks to him in an unknown language. He answers her in English, and she continues in that tongue, saying:

"You learn. I make. I have created languages that were dust in the mouths of skulls before you were born. Have you forgotten? The gift you have was an apology, because you have nothing of your own. Have you forgotten, then?"

Bonner replies, "I forget nothing,...I don't think I can." Sia makes "a sound in her throat like hard snow underfoot," and says to him, "In Augsburg, I thought that was the last time." When he suggests that she always underestimates him, she corrects him. "No, never you. Human stupidity, human longing, human madness, I have underestimated those forever."

Bonner always returns to where Sia is, and each time he perceives she is weaker, more imaginary. "I could walk into your house now, if I wanted to," he challenges her. But Sia knows better.

"You? Idiot wizards, drunken priests, any tinker woman with a grudge can banish you from this world; any spiteful child can call you back again. The yo-yo of the universe!...In my house, you? To walk through my shadow would destroy you."

She adds something in the other language, and Farrell wonders if she is calling Bonner by his true name.

Sia retains enough power, even in her diminished state, to keep him out of her house, and while she cannot change him for the better she can change him for the worse by preventing him from ever wearing beauty again. Bonner, however, has engaged Aiffe's powers, and has shown her how to cast the spell that would allow him to enter. When he attempts to force her to do so, Farrell (and through him, the reader) again sees Sia as she really is, a being of unknown and unmatched power. "You see," she tells Bonner when he has failed, "You cannot come in. Not even with her to make the way."

While Aiffe failed, however, she pushed Sia to the limit. Bonner tells Sia, "She has no idea how close she came. You and I know.... That kind of power. She almost broke you. Ignorant, unpracticed, frightened out of her wits, she almost walked over you. You aren't quite senile enough not to know,"

Farrell next sees Aiffe and Bonner at a League wedding reception held at one of the actual castles built on a hillside overlooking Avicenna, where they use a silent spell to torture a kitten which has good-naturedly attacked Bonner's leg as kittens will. It is at this event also that Farrell and Julie see Prester John.

Prester John is the League name of Micah Willows, the tall black man who, it turns out, has been possessed by the spirit of Mansa Kaskan Musa, Emperor of Mali in the early fourteenth century. Aiffe had called up the spirit at the Whalemas Tournament two years previously, while Micah had been challenging her father for the kingship, and it had lodged in Micah's body. Farrell and Julie discover the possession by accident one night after another League event when they come upon Micah being mugged and chase away his attackers. When he asks for the Lady, Farrell knows who is talking about and they take him to Sia. She speaks to him in medieval Arabic and asks why they have brought him to her. Julie has an immediate reply: "You're supposed to be a healer. He needs to be healed." She tries to do so, not with witch-spells and potions as Aiffe would have done, for Sia is no mere witch, but with a miracle. Magic will no longer do. She tells Julie, "Oh, more people than not have some magic, they just forget about it. Children use it all the time—what do you think jump rope rhymes are, or ball-bouncing games, or cat's cradles? Where do you think that girl, that Aiffe, draws her power? Because she refuses to forget, that's all it is."

But Sia fails to heal Micah. As she explains it, "For every action, an equal and opposite reaction—this is true for gods and demons as well as rocket ships. If you bend the universe the wrong way, even for the smallest instant—which is what you would call a miracle—and you lose your hold, the universe snaps back at you, you get something you did not ask for. I was punished so once before." More than that she will not say, for now.

Julie begs her to try again, with her help, for when she was a child her grandmother consecrated her to the Japanese goddess Kannon. Sia agrees, and in doing so explains to Farrell and Julie what her purpose is. "My responsibility is to see that certain laws are kept, certain gates are only allowed to swing one way. However tired or weak or frightened I am, this is still what I am for." She tells Julie, "Never mind Kannon;...Try calling your grandmother." Julie calls for Kannon, and the goddess, an old friend of Sia, comes to them. "Farrell saw her bow slightly to Julie, saluting and acknowledging her. When she looked at him, he wiped his mouth weakly, ashamed that she should have seen him so, but Kannon smiled. Farrell wept—not then, but later—because Kannon's smile allowed him to, as it allowed him to forgive himself for several quite terrible things." Sia asks Kannon to use her strength to heal Micah, and Kannon does so, then departs, leaving Farrell thinking entirely about her smile.

At a meeting of the Falconer's Guild, where everyone is in costume and six birds are being flown, Farrell and Julie are nervous because Aiffe is not present. Bonner is there, brandishing an owl on a perch, and Aiffe eventually arrives. Farrell notices that "there was the slightest questioning tilt to [her] words, the smallest temblor of vulnerability touching [him] by surprise. *She wants in so terribly.*" Aiffe claims the owl is a wood-devil she has raised. The owl flies, either at her command or at Bonner's or on its own volition, and takes Micaela, a

Canadian gyrfalcon who is a particular favorite of the Guild. Farrell remembers seeing Aiffe's hands seeming to control the bird as it killed. He thinks, while he takes her seriously, Aiffe didn't really mean to kill the falcon; she was just showing off. Julie, though, knows better. "The point," she tells him, "is power. Power doesn't need to explain itself, power is all about not explaining. Power just does because it can."

> "Aiffe is a lot more dangerous than her ambitions. You dismiss her because all she wants right now is to reign over something called the League for Archaic Pleasures. But what matters, Joe, what matters is how badly she wants it.... You know how people say, 'I'd kill to have legs like that, I'd kill to get that job, to get next to him'? Yes, well, Aiffe means it. To wear a crown that looks like a damn sand castle, to lead galliards, to go in to dinner ahead of a lot of fools in fancy long johns—Rosanna Berry would indeed kill for that. Maybe tomorrow she'll kill to be Homecoming Queen.... I once saw her do something that was worse than killing, and I'll never forgive her for it."

Farrell is fired from his job at the zoo when he is "discovered early one morning in the Nocturnal Animal House, curled up on a ledge between a couple of drowsily annoyed kinkajous." He quickly finds another job at an antique automobile restoration shop, which he enjoys in part because it exposes him to "people who mess with time, whether they know it or not.... [M]aybe there's really no present, just the past looping on and on."

The League was to have a mock war, wherein the King and his supporters would be besieged by the forces loyal to the opposition, including Aiffe. Farrell wishes to be a noncombatant but is informed that there are no guarantees. A League war is fought under the same rules as any other League tournament, but each party is allowed to use one weapon customarily forbidden, such as the longbow (with special blunted arrows easily turned aside by helmets and body armor) and the morgenstern, a flail-crowned mace. The war takes place each summer on an island provided to the League, and the defending side gets a week to fortify their positions. William the Dubious, preparing for the war with Farrell, tells him:

> "I just think it's a great outlet for so much bad stuff—all your aggressions, your violence, phony be-havior, the whole thing of choosing sides, winning. I think all wars will have to be like that pretty soon, like ours. Nobody can afford the real ones anymore, but people still have to have them.... Okay, *men* have to have them. See, I'm trained."

The war is to be called the War of the Witch. The plan is to "[p]ound 'em on the head, stay out of the poison oak, and run like hell when Aiffe shows up." The other side plans for it "to be a one-woman extravaganza, live from Las Vegas, and when it's over there won't be any more wondering, any uncertainty about just who is the star around this League. And there is to be a death." So prophecies Hamid ibn Shanfara in full bardic mode. "[I]t just happens like that once in a while, with bards," he tells Farrell. Farrell believes the prophecy to be their busi-ness; they should pay attention. Hamid agrees that they should do whatever they can.

Hamid also makes an observation about witchcraft appli-cable far beyond the confines of the novel. He and Farrell had seen what Aiffe had done to Micah, changing him to fit the story, and Hamid had also seen "more than a hundred intel-ligent people steadily denying something she pulled off right in front of their eyes.... You ever want to see the real witch-craft, you watch people protecting their comfort, their beliefs. That's where it is." It does not take too much of a stretch to apply Micah's comments to the HUAC hearings and Senator McCarthy in the fifties.

Julie insists that Farrell take the mail shirt she made with him to the war, and he takes it and his lute with him when William the Dubious picks him up the next morning. Ben is also in the van, "dressed in full Viking battle gear, all studded leather and painted steel, with heavy arm rings and a bear-claw necklace. Only the battle-axe and horned helmet were familiar to Farrell." Farrell is unsure at first whether it is his friend or the real Viking who sits across from him, but Ben makes himself known with a grin and "a uniquely obscene gesture they had both learned from a Sicilian classmate." Sia sent him to keep Farrell out of trouble, and the last thing he tells Farrell before the war begins reinforces what Julie told him: "Be careful. You hear me, Joe? Be really careful." Such double foreshadowing clearly indicates to readers that there is good reason for Farrell to be careful, and we should at least suspect that the mail shirt will play an important role.

Sia had literally dumped Ben out of bed, nearly dressed him, and shoved him into the van. All the while she kept saying that something terrible was going to happen, and that Ben should stay with Farrell all day. Farrell tells Ben about Hamid's warning, and wonders whether that might be what Sia was talking about. Ben wryly replies, "She's not always right, you know. And sometimes when she *is* right, it's not in any way you could have imagined. Who knows what Sia means by death?"

The attack begins with a hail of arrows, which catches the defenders somewhat off guard and immediately (in League reckoning) wounds or kills several. Farrell and Hamid maintain noncombatant roles at first, with the bard "str[iding] the island tirelessly in his white robes and turban, wailing Moorish and Celtic battle songs and constantly inventing immediate rhymed accounts of events that were still going on as he chanted them," and with Farrell cheering his lord, bearing messages for him, "and casting increasingly wistful glances at the refreshment table each time he swept past it." Aiffe and Nicholas Bonner are nowhere to be seen, but soon unnatural accidents and illnesses begin to take a toll on the defenders. Wandering idly and playing his lute, Farrell comes upon her in the woods, arguing with Bonner. She minimizes his contribution, and he calls her a "greedy, thankless child" who wounds his heart. He challenges her to use the war to find out what she can do.

Bonner wishes to have sex with her, but Aiffe knows he gets nothing from it. When she asks him why he wants it, he replies:

> "Dear love, I enjoy exactly what you enjoy, and that is the sensuality of power. There is no other pleasure I can take, even if I would. Yet each time we couple, you and I, something moves, something is born, as it is with real people. I am well content."

While Bonner is correct and monsters are born from their coupling, what is born flies through the air (and is thus the true folk of the air of the title) but as yet has no effect upon the world. Ben sums things up well: "She's very good.... If he hadn't been pushing her a bit too hard, we'd have been in big trouble." Farrell catches on, too. "Those things aren't real." Ben confirms the thought, for the moment. "Not quite, not yet. They will be. Another month, another week. The least little bit overtrained, that's all.... I certainly wonder what she'll try now."

Farrell is sent by the King with Crof Grant to find out, they being the two least likely to be missed if fighting breaks out again. They find Aiffe surrounded by five men who look like participants in the mock war but are instead real knights whom Aiffe has summoned and who kill for real and not in jest. One is Norman, one Venetian free-lance, and two are early Crusaders. One of them sends a real arrow towards Farrell's head, and as he runs away he finds himself asking the Lady Kannon for pity. Just as Farrell is attacked by one of the knights with his sword, Crof Grant steps in to protect him from, as he believes, a League member who isn't following the rules and is using a metal sword. He is killed in Farrell's place for his trouble. The Lady Kannon's pity has come at a price.

The final siege brings the attacking forces, including Aiffe, Bonner, and the five summoned knights, to the King's fortification. The King urges his supporters to defend him, but Aiffe knocks the gates down flat with blown kisses she sends on their way with a wave of her arms. The five real knights, whom Farrell dubs "realies," operate as efficient killing machines, and would have destroyed all of the pretended knights had Farrell and Hamid not distracted them in the nick of time, Farrell smashing his lute on the head of the Norman as he was about to kill William the Dubious. He escapes with a blow to the chest that drives Julie's chain mail deep into his flesh, "leaving the ring-pattern visible—and breathing an activity not to be engaged in lightly—for more than a week." It was clear that, whatever she believed, Aiffe was unable to control her summonings.

What saves them all is the coming of Egil Eyvindsson, roaring and swinging his axe.

> "Farrell realized later that they must surely have known the terror of the berserker in their own time, and it was this that had routed them, and not so much the fact that Ben knocked the Venetian briefly sense-less with one end of the longaxe, then caught the Nor-man full amidships with the other and drove him out through the gate like a croquet ball. That was the true end of the War of the Witch; the other four simply fol-lowed him, professionals cutting their losses."

Farrell never saw them again, but he never quite stopped looking.

Crof Grant is not the only casualty; Ben tells Farrell that Egil is dead as well, back in his own time. Ben doesn't know what he died of, but he will always believe that Egil died of him; of what he did to him, what he made him do. There are no marks on Crof and no blood; the death is put down as due to a heart attack. His widow threatens to sue the League for thirty-five million dollars for its role in his death and his life, but never gets around to filing suit. Crof was just one more obsessed role-playing League member. There are, however, several resigna-tions; there had been too many unexplained serious wounds, and too many nightmares about flying monsters.

Farrell tells Julie what he saw, and she, the only person Farrell sees cry for Crof's death, is infuriated that Aiffe has gotten away with murder. She resigns from the League, and sends Farrell away until she can decide she wants to see him again. Ben's very tenure is at stake, since he has allowed his grief over Egil's death to interfere with his teaching and his students ominously predict that "[t]hey're going to find out about him." More even than Ben, Sia begins "slipping into a chilling solitude, neglecting her counseling work, her weaving, her carving, to stomp through the house in ponderous silence, attended always by the wistful clicking of Briseis' claws." She appears to be looking for something she needs badly but cannot find.

Farrell and Hamid busy themselves with preparing for the next League event, the Whalemas tournament, at which a new King will be crowned, a bunch of squires will be made knights, and there will be the usual singing and dancing and probably even a mummers' play in the evening. There will be plenty of work for musicians (Farrell's lute having been repaired), and afterwards they both plan to resign from the League.

About two weeks later Briseis summons Farrell to Sia's house, but after a thorough search he cannot find her. Briseis leads him to the linen closet, which has been stretched beyond recognition into a courtyard leading into a windowless room and up a stairway that soon leads down and sideways. They find Sia behind another door. Farrell recognizes her for what she is, dressed as he had never seen before, and bows to her, saying, "Great Queen of Heaven."

> "Don't be stupid," she replies, breaking the mood.
> "I am no queen—no more, never again—and
> there is no heaven, not the way you mean. And
> as for greatness...I sent Briseis to bring you here
> because I was lonely. Very tired, too, and very
> frightened, but mostly lonely. Do you think a

great queen would do that?"

Sia goes on to explain that the room is a duplicate of a place she was quite happy once. It's not exactly in the same place as the house, but is as much a part of the house as anything else is. It is just hard to find, even for her. It was the thing she had been looking for, and Briseis had helped her find it, as had Farrell.

When he looks out the windows, Farrell sees what Sia sees; the windows are her eyes, in a way. The vision is disturbing to him, containing a world full of suffering men, women, and children, and he begs her to make it stop. She does, although she laughs. Farrell finally asks her straightforwardly who she is. She replies:

> "I am a black stone, the size of a kitchen stove. They wash me in the stream every summer and sing over me. I am skulls and cocks, spring rain and the blood of the bull. Virgins lie with strangers in my name, the young priests throw pieces of themselves at my stone feet. I am white corn, and the wind in the corn, and the earth whereof the corn stands up, and the blind worms rolled in an oozy ball of love at the corn's roots. I am rut and flood and honeybees. Since you asked."

Farrell is surprised and angered; he had thought she was wonderful, like the Lady Kannon. Sia sets him straight:

> "Like the Lady Kannon? Is that what you thought, that I was a goddess of mercy with a thousand arms, to save a world with each one? No, no, the Lady Kannon really is a queen, and I really am only a black stone. That was my first nature, and I have not changed so much.... Not as much as perhaps I would have liked. I am stone that has washed dishes, slept in human beds, seen too many movies, but I am still stone. Stone can never be wonderful, I'm afraid."

Sia believes her power now is limited to the house, and perhaps to that very room. She could not have done what she did for Micah without help from Julie. Farrell wishes he could have seen her when she was a black stone, and Sia replies:

> "Oh, I was certainly something.... It was nice, I think, the flutes and the smoky prayers and the screaming—a long time ago, that must have been what pleased me. I intervened everywhere, absolutely everywhere, in everything, just to be doing it, just because I could.... I would have been more use to those children if I had remained all stone."

When Farrell remarks that he doesn't understand how a goddess can lose her power, she draws back slightly and looks at him with a kind a dangerous wonder before smiling:

> "Oh, very good. I never thought you would ever use that word. Well, with power it is the same for everyone—if you don't want it quite enough, it just leaves you. Power always knows, you see. And gods always lose their power, because we lose our pleasure in it, we all come to want other things, sooner or later. This is where we are different from human beings."

Farrell of course cannot resist the temptation, and he asks her what it was she wanted more than being a goddess. In reply Sia takes down her hair, as she had done on the night she tried to bend the universe for Micah Willows, and asks him to brush it for her. He does so, as he has always wanted to, and Sia reveals the secret of the universe to him.

> "I like it here.... Of all worlds, this one was made for me, with its silliness and its cruelty. And its fine trees. Nothing ever changes. For every understanding, a new terror—for each foolishness at last pulled down,

three little new insanities sprouting. Such mess, such beauty, such hopelessness. I talk to my clients, but I can never know how they get up in the morning, how any of you can ever get out of bed. One day, nobody will bother.

And still you desire one another.... And still you invent and reinvent yourselves, you manufacture entire universes, just as real and fatal as this one, all for an excuse to stumble against one another for a moment. I know gods who have come into existence only because two of you wanted there to be a reason for what they were about to do that afternoon. Listen, I tell you that on the stars they can smell your desire—there are ears of a shape you have no word for listening to your dreams and lies, tears and gruntings. There is nothing like you anywhere among all the stones in the sky, do you realize that? You are the wonder of the cosmos, possibly for embarrassing reasons, but anyway a wonder. You are the home of hunger and of boredom, and I roll in you like a dog."

She kisses him then and they make love, at the end of which he has a revelation: "Nicholas Bonner is your son." It is not a question, just a simple statement of fact. Her initial response is: "Sleep with a mortal and lose your secrets. Ben wakes up each morning knowing one more thing that I did not tell him." She shortly admits he is right.

"I was lonely. It is an occupational hazard for us, and we deal with it in different way. Some gods create worlds, entire galaxies, just to have someone intelligent and sympathetic to talk to. They are usually disappointed. Others go in for having children—they mate with each other, with humans, animals, trees, oceans, even with the elements. It is all very exhausting and takes up most of their time. But they do have the children in the end. Some of them have thousands.

I am not sure what I wanted anymore. It was long ago, and I was different. Your world existed, I remember that, but it was all fire and water then, nothing else. I had no idea that I would come to love it so much.... We have no word for love, you know. *Hunger*, degrees of hunger, that is as close as we can come. If you were a god, we would have been making hunger together."

As for Bonner, Sia tells Farrell:

"He knows I did not *have* him.... He knows I *made* him. Do you understand me?... What he knows is that I made him in myself, by myself, not even really out of loneliness, but out of contempt, such contempt for mysteries, oracles, temples, all those warrens of little half-gods and quarter-gods, that helpless vampire need that illusions have for adoration. I was going to make a child who could exist without fraudulence, who would be a god if nothing in the universe ever worshiped him. Contempt and vanity, you see. Even for a goddess, I have always been vain."

"He is not anything. You cannot make anything useful out of contempt and vanity, no matter who you are. Nicholas Bonner is not a god, not human, not a spirit of power—he is nothing, nothing but immortal and eternally enraged at me. As he should be. Can you begin to imagine what I did to him?... Can you imagine what it might be like to know certainly that you have no business existing anywhere—that there is no possible place for you from one end of the universe to the other? Can you imagine how that would feel, Joe? Knowing that you can never even die and be free of this terrible not-life, never? That is what I did to my son, Nicholas Bonner."

Sia had tried to unmake Bonner, but she lacked the power. The most she was ever able to do was to send him very far away, to limbo, but someone always summons him by mistake. While her body continuously grows older and uglier, he remains eternally fourteen.

Ben's bride Sia is thus revealed to be one of the immortal ancient gods engaged in a battle for supremacy with her son, Bonner. It is Farrell's discovery of Sia's true identity that has driven the movement of the novel, and now that all the information needed is provided to Farrell (and through him, to the reader) the climax is at hand. Bonner and Aiffe will again try to come into Sia's house, and try to send her where she has sent Bonner before. Sia believes Aiffe may be strong enough to enter the house, but perhaps not that room. She asks Farrell to stay with her until Ben returns, and he does so. "I will miss it," she tells him.

> "This hell of a place. I will miss it so much. This fat body, walking mud puddle, deceived by everything, this impossible, ruinous accident of a world, these people who would truly rather hurt one another than eat—oh, there is nothing, nothing, nothing I would not do to stay here ten minutes longer. Oh, I will leave clawmarks, I will drag mountains and forests away under my fingernails when I am dragged off. Such a stupid way to feel. I will be all dirty from clutching at this stupid planet, and the gods will laugh at me."

Farrell finally understands, and asks his last question: "When we made love, it wasn't really me, was it?... Clutching at the whole stupid planet?... I'm honored."

Sex has power in *The Folk of the Air*. Farrell first wonders what sex must be like for Ben and Sia, but dismisses the thought with a quotation from *Macbeth*: "These deeds must not be thought after these ways—so, it will make us mad." The same night he senses the power by merely being in the same house while Ben and Sia make love, but he doesn't know what it means.

> "This was an understanding intensely beyond cries or creaking springs, an awareness so strong that he sat up, sweating in the dark, smelling her pleasure, feeling Ben's laughter on his skin as if he were caught up in bed with the two of them. He tried to sleep again, but the wicked sharing invaded him from all quarters, tumbling him in his own bed like a pebble in a flash flood. Shamed and terrified, he bit his mouth and clenched around himself, but the cry clawed free of him at the last, as his body shook loose from his will, resonating helplessly to the alien joy that used him in order to savor itself that much more and had already forgotten him as it let him go."

Farrell later discovers Aiffe and Bonner having sex, and their coupling produces frightening spirits that fly through the air but ultimately have no effect on this world. Farrell thought of them as "*Aiffe's children.*" He tells Ben, "That's not just your garden-variety quickie going on back there. That is machinery." Ben more accurately describes it as "Tantric sorcery. Sex magic. Really effective if you know what you're doing. Sort of like Leg-O's—you can make all kinds of really unpleasant stuff with it. Sia said they'd be using that."

The first sending from Aiffe and Bonner's coupling "looked like a raw, bloody stomach with a crocodile's head, and it flew at them on wings edged with tiny mouths.... It had ridiculously bright blue eyes." The second monster was half-toad, half game-cock, and the third was something like a pulpy *Nutcracker Suite* mushroom with yellow human teeth and a snake's tongue. More sendings came: "goat-legged viscera, fanged cacti, huge, hound-faced slugs, creatures like stuffed toys oozing sewage, creatures like tall skeletal birds with fire pulsing between their ribs." They kept coming, "inexhaustible nightmare hybrids, chattering like parakeets, snuffling like bears." The folk of the air are not pretty, as Farrell had previously thought.

Finally, though, when Sia and Farrell make love he discovers fully the ancient power of the act.

> "Abruptly she turned, took hard hold of his shoulders, and kissed him on the mouth, pulling herself to her feet as she did so. Farrell, who had wondered often enough what that could be like and flinched slightly in his imagination from the muscular contact, dry as cast snakeskin, found that the breath was noisy and curious and full of flowers, and that kissing her was as shocking and undoing a revelation as the first chocolate he had ever tasted. The chair purred under them, pouring itself across the floor. Farrell sank through the night-colored gown to swim in Sia's absolute welcome with the frightened ease and eagerness of the small four-handed land creature that remembered the sea and became the grandfather of whales. Her breasts were as softly shapeless as he had supposed, her belly as mottled, and Farrell kissed and prowled her, laughing as she did in bedazzlement at such bounty until she put her arm around his neck and told him, 'Now look at me, now don't stop looking at me.' That became quickly hard to do, but they held tightly to each other, and Farrell never looked away from her, even when he saw the black stone and what lay before it. He only closed his eyes at the last, when her face became too beautiful and sorrowful to bear. But she smiled straight into his head *like someone else*, and all his bones went up in sunlight."

Sia sends Ben with Farrell to the Michelmas Tourney, and there he confronts Aiffe directly. "I know who you are, anyway," he tells her.

"You're Rosanna Berry and you have to take algebra over this year and you had too many cuts in P.E. and you still break out if you eat one candy bar and you still bite your nails. And a man is dead because of you, and you really think you're magic."

She replies in a chilling whisper, her immaturity showing despite her best efforts: "You are so fucking right, I'm magic. You wait, okay, you wait, you'll see how magic I am." Bonner, dressed as a juggler, merely bides his time, but Aiffe assists her father, Garth de Montfaucon, in defeating King Bohemond to become the new King.

"As long as he lived, Farrell held that strange moment motionless in his head—a stained-glass window in which a transfigured, bride-faced Aiffe forever leaned down to crown her father, as the falcons banked low above them and Leonora supported her defeated lord. In the background, the nobles of the League of Archaic Pleasures swayed close, painted in forgotten colors and looking on with unreadable, obsolete expressions. It was his last vision of many people he never saw again."

The new King, however, is immediately challenged by the Ronin Benkei, an unidentified knight who earlier defeated all comers but refused to challenge King Behemond. Beagle never explicitly identifies the Ronin Benkei, but we may presume it is the rehabilitated Micah Willows in disguise. He easily humiliates King Garth, despite Aiffe's protective spell, and then exposes what everyone present, including Farrell until the very end, took to be Aiffe and Bonner as simulacra. Ben and Farrell, knowing that Aiffe only wanted to hold them at the tournament while she and Bonner went to destroy Sia, race to the house, accompanied by Julie on her bike. Along the way they are ambushed by a freak storm summoned by Aiffe, with torrential rain, hurricane-force wind, hail, and black ice, resulting in Julie's bike in a ditch by the side of the road and Farrell's car on its last legs. Julie, who had been cursing in Japanese as Farrell had never heard her do, sums up everyone's attitude about Aiffe: "Black ice,...black ice in fucking September, and both forks bent to hell. Okay, *now* the bitch dies."

When they arrive they immediately notice a hole in the house; Aiffe is indeed strong enough to enter. Briseis is not there to lead them, so they search for Sia's room, with Ben leading them through windows, up and down stairs, past the ghosts of rooms Sia had once imagined and then forgotten about. In the end, the room found them, the doorway seeming to come roaring up to them, visibly slow down, and stop where they stand. Inside the room is full of vines and flowers like unpleasant human faces, with a clearing in which Aiffe, for want of a better word, dances. She calls Sia out of hiding with her dance, and Sia comes trudging across the clearing to her. Bonner appears and taunts Sia, who grows visibly older. Bonner sings:

> "But now you must go where I will never go again, to lie down howling in that place where you have sent me time and time, and you must wait for someone to call you back to light and warmth and pity, and no one ever will, not you, never. And this is nothing but the least bare justice of the gods, and you know that better than anyone except your son."

Aiffe continues her dance, weaving not circles but hexagons, octagons, dodecahedrons around Sia, who shuffles from foot to foot. Farrell and Julie cry. At the end, Aiffe raises her arms, with Bonner's laughter soaring as her arms fall. Farrell hides his face against Julie's wet cheek as Aiffe completes the gesture that would banish Sia, while Ben tries to save her but one of the vines catches him at the shins and drops him flat on his face. It is Briseis who stops it, crashing full tilt into Bonner and knocking him to the floor with a stone beneath his head that had not been there a second before. Farrell keeps his face hidden until he hears Sia's own laughter, a sound he would have known anywhere.

> "Young and rough, and as much of the earth as Nicholas Bonner's laugh was of that part of the universe where the stars end, she shook the green vines like a wild wind and set birds fluttering and calling where there had been no hint of any other life in the clearing. Sia said, 'The justice of the gods. As old as he is, and he still believes that.' Farrell thought he heard Briseis whine, but it was Aiffe."

She and Sia are standing so close together they almost touch. Aiffe tries to back away but cannot. Sia tells her,

> "No, no, child, it was your magic that bound me to you. A very pretty spell, beautiful even, but you let yourself be distracted. Magic is easily offended.... You see, you never would have let me near you if I looked even a little bit threatening. And I am only really good at very close range these days. I think I must need contact lenses."

An epic battle between Sia and Aiffe follows, with each side seeming to take the upper hand until, finally, inevitably, Aiffe is spent. She had,

> "in one afternoon, created illusory beings and real storms, hurled thunderbolts, torn rocks and trees to pieces, and broken into a goddess' sky, where Aiffe had flown as high as any hawk. Now she trudged through stillborn spells on stumbling feet, reduced to picking up handfuls of dirt and hurtling them into the air, kicking stones and sand away on all sides."

With that, Sia declares, "no more," and "with those words the great forest fled, and they were back in the vaguely pleasant little room that Farrell remembered, with the windows full of nothing but Avicenna twilight and an old man and woman laughing on a street corner." Sia, unlike the Lady Kannon and merciless as the stone she claims to be, begins to unravel and erase Aiffe's life, "to punish that girl in the way that we punish, that *we* have to punish such pride. I meant to strip her of every memory except that she had offended the gods and must do penance forever." Distracted by Farrell's cry of protest as he realizes what she is doing, Sia allows Bonner to intervene and he takes for himself the banishment Sia had meant for Aiffe, to Sia's great despair. She tries to save him, but is unable to do so. He was, after all, her son.

Farrell, Ben, and Julie watch the unrolling of this drama, unable to affect or alter it in any way. Sia tells them to leave, and gives Farrell a gold ring from her finger. "It is not magic, it has absolutely no useful powers. It will do nothing at all for you but remind you of me." Farrell accepts it gratefully. Sia takes the face of the young woman who had been Aiffe between her hands and addresses her and all of them in the most thematically significant passage in the novel:

> "Let's see. You have conspired against me with my son, you have tried twice to destroy me, and the second time you had visions of stealing my immortality, which is probably the worst kind of blasphemy, when I think about it. In addition to that, you have used your beautiful little gift for nothing but stupid nastiness. You have caused one man's death, another's madness and possession, and you have done worse damage that you do not even know about to people who you dragged back and forth across time for the sake of your pride, your play, your revenge. And I am expected to pardon you for no reason but to show off to a friend whose idea of

interceding is to tell me that she hates the gods.... What have I come to, indeed, for my last act in this world?"

After warning them that the house is falling and they must leave or die, she continues. "The girl will stay with me, I will do what I can do. What are you waiting for, good-bye kisses? I am done with hellos and good-byes, done with this place, done with you. Get out of my house now!" Briseis leads them out.

Sia's will, written years before Ben even met her, leaves him everything except Briseis, whom Sia gives to Farrell. Bonner was the only reason she remained in human shape; he was her responsibility. Now that he is gone, as Sia said she is done with all of them. Farrell continues to dream about Sia, though, and eventually Julie tells him he has to go to her, wherever and whatever she is. Neither Julie nor Ben can join him on his quest, but Briseis can and does. On his way out of town he sees Rosanna, who used to be Aiffe, who recognizes him but remembers nothing of the witchcraft in her past or her struggle with Sia. In response to Farrell's question all she can say is, "I was sick. I'm fine now. I was really sick.... I was pretty delirious,...I don't remember a whole lot." She does not remember Nicholas Bonner, either: "Actually, there's a whole lot of people in the League I don't know anymore. I'm not as much into that whole thing as I used to be." When he presses her on what Sia said to her in that room, she exhibits bewildered tears, and Farrell wisely leaves her before he can be arrested for harassment. Briseis will lead him to Sia, if anyone can.

While on one level *The Folk of the Air* is a novel about sex, and on another level a novel about power, ultimately it is a novel about the power of forgiveness. Sia tells Julie, upon learning that the young woman has been consecrated to the Japanese goddess Kannon, "Your grandmother was very wise. She had no idea what gift to give you for your life in this country that was already snatching you away from her, but she knew that human beings everywhere need mercy most of all." The goddess Kannon's great gift to Farrell through her smile is the ability to forgive himself for several very terrible if unnamed things. As he later runs from the demon knights bent on killing, he prays to Kannon for her pity, and he receives it although at great cost. The *denouement* of the novel shows us the teen-aged girl who had been Aiffe, laughing and whispering with her girlfriends as teen-aged girls have done from the beginning of time. Although she had conjured a demon and caused pain and even death, she is forgiven. Sia is gone, but she forgives her son and grieves for him even as she banishes him eternally.

Beagle has created a fascinating world in which the ancient gods survive, and in which they envy and admire human beings for our capacity to love. Since, in *The Folk of the Air*, there is no heaven and there is no hell, here and now is all that we have. We should forgive and be forgiven in turn. Farrell, Ben, and Julie strive to do so and to make the most of their time here. Beagle suggests that we should do the same.

Beagle has promised a substantial rewrite of *The Folk of the Air*, to be called *Avicenna*. Its publication has not yet been announced at the time of the publication of this book, and no information regarding the nature of the revisions is available.

CHAPTER FOUR:
THE INNKEEPER'S SONG

While in his first three novels Beagle uses the omniscient third person narrator, in *The Innkeeper's Song* he experiments with a variety of narrative voices. The Prologue is written in the familiar third person, but the succeeding chapters are each written from the point of view of one of the characters, not in strictly chronological order and not always by the character most central to the action. The plot is thus revealed in the form of a report compiled after the fact from disparate sources. That this experiment not only succeeds but succeeds seamlessly and brilliantly is a tribute to Beagle's developing skill. While he may remain best-known for *The Last Unicorn*, in part because it was made into a successful animated film, *The Innkeeper's Song* is both his personal favorite and his best novel. He loves the characters and landscape he created so much he keeps returning to them with independent stories and novellas; the novel simply didn't tell enough of the story to satisfy him.

The Prologue begins with a variation of the beginning of the nursery rhyme's "Once upon a time," but this is not to be a fairy tale (or even a homage to fairy tales like *The Last Unicorn*). Readers learn that this is a world in which magic exists, but this is not a comically magical world but a serious one: a girl dies. Readers also learn that that music, particularly singing, has power here, and that there are strange and powerful beasts abroad; we may not yet know what a *sheknath* is, but we know that it roars and scares the sheep. Finally, readers learn of a black woman on a horse, dressed in shirt and leggings of rough leather, and carrying no weapon save a walking stick slung at her saddlebow. We do not yet know her name, but we know she is important (if for no other reason than the narrator spends a lot of time in the Prologue describing her), and she sings. Her singing literally raises the dead girl, whose name we also learn was Lukassa, and the black woman places her ring on the dead girl's finger. The boy who loves Lukassa, named Tikat, sets out on a quest to retrieve her. Three of the main characters—Lukassa, Tikat, and the yet un-named black woman—are thus introduced in the Prologue, and the outline of the story—a quest in a magical world—is established.

The chapters in *The Innkeeper's Song* are not numbered, but each is named for the character who narrates it. The sixteen-year-old Stable Boy is the first narrator, and he tells us that he was the first to see "them," but he doesn't immediately tell us who "they" are. Instead we find out that the stable boy is named Rosseth, that he is lusts after a slightly older brown woman named Marinesha (which means *scent of the morning*), and that he works for "old Karsh," who is fat and kind to animals, and who named him. Names, it seems, are important in this world.

In his own time Rosseth tells us that "they" are three women on horseback, one black, one brown, and one "so pale that to call her 'white' has no meaning." We are prepared for the black woman and the pale girl, but do not expect a brown woman to be with them. The black woman is named Lal, but she has a longer name which Rosseth does not know how to say. Lal is the first black woman he has ever seen, and previously he had believed, along with most other people, that there were none, although he had occasionally seen black men. She asks him if there is an inn where the three of them can stay, and since Rosseth works at Karsh's inn his answer is obvious even if he is tongue-tied. Rosseth then notices a fox riding in the brown woman's saddlebag, looking at him as though it knew his real name, the one he himself does not know. Lal invites Rosseth to accompany them to the inn, and he rides with her on her horse, smelling the scent of the sea in her leather clothing but mostly registering her own scent. He forgets about Marinesha for the rest of the day.

The Innkeeper, Karsh, is the next narrator, and his voice is honest and ironic. We learn that his inn is called The Gaff and Slasher, that Karsh was born in another country, and that his father and grandfather before him were also innkeepers. He is neither a soldier nor a bard, but he tells us that some time after the events of the novel take place, someone composed a song about the three women, in which Karsh plays a major and possibly martial role. He will clearly be a major character, if not **the** major character; after all, he is the Innkeeper of the title of the novel, and it is his song (or the song about him?) with which we are concerned. And apparently the fox will figure prominently in the action as well; Karsh tells us, "That bloody fox is in the song, too."

The song, although not part of the novel proper, is set out as a frontispiece and deserves citing at length.

> "There came three ladies at sundown:
> one was as brown as bread is brown,
> one was black, with a sailor's sway,
> and one was pale as the moon by day.
>
> The white one wore an emerald ring,
> the brown led a fox on a silver string,
> and the black one carried a rosewood cane
> with a sword inside, for I saw it plain.
>
> They took my own room, they barred the door,
> they sang songs I never had heard before.
> My cheese and mutton they did destroy,
> and they called for wine and the stable boy.
>
> And once they quarreled and twice they cried—
> Their laughter blazed through the countryside.

The ceiling shook and the plaster flew,
and the fox ate my chickens, all but two.

They rode away with the morning sun,
the white like a queen, the black like a nun,
and the brown one singing with scarlet joy,
and I'll have to get a new stable boy."

The song is reminiscent of the songs from *The Last Unicorn* in many ways; each stanza uses Beagle's favorite AABB rhyme scheme, and the incongruous elements are foregrounded. It seems clear that although he claims not to be a bard, the composer of the song is Karsh.

In any case, when he first meets them some instinct tells Karsh that the three women are trouble, and he tries to send them elsewhere. When Lal carefully reveals the sword concealed within her walking stick and the fox kills one of his chickens, however, he relents. He first shows them a room he usually keeps for tanners and fur traders, then a room where a prostitute once plied her trade, but the black one rejects the first with a raised eyebrow and the white one rejects the second when she senses death and madness there. He offers them his own room and they accept. There in fact had been madness and death in the second room, and Karsh is somewhat afraid of what the white one knows and how she knows it, although he merely marks her down as mad for the moment.

Tikat is the next narrator, and he has begun to develop the traits of a hero while on his quest to recover Lukassa from Lal. His chase of them is reminiscent of the chase of Aragorn, Gimli, and Legolas of the orcs bearing Merry and Pippin in Book Three of *The Lord of the Rings*: he never gains, and no matter whether he rests or gallops all night they are always beyond his sight come dawn. He begins to starve, and after the eleventh, twelfth, or perhaps fifteenth day (he honestly cannot tell) his horse dies under him. He cannot eat the horse (not for reasons of daintiness or loyalty; he simply cannot cut through her tough hide), but he does eat the first bird that comes to feed on her. The bird sustains him for two more days, and brings him to his senses for long enough to realize where he is, but he retreats more and more into dreams. In one of the dreams is an old man wearing a faded scarlet coat riding a black horse and whispering to it as he leans upon its neck. The old man looks directly into Tikat's face, and his eyes laugh with such laughter that Tikat never hopes to see again in his life. The vision jars him awake, and he is able then to sleep with more settled dreams, of four hounds riding horses past him.

When Tikat wakes again he finds that his dreams have come true, in that the hounds he dreamt of chasing the man in the scarlet coat are actually four Mildasis, northern warriors who raid into the south and who pride themselves on their horses. The Mildasis have caught the man in the scarlet coat and accuse him of stealing one of their prize horses. They savagely beat him while threatening worse for anyone foolish enough to do what he has done. The man has rolled himself up into a ball and is being kicked from one to another. Tikat needs a horse, and knows that the religious Mildasis will probably kill the old man as a sacrifice to their sun god at sunset. As the Mildasis complete their ceremony he steals a gray horse he has picked out and scatters the others, galloping away clutching the horse's back. At the last moment the old man in the scarlet coat jumps up behind him and they both escape on Rabbit, as Tikat thereafter calls the gray horse, with the old man taunting the Mildasis as he rides to freedom.

Tikat acknowledges that it is the old man who saves him, who holds onto him as he falls asleep in the saddle, who guides the Rabbit through the night ride. When he wakes Tikat is on the ground, wrapped in the old man's coat. The old man is gone. Tikat vows that he will not die until he finds Lukassa, and then sees a fox, trotting up with a bird in his mouth. The fox waits until he is certain Tikat sees him, then changes into the old man. He will not say if he is a fox who can turn into a man, or a man who can turn into a fox; he simply tells Tikat, "The bird can turn into us. That's what matters."

The shape-changer tells Tikat that he is the companion of a great lady from a far shore—not a black one, but a brown one—named Nyateneri. Readers thus learn the name of the remaining major character. He does not serve, but is her comrade, her equal. The business with the Mildasis was merely his sport; regardless of how it might have looked, he was never in any danger. He then surprises Tikat by telling him that he will never catch them, not on a Mildasi horse nor on any other. And if he did, he would soon wish he hadn't. Responding to Tikat's suggestion that the black woman must be a great wizard, the old man tells him:

> "The woman's no more magical than you are, but what she does not know about flight and following, about tracking and covering tracks, about sending the hounds howling off after their own smell, even I do not know. And now my lady Nyateneri has joined her—yes, as you guessed—and between the pair of them, a poor fox can only chew his paws and pray not to be too corrupted by their subtlety. Give over, boy, go home."

Tikat tells him to tell them both that Lukassa's man is coming after her, but the old man knows that Tikat can never find them without his help. He demands the locket Tikat wears around his neck as payment for his help, and although reluctant because it was Lukassa's gift for his thirteenth name-day, he gives it to him. The old man turns back into the fox, and is off the find the black Mildasi horse again. He will leave Tikat a trail to follow.

Lal narrates the next chapter, and we learn that she has had a dream sent by someone she refers to as *my friend* without being more specific, and that she has had more dreams since she put her ring on Lukassa's finger. These are not the bad dreams, but merely the way *her friend* talks to her. The bad dreams are far older, and are the way she bleeds. She is Lalkhamsin-lhamsolal, sleek and lean and fearless, known as Sailor Lal and Swordcane Lal and Lal-Alone. She had wept and screamed in the night, every night from the time she was twelve years old, until *her friend* gave her the emerald ring. She was to keep it until she found one whose need was greater than her own, and she had given it to Lukassa. *Her friend* promised her that she would then need the ring no longer, but it had not proven so. All of the old rape terrors had returned:

> "Jaejan, with his mouth like a hot mudhole. Jaejan and his nameless friend, and me not three hours stolen from my home. Shavak, Daradara, who killed him, and what she did to me in his blood. Loum, that little boy, I could not have helped him, I could not have helped, I was little too. Unavavia, with his striped nightgowns and his knives. Edkilos, who pretended to be kind. Bismaya, who sold me."

Lal had been raised from birth to be a storyteller, a chronicler, a rememberer; the word is *inbarati*. By the time she was nine years old Lal could sing the history of every family in her province, both in the formal tongue and the market speech her teachers whipped her for using. She knew every battle song, beast-tale, every version of the founding of the city and their floods and plagues and droughts, not to mention every legend, love story, and tale of magic. Bismaya had been her cousin, her playmate, and her best friend, and she had arranged for Lal to be stolen and sold out of a child's boredom. She dreamt of her, dead of childbirth before Lal could kill her, more than any of the others. Lal dealt with her nightmares before receiving the ring from *her friend* by telling herself stories from sunset to sunrise.

Lal had received two dreams from *her friend*, the second of such intensity that she could not ignore it, and she immediately set out to save Lukassa. She felt she owed *her friend* her very soul; he had found her, "an escaped never-mind-what...hiding naked under a fish basket at the wharf at Lameddin." He was "a magus powerful enough to crumble great ships of war into the sea like biscuits in soup (and kind enough to send dolphins to bear the sailors home)." After her rescue, at first Lukassa sleeps at night like the dead she had been, while Lal waits for another message from *her friend*. It finally comes to her in the Barrens, on the night they ran out of road, not as a dream but as a vision rising out of the fire. *Her friend* has just enough strength to call to her for help, but no one else. He points northerly, and a ribbon of light streams from his finger across the Barrens and to the mountains beyond. She swears she will come to find him, and he vanishes, the glowing green trail lingering on the hills.

Lukassa remembers nothing of her life before her death, but insists that Lal tell her the story of being saved over and over again. Lal explains also that *her friend* is not her lover but her teacher, who helped her when there was no help for her in the world. Lal tells Lukassa also about Lukassa's lover, who has been doggedly following them since the night Lal took her away. Lal suggests that Lukassa should simply wait for him to catch up, but Lukassa knows only death and Lal and would stay with her. So they continue on together.

Nyateneri came to them on their fourth day in the hills. Lal sensed magic about her, with a skill enhanced by spending as much time with a magician as she had. That was how Nyateneri was able to surprise Lal despite making no effort to muffle her horse's hoofbeats or to take other stealth precautions. It was not Nyateneri's own magic—she was no wizard, whatever else she was—but there was surely some sort of spell upon her.

Nyateneri was the color of strong tea, taller than Lal, powerful, left-handed, and she carried a bow. Her clothing was common west-country stuff, nothing matching. She road a roan and trailed a shaggy little black horse with the far-away yellow eyes of a carnivore. Lal had never seen a horse like that. It is, we soon discover, the black horse of the Mildasis that the shape-changer stole.

Lal greets Nyateneri in the tongue of her people, but the

brown woman answers in a different language. Nyateneri tells Lal her name and that she is daughter of Lomadis, daughter of Tyrrin, and surprises Lal by calling her Sailor Lal, Lal-after-dark. When Lal denies her identity and gives Nyateneri one of her traveling names, Nyateneri merely recites the evidence: a black woman with a swordcane at her saddle, following a green night trail to the aid of a great wizard in greater trouble, when it is widely known that "Lalkhamsin-khamsolal—she almost had it correctly—was once the adopted companion and student of the magician—" At that Lal cuts her off by interjecting, "The magician whose name is not spoken.... Some call him the Teacher; some the Hidden One; some, just the Old Man. I call him—what I call him."

"And I have always called him the *Man Who Laughs*. One who knows him as you do may understand." Lal does understand and knows that, whoever she may be, Nyateneri knows *her friend*. She welcomes Nyateneri, but notices when the brown woman's hood falls back when she alights that her graying brown hair was chopped into random patterns of tufts and whorls and spearpoint strips, in the style of a convent. Lal knows a convent cut when she sees it, but she does not know this one.

The fox soon follows his nose out of the saddlebag, and Nyateneri introduces him as her traveling companion of many years. Lukassa immediately takes to the fox, carrying him everywhere, feeding him scraps, and singing to him. She begs to be allowed to have the fox sleep with her, and after a sharp call to him in his own language Nyateneri assures Lal that he will not harm her. Lal confronts Nyateneri regarding her convent past, but the brown woman assures the black one that there is no price on her head, and that no one wants her back, anywhere in the world. Satisfied, Lal tells Nyateneri the name she has always called *her friend*.

The fox takes up the narrative at this point. His voice is rapid, self-centered, untrustworthy, and unmistakable for any other we have heard so far. He tells us that he knows things about

Nyateneri that no one else knows—for example, how she is always ready for the two men who are following. Not the boy—she does not worry about him—but two men, following for so long, running swiftly. If they catch up, there will be at least two dead. The fox would prefer that the dead not include Nyateneri; without her there would be no more riding in saddlebags, no more fire on cold nights.

The fox begins his part of the story while they are staying at the inn. In his man-shape, the fox had told Tikat that there would be a trail, but it is the fox that leaves the trail, not the man-shape, about whom the fox speaks in third person. He takes the man-shape when Nyateneri is not looking, and the white-whiskered grandfatherly old man sits in the bar of the inn and obtains intelligence from Rosseth and Marinesha. Karsh, however, does not like man-shape. Rosseth admires Lal, but the porter Gatti admires Nyateneri, and becomes obsessed with her. When the brown woman notices him noticing her she asks Karsh about him and seems angry that he has been at the inn for eighteen years. He is not who she is looking for.

Each day for twelve days Lal and Nyateneri ride off, looking for the old wizard, leaving Lukassa at the inn. The fox over-hears Nyateneri tell Lal that he is here, and that tomorrow they will find him. He is too weak, she says, to come to them in another dream. When she tentatively suggests that magicians, too, die, Lal challenges the thought: "Not this one. Not this way. Magicians die sometimes because they grow greedy, because they become frightened, but this one wants nothing, fears nothing, laughs at everything. No power has any hold on him." Nyateneri responds sharply, "You don't know that. You know nothing about him, and no more do I. Tell me how old he is, tell me where he came from, tell me about his family, his own teacher, his real home.... Tell me whom he loves."

Lal concedes the truth of it, but insists, "He loves somebody. Somebody knows his name." Knowing someone's true name is a sign of love in this world, and it is also a sign of power. Lal continues: "You saw him. No one could have done from a distance what has been done to him. Whoever has broken his magic was deeply trusted, greatly loved. It must be so." They further agree it was no one whom either of them knows.

Rosseth brings them dinner, having observed that they came in late, and they send him away with little thought. The fox, though, sees everything—how Rosseth can't breathe in Lal's presence, how her smallest touch captivates him. Lal merely remarks, "A good child. He is full of wonder, and he really does work very hard.... I suppose my—I suppose our friend has said exactly the same thing about us, many times. To whomever he loved."

Lukassa, who has also been present but silent, now tells Lal and Nyateneri that they found the wizard today, not tomorrow. They have been where he was, where something happened. They were at a place of death—she smells it on them. When Nyateneri points out that Lukassa used the same trick with Karsh on the day they arrived, Lal counters with: "It is no trick.... She knows death as we do not, she can tell where it has passed. And you will have to take my word for this." Nyateneri agrees.

The two women finally decide that the place to which Lukassa refers must be the tower, and they agree to investigate further the next day. Lukassa is to come with them: "Our very own little deathstalker," as Nyateneri calls her. But Lukassa surprises them both by walking up to Nyateneri and saying to her, while looking directly into her eyes:

> "I belong to no one. Lal told me. I am not a hat, not a pet fox, not somebody who does a trick. I am your companion, and Lal's, or I am not, and if I am, then from tomorrow I go where you go, and there's an end to that.... For I have come a longer journey than you have."

Nyateneri accepts the rebuke, and restrings her bow in preparation for the morrow. The fox's final report of the night is that, before she sleeps, Lukassa asks him for his name, and tells him they call her Lukassa, but she doesn't know. Nyateneri speaks to him in their private language, and tells him that the old man is to drink no more ale downstairs.

Marinesha continues the tale, describing how the fox jumped out the window and ran away the next morning. She thinks Rosseth "can be quite pleasant, in his way, but he is simply an irresponsible boy." By the time the action of the novel is completed she will change her mind, just as the reader will.

Marinesha tells us a couple more local names: a *tharakki* is an unpleasant small animal that once or twice has emerged from under the bathhouse, and one of the trees is a *maril* tree, upon which she likes to hang the wash. But her primary purpose in this chapter is to narrate the arrival of two small, thin, brown men whose feet make no sound and who are asking after a tall woman with a bow and arrow and a pet fox, and whose "pet name" is Nyateneri. They have a foreign accent which makes her nervous, and when one of them put his hand on her shoulder she cries out with the heat of it and feels it for a week afterward. Without quite knowing why, Marinesha lies to the strangers and says there is no such person there, and none has come through recently. They ask to see the landlord, and she takes them to where they can wait for Karsh. When she goes back to hang up her washing she doesn't even know she is crying until she is done.

Although a reader might expect Karsh to be the next narrator, Beagle gives us Rosseth instead, a hint that the erstwhile stable boy may be more important than we thought. Rosseth tells how that morning all three women rode out together for the first time. They appear to him as

> "sudden strangers beyond my conception of forgiveness, alien as I had never imagined them, although I should have. I was too young then to see past my own skin, and my skin was in love with them, all three. Yet I never saw them more truly than I did that morning."

Rosseth is reciting his account from far in the future, when he has gained insight into himself and others. He tells us,

> "Lal and Nyateneri and Lukassa were shadows of the future, although I didn't know it, and what I feared and adored and hungered for in them was myself-to-be, as you might say. But I didn't know that either, of course: only that I had never in my life been hurt so by the sound of women laughing in a little rented room upstairs."

Rosseth soon tells us why his account follows that of Marinesha; he witnesses her confrontation with the two small, silent men. She cannot speak, merely clings to him and whimpers, which in turn frightens him. When he hoists his trusty spade (he has been mucking out stalls) and goes inside, he sees the two strangers: "Small men and slender, graceful in their movements, almost dainty, their plain brown clothes fitting them like fur. They reminded me of *shakris*, those hot, rippling little animals that follow the smell of blood down holes, up trees, anywhere, endlessly." Although he is frightened nearly out of his wits, he resists their questioning; his fear makes him angry. Had they allowed him to, he would have told them everything; Nyateneri told him afterward that it was brave of him to keep silent but he knew better. He has just enough of Karsh's "idiot-stubbornness," as he calls it, to behave like an idiot, like a rock, "even when [his] bowels are falling to the floor." At that point Karsh comes back from the market.

The innkeeper takes up the tale, but not without a diversion in his inimitable style. Karsh tells us of having gone to the market with his father when he was a child, setting the stage for his own mood at that point. "There have been times," he tells us,

> "when I wouldn't have minded walking into The Gaff and Slasher to look up the stairs and see that fool of a boy pinned to the wall with his neck half-wrung, but

all I wanted to deal with then was a gallon of my own red ale, and this was one plaguey annoyance too many, especially from outlanders."

He tells the men to put the boy down, and when they do so they tell him they are looking for a woman who is a friend of theirs, "A good, *good* friend? It is most, most urgent?" Karsh registers the voice as "[a] southern voice, like hers, but with something else to it, a kind of restless twitch that isn't southern at all." He knows they mean Nyateneri, and has no reason not to tell them she is not staying there, but instead he asks Rosseth if she is here. He replies, truthfully enough, "They went out this morning. I don't know when they'll be back." The men say they will wait in her room, but Karsh pulls them up short; the rooms are private. He does not shout, but they hear him just the same; his father had taught him how to catch a guest's ear without losing either the guest or his own ear. He tells them they can wait in the taproom, and offers to stand each of them a pint of ale; he has learned that a joke and a free drink take care of most misunderstandings. When Gatti and some itinerant actors in search of a card game come in, and Rosseth moves to his side, the two men look at each other and at the assemblage. There is no doubt in Karsh's mind that the two men could kill them all barely raising a sweat, but apparently it isn't worth either the sweat or the clamor to them and they leave as silently as they came.

Rosseth offers to go after Nyateneri to warn her and tell her the men are looking for her, "red and pale by turns, sweating, and shaking, the way it happens when you're either going to soil your breeches or kill people." Karsh catches him at the door.

Nyateneri takes up the narrative for the first time, at the point in the morning when the three women ride out. Having been the subject of much discussion by and among the other characters, her narrative voice is highly anticipated by the reader, and Beagle does not disappoint. She first tells us that she sees Rosseth watching them from hiding, finding it odd since there was never anything furtive about him when it came to them:

"he wore his worship on his sleeve as a bird wears its feathers, and it gave him color and flight, as feathers will." The other two did not see him; Lal was singing one of her long, incredibly tuneless songs to herself, and Lukassa's presence "changed even my smell and set the hairs of my body at war with each other. I know why now, of course, but then all I could imagine was that I had been far too long away from ordinary human company."

Nyateneri likes Corcorua, the nearest to a proper town that she ever saw in the northern wilderness, with its tired soil but interesting apple brandy. She could have come to like the people there as much as the brandy, and she bought a fine dagger at the market "at a price that was shameful but almost fair." As they ride out of town, Nyateneri and Lal talk about their friend, who also liked places like the town and has a revolting passion for *limbri*, "that awful tooth-melting candied fruit from Sharan-Zek." Nyateneri is certain that, although he may be gone now, he has been there recently. Lal believes her, but is going to look at the old red tower, on Lukassa's advice.

Lal tells Lukassa to lead them, and Lukassa's horse is off and running before Lal and Nyateneri even know she has gone. When they catch up with her in the hills outside of town, Lukassa continues straight to the red tower as if she knows the way of old. The tower is as much a ruin as a building could be without falling down, but it stands out in the lonely hills as just the sort of place he would have made for himself. Nyateneri blames herself for not having thought of that earlier.

Lukassa leads the way on foot, Lal and Nyateneri following silently. It was as long, tiring, and smelly an ascent as it had been the first time they were there, and Nyateneri fondly recalls the look in Rosseth's eyes as he watched them leave on their presumably heroic quest that morning. There is too much going on in his head, she thinks, and he has no idea of his own worldly beauty. There was no combination more attractive, although she needs no more trouble than she has.

While Nyateneri and Lal have trouble keeping to the path,

it is not so for Lukassa. Nyateneri asks Lal to explain exactly how Lukassa knows about their friend, when they are done with their journey; it is the least she can do. Lal declines, however; it is not hers to tell. The tower is double built, with a strong core inside the failing exterior, and it is here that Lukassa goes, straight to an inner chamber.

The chamber is cold. Magic does not have a smell, but it leaves a place where it has been very cold. Her friend had told her that it the cold was the breath of the other side, the place from which magic visits us, "like a neighbor's cat, whom we coax over the fence with bits of chicken to hunt out mice." There has been a struggle in the room, and the floor is covered with trampled chalk and charcoal marks neither Lal nor Nyateneri could interpret. Lukassa, who has always before been mild as the grave, shows them a contorted face and screams at them, "Can you see nothing, can you feel nothing? It was here—it was here!" Responding to Lal's question, Lukassa tells them that their friend had been in the room, and that with him was *his* friend, and that the Others had come from the corner. Lal and Nyateneri know immediately that it is not a corner, but a door, an open door, which will remain long after the tower is rubble. The two men fought, and then the Others came.

Nyateneri knows that the Others do not come without a call, and asks Lukassa who summoned them. But Lukassa could not, or would not, say. Lal states the obvious: "Magic. They fought with magic." Lal then puts the question:

> "Lukassa, one of those two men was the man we have sought so long, the old man who sang over his vegetable garden. If it were not for him—. No one but you can help us to find him, and you would be dead at the bottom of a river but for him. What happens from this moment is your choice."

Lukassa returns to herself in that moment, and tells them that the old man battled someone called Arshadin. He became terrible with fear and sorrow and loneliness, and he struck back with such bitter thunder that the one called Arshadin lost power for that moment. In his fear Arshadin called upon the Others for aid. Lukassa reads it all in the stones; it is written everywhere. The friend of their friend died, but he rose again; the Others whom he summoned killed him, but he did not die. The old man fled, and his friend pursued him. Lukassa did not know where.

An actress staying at the inn, Lisonje, takes up the tale from there with a bit of comic relief. She witnessed Tikat's arrival, exhausted, asking for Lukassa. Lisonje knew the name, since she had heard Rosseth talking in his sleep about Lukassa, Lal, and Nyateneri, dreaming of sweet nights with all three. Lisonje tells Tikat that Lukassa has ridden out with her friends, and goes to find Rosseth, who scrounges some soup for Tikat. She tells Tikat that Lukassa's friends were a black woman and a brown warrior. Tikat can barely keep awake, and they must peel his clothes that are caked with his own blood off of him, but he tells them that he has come for Lukassa, and they are to tell her so. Although Tikat has no money, Rosseth thinks Karsh will take him on as an employee and allow him to sleep in the barn.

Tikat continues, telling us that when he awoke he asked about the Rabbit, and was told he had already bitten two horses and one actor, so everything was all right. Rosseth tries to help him, but Tikat refuses and the two form a bond of sorts. Rosseth takes Tikat to Karsh, and Tikat notices Karsh's gingerbread body but piercing eyes. There is more to him, Tikat realizes, than bread pudding. While agreeing to feed Tikat and give him shelter, Karsh casually asks Rosseth about the two men, but receives no reply.

Rosseth of course goes on from there, narrating the return of Lal, Nyateneri, and Lukassa. Rosseth's only concern is to warn Nyateneri about the two men, but Tikat has eyes only for Lukassa. Nyateneri was neither frightened nor surprised, although for a moment her hand tightened on Rosseth's shoulder as he leaned against her horse to tell her everything the men had said and done. Lukassa, meanwhile, who remembers nothing of Tikat from before her death, tries to get away from him and insists that they make him stop saying who he is as if she should know him. Lal salutes him for his tracking ability as well as his ability to love, and tells Nyateneri that he is Lukassa's betrothed. Lukassa bolts through the inn door, and Tikat reluctantly allows her to go. Rosseth, who has known Tikat, proud and stubborn and cranky, less than three hours, and whose heart would break for him, takes Tikat and the horses to the barn. It is while he is on his way to help Marinesha clear away dinner that he is accosted by the fox, in man-shape, whom he does not yet know. The grandfatherly figure tells him that Nyateneri has gone to the bathhouse and wishes Rosseth to attend her there. The request does not strike him as unusual, although Nyateneri is the only guest to use the steam-bath that Rosseth knows of, and he savors an opportunity to see her naked through a crack in the wall. Instead, he sees her attacked by the two strange men who had been following her. She has a dagger in her left hand and a towel wrapped around her right arm, and the men, whom Rosseth dubs Blue Eyes and Half-Mouth, are unarmed.

What follows is an epic fight, with first one side and then the other ascendant. "Nyateneri," says Rosseth, "plainly had no desire to come to close quarters with Blue Eyes and Half-Mouth, unarmed or no: her goal was the door and the night beyond. For their part, they wanted nothing but to get past her dagger, and room to use their long, thin hands." She cannot kill them, and elude them as she might she cannot get out of the bathhouse; the end seems certain. The wild card in the fight, though, is the fire trench in the middle of the bathhouse, and Nyateneri uses it to her advantage. Things still go against her, however, and she courageously prepares her final stand, with one hand dangling uselessly but with defiance on her lips. At the final instant Rosseth realizes that he is something more than a pair of eyes peering through a crack in a wall, and he pours the water he has brought to make steam. In the subsequent confusion Nyateneri kills one of the men with a single dagger thrust; Rosseth, as he says, "promptly began my new life of active stupidity by pushing the door open"; and both Blue Eyes and Nyateneri tumble on top of him, Rosseth kicking the man in the stomach and Nyateneri killing him with her bare hands. Nyateneri thanks him in a quiet, tired voice, and tells him that until he opened that door, she was finished.

Rosseth's nose is broken, and Nyateneri strokes his head in her lap until the bleeding stops. She then fetches her robe, while Rosseth wonders that nothing ever happens the way he imagines it. When asked why he was carrying the water rather than Marinesha, whom she had requested, Rosseth tells Nyateneri that it was the old man who had told him to come. In answer to his question as to why the men had come looking for her, Nyateneri crouches beside him, looking into his eyes and putting her injured hand lightly on the side of his neck, saying, "Rosseth, if one thing goes against my nature more than any other, it is lying to a person who has just saved my life. Please don't make me do it." He does not, so long as she will tell him some day, which she promises to do. And then she kisses him on his injured nose.

Karsh continues at this point, with a diversion about the queen, or perhaps king now, who rules the country. Or perhaps there has been another military coup. It doesn't really matter who is in power; the tax collectors stay the same, whoever rules. Nyateneri has reported the two killers to him, and rather than wait for the county magistrate in four or five days, Karsh suggests that what is wanted is a shovel and silence; he deals in forgetfulness. Lal, who has joined them along with Lukassa, dismisses both Karsh and Rosseth, much to the stable boy's dismay, and says that the three women will handle the problem.

Lal then narrates the next chapter, and we discover that when she and Lukassa are summoned to the bathhouse she has been drinking, which has caused her to become sullen, brooding, and resentful. After they bury the two bodies and return to the inn she rounds on Nyateneri, angry with her because she had deceived them and endangered their lives when she said no one pursued her. Nyateneri, although younger and stronger than Lal, puts the bed between them and holds up her hands for peace. She points out that she is not the only one with secrets; they never told her about Lukassa's death and resurrection. That was something Lal had not learned from her friend, who knew that there was no way of raising the dead that was not wrong in its very nature.

This reference to her friend so infuriates Lal that she reverts to her oldest childhood tongue, and of course Nyateneri cannot understand her. She repeats what she said in the common tongue, informing Nyateneri that she had resurrected Lukassa by using her friend's old gardening spell. At this Nyateneri collapses on the bed in laughter, joined by the fox and ultimately by both Lal and Lukassa. The tension had been so strong that something was needed to break it, and Lal's disclosure did the trick.

Lukassa then explains to Nyateneri what it had been like to die, and to live again. She remained Lukassa throughout, yet when she rose again she was different. She had no name, and no one could call her. The thought of having no name brings tears to Lal, the first time she has cried in a long time, and the first time any living person except her friend if he still lived has seen her cry.

While Nyateneri goes to fetch more wine from Karsh, Lal tells Lukassa that there is in fact one person who can still call her back: Tikat. Lukassa shudders at the thought, but Lal knows that if Lukassa wants that part of herself back it must be Tikat who gives it to her. Lukassa tells Lal that she does not know if she wants that part of herself back.

When Nyateneri returns with the wine, it takes less than one bottle for her to begin to tell them about the convent she has fled. She had been there twenty-one years, from the time she was nine. She has been fleeing them for eleven years, which makes her forty-one years old. The first trackers caught her in less than a year. There had been two other teams since. They hunt in teams, and there is no losing them; they must be killed. When word gets back to the convent, another team is sent. She was the first ever to survive three teams. They do not allow anyone to leave and survive because the place has too many secrets. Everyone who enters must have at least one secret to tell; Nyateneri had secrets enough for them. They were happy to take her in, and she was content there. She grew strong there, and she learned a great deal.

Although Nyateneri knew something about pain when she entered the convent, they taught her a great deal more. Lal, though, knows a South Islands trick to fool pain, a little, and she works it on Nyateneri's broken hand.

Nyateneri left the convent because they offered her power, indeed had been training her for it since childhood. They wanted her to take her place among them, a superior being among superior beings, and in the instant of the offer she knew that power was not what she wanted. Since she could not say no to such an offer, she said yes, and she ran away that very night. She has been running ever since.

Nyateneri finally reveals her most important secret: there are always three on the hunting team. The third moves away from the other two, watching but not with them. He is always the cleverest, and he is never far away. At that moment, there is a very gentle knock at the door.

The reader has been led, perhaps, to expect the entrance of the third assassin at this point, followed by another epic battle, but what we get instead is a rapid sequence of fourteen chapters, ranging in length from one line to two pages. The point of view shifts quickly from Nyateneri, to Lal, to the Fox, to Rosseth, to Nyateneri, to Lal, to the Fox, to Rosseth, to Nyateneri, to Lal, to the Fox, to Rosseth, to Nyateneri, to Lal. For it is Rosseth who enters, and what follows is an uninhibited and entirely unexpected group sex scene. The participants are Rosseth, Nyateneri, Lal, and even Lukassa, while the Fox watches and reports and seeks pigeons in the rafters. The bodies are so mixed and matched that not even the participants are sure what is going on, but the love is both sweet and necessary for all of them.

But if the group sex scene is a surprise to the reader, even more surprising is what is revealed during it: Nyateneri is a man, not a woman. He has been under an enchantment for eleven years, disguised well enough to live and travel with real women on terms of daily intimacy without arousing the slightest suspicion but not transformed. When Lal discovers the truth, he informs her that it was her friend, The Man Who Laughs, who taught him how. He always knew he was a man, and it was Rosseth's innocent desire that brought his own growling out of a long winter sleep. "All I know," says Nyateneri, "is that I kissed them all, woke to their kisses, no more or no less as Nyateneri than as the man who was not Rosseth when Lal cried out and buried her hands in his hair. There were no census-takers in that bed that night, no border patrols."

The Fox moves the narrative forward, revealing that the three women continue to ride out each day, and that he cannot take man-shape because Tikat might recognize him. Even the convent was better than this, except for the nasty food. One day while out hunting, the Fox is pursued by a dog with no smell through a great storm, right into the arms of Lal's friend, the magician. It is he who raised the storm, with his magic, and the dog was just part of it. All of it was designed to drive the Fox to him, so that he could ask the Fox, his old friend, to take him to Lal and Nyateneri. The storm took the last of his strength, and he needs the man-shape to lean on to get the last few miles to them. The Fox tries to refuse and run away, but Lal's friend still has enough strength to haul him back without touching him, and the man-shape carries the magician as he wishes.

Tikat, the next narrator, recognizes the man-shape immediately and rushes to him as he sets the old wizard down. Tikat picks him up, and is astonished at his weight; the old man looks like he weighs nothing at all but is in fact quite substantial. Rosseth helps him get the old man upstairs to the room of the three women, but Tikat cannot enter even though Rosseth assures him Lukassa is not there. Instead he goes to find Marinesha and send her to help.

Marinesha tells us that when Tikat finds her she smashes a

porringer and slaps him for it. She is attracted to him and his manners, but this time he is different. She goes to Rosseth, who is with the oldest man she has ever seen. He looks as though he is dying, and Rosseth asks her to tell him what to do to heal him. She looks again at the old man, past the grayness, past the features, past everything, and just looking at him begins to make her happy, in a funny way. It makes her want to cry, too. When Rosseth goes to answer Karsh's call, Marinesha cleans the old man's face, and waking up he recognizes her although they have never met before. His laughter makes her want to hear it again. When the three women enter the room, it is Lukassa who goes to the old man and is welcomed by him. Marinesha is forgotten and leaves unnoticed.

Lal, although jealous, explains that he always goes where the need is greatest, immediately and without being told. Over Lukassa's head he tells them that the other's name is Arshadin, and in response Lal tells him that Nyateneri's name is Soukyan, and she doesn't like it much. Her friend says that he will continue to call him Nyateneri, unless he objects very strongly.

Since the night of their lovemaking none of them had so much as looked at the others. Nyateneri had resumed his woman's guise, mostly for the sake of Karsh's sanity, and had moved into the room next door. Rosseth could neither stay away from them nor speak to them, Lukassa remembered the events as if in a dream, but for Lal they represented an annoying complication. She had broken the rules of a lifetime, and could not trust Nyateneri/Soukyan, but she felt regret, even rarer in her life than trust. Her friend gave his blessing to Nyateneri, and beckoned to her, but she could not go to him.

Both Lal and Nyateneri think they know Arshadin, but in truth no one knows him. Her friend missed Lal after she left him, and he was not prepared for that at his age. It was disconcerting. He had neither embraced her nor so much as waited to watch her go, that day she set out alone again because he said it was time. She had cried for him many a night, but it had never occurred to her to wonder whether he felt at all lessened or lonely without her. Arshadin had appeared at his door when he was at a low ebb, a bit at loose ends. Arshadin's one ambition was to be the greatest magician who ever walked the earth, and he achieved it. As a teacher her friend had always wondered how he would react when one day he met someone with a greater gift than his. He knew him on the instant, just as Lal will one day meet a better swordsman and give him a salute with her blades. He told them, "We all meet our masters, all of us—why do you think we are in this world?"

If you are a wizard, nothing in the world is more important than how you die. A wizard must die at peace, a drawing-in, a particular sitting still that can requires great preparation and that a magician can only achieve by means of a long, motionless journey, called the *lamisetha*. He had been occupied in preparing his when he met Arshadin. And yet he took in Nyateneri, with no question about it, ever. The magician had allowed himself to be distracted from his task of arranging his soul before Nyateneri, but after her he resolved that he would never be again.

Arshadin became his son, not of the body but of the search, the voyage. Wizards do not fear death as others do, perhaps because they know transcience better than most. Perhaps for that reason they hunger even more deeply to leave behind them some small suggestion of their passage. For some that may be achievements that appear to be commandings and shapings of the very earth itself, but for most it is nothing more than the handing on of knowledge to someone who at least understands how painfully it was come by and who can be trusted not to let it slip away into the darkness with them.

He had been the greatest magician he ever knew, and he always knew he deserved a true heir. He felt it was his right to be father to one wiser and mightier than he; as different in kind from him as a bird is from the shards of its broken egg. He was given Arshadin, exactly what his pride and foolishness deserved.

Nyateneri interrupted him, meaning no disrespect, to point

out that while it may have been Arshadin who summoned what-ever he summoned, Arshadin was slain while he survived. They could not make out how that makes Arshadin his master and the greatest of all magicians.

The magician explained to them that while most people are awake only on special occasions, magicians are awake all the time, never more so than at the moments of their own deaths. If a magician's death is unquiet, if he has not had time to make his *lamisetha*, his wide-awakeness can become something quite dreadful. As there is for everything in their world, there is a word for it, and words to command it. There were words the magician did not want Arshadin to learn, but he learned them anyway. Others taught him things the magician would not. At that, the magician began to cry. He had loved Arshadin as himself, but that had been his mistake; there was no Arshadin to love. There was only a wondrous gift and a glorious desire; it had been the magician's vanity that made him think he could make a real Arshadin grow around those things.

After Arshadin left the magician, Nyateneri appeared and distracted him again from preparing a proper wizard's funeral. He forgot all about Arshadin, except now and then, until the sendings began. At first they were not so bad, a few night-mares, a bad memory or two made visible, a few rather tremu-lous midnight scratchings at the door. The magician recognized them for what they were, and summoned Arshadin to him; he could still do that then. Arshadin told him how unhappy he was that it was going to be necessary to destroy him.

What Arshadin had wanted to learn had not come cheaply or simply. There were powers to be supplicated, principalities to be appeased; certain unpleasantnesses and advanced payments had to be endured. Arshadin had felt what he had learned was worth the price; the magician himself had made similar bargains in his time. The true price of Arshadin's education was the magician's *lamisetha*; Arshadin was to make sure that when he dies, he dies such a troubled, peaceless death that he becomes a *griga'ath*, a wandering spirit of malice and wickedness, without a home, without a body, without rest or ending.

The magician had taught Nyateneri a charm against the *griga'ath*, but he had made it up because Nyateneri was always so frightened of the bloody creatures, even though she/he had never seen one. The magician had, and so might they all. Lal bravely tells him that she will not allow it to happen, but the magician knows that even the mighty Lal is no match for a *griga'ath* that had been a magician during its lifetime. There would be nothing such a spirit could not do, and no defense against it, when it came at the call of Arshadin or those whom he imagines he is using. Arshadin's only weakness is that he has no sense of irony.

Tikat takes up the story, interrupting at that point after knocking on the door and hiding in the hallway. He eavesdrops from outside the door, and hears the magician say that Arshadin knew him well enough to take advantage of his arrogance as no one had ever done. The magician ignored the continued sendings, and did not try to humiliate Arshadin, but the sendings got worse, a little at a time. At last the magician found himself at bay in evil dreams and unable to awaken. He went to Arshadin, and it took the best part of his strength. They came to an agreement, and the magician left although Arshadin tried to stop him. He fled to the red tower and tried to reinforce it against Arshadin, who followed, first in spirit, then in the body. The rest Lukassa knows. The dreams, though, were not dreams, but real things that happened to him. No mere dream could have made him as they saw him. At the very end of the chapter, something touches Tikat on the shoulder, very lightly.

Nyateneri narrates the next chapter, and brings up the Others that Lukassa told them about. She says the Others killed Arshadin after he summoned them for help, but he came back to life again. The magician tells them that there was a great deal of confusion, and he took that one moment of inattention to escape. He has been fleeing Arshadin ever since, never daring to contact them for fear of betraying his presence. When he became too weary, however, he summoned the Fox, which may have already alerted Arshadin.

Nyateneri demands to know where Arshadin's castle lies, so that she/he and Lal can go there, and the magician forbids it utterly. This causes Lal and Nyateneri to burst into sustained laughter, but the magician is serious; this is wizards' business, and they cannot help, not in that way. Nyateneri explains that one of the most important lessons she learned from the magician was when to ignore him, and she asks again where Arshadin lives. The magician ignores them both, but Lukassa provides the clue that they need: the white teeth of the river in the mountains. The magician then tells them that Tikat lies injured outside the door, and they should see to him.

Rosseth wishes to accompany them the next morning, but Lal refuses and tries to bully him into staying at the inn to help care for the magician. Nyateneri also opposes Rosseth's joining them, but uses more reasonable methods of persuasion; Arshadin will find the magician, sooner or later, and he will need someone to protect him. Lal also reveals the existence of the third tracker, and the fact that it was probably he who injured Tikat the night before. Rosseth knows when he is beaten, and returns to the stable and Karsh's calls for him.

The Innkeeper continues the story, telling Rosseth not to ask but just to go next time. Karsh sees the fox watching him as he beats the stable boy while advising him.

When Nyateneri takes up the tale the next day, she and Lal are on their way. Lal apologizes for her continual singing, and wonders why she has never heard Nyateneri sing. Nyateneri gives an answer that is not an answer, that the air is thin and she saves her breath for breathing. The air is thin, as they are climbing the mountains in search of Arshadin, but that is no excuse; for Lal, singing is breathing. She does not understand people who do not sing. On the other hand, she refuses to discuss what happened between them. Nyateneri/Soukyan's life has not led him easily to ask about such things, and Lal's has not taught her to answer such questions, so they proceed without discussion. The third hunter is following them, they know, and could have picked them off with a bowshot at any time, but the hunters never use weapons of any sort. Nyateneri knows that the hunter's vanity and carelessness will lead to his demise, as it did to those of his two colleagues.

They eat fresh fish from the stream, cooked in oil and a bit of their precious flour, and Lal makes the tea they were both taught to make by the magician. Nyateneri will take the first watch, and they agree that it will take them almost two weeks to reach Arshadin. Lal believes they may not have that much time; sorcerers who die and are resurrected always come back stronger and meaner than they were, and their friend's true power has not returned and may never return. They dare not give away two weeks to Arshadin, or to the hunter following them.

Nyateneri knows what Lal is suggesting; she is not called Sailor Lal for nothing. They find the Susathi River a day and a half later, flowing west to east.

Tikat is the next narrator, picking up the story from his recovery from the attack of the third hunter outside the door in the inn. Although he is two years older than Rosseth, somehow Rosseth has found out as much about him as he has found out about Rosseth. The stable boy continuously reassures him about Lukassa, and rather than tell him not to talk about her Tikat begins to spend more and more time with the old man, whom he calls *tafiya*: one who is seen to have a certain kind of power, dignity, or stature. He called his teacher *tafiya*, but not the blacksmith. The town whore is not called *tafiya* but her mother is, as is one of the two priests in town but not the other. Two or three farmers are worthy of the name, but not the headman or the doctor.

The old man is very weak, but whether it was a weakness from which he could recover is still to be seen. With Karsh keeping Rosseth busy elsewhere in the inn, and with Marinesha recovering from a twisted ankle, Tikat becomes his primary caretaker. It is hard for him, since Lukassa spends much time in the old man's room, and he still cannot understand why she will not recognize him. The old man tells him that she will never remember; if he wants her, he must go where she is, for she will never come back to him. That is a place that is neither here nor there, a country where Lal and Nyateneri are her sisters and the old man is her grandfather, where Tikat never existed. He cannot go back to a world and a life that never was. Nor can he ask the old man what he must do; instead, he must tell him what he will do, so that they can argue properly. Tikat tells him that he will go to Lukassa the next day and speak to her as gently as he would to any stranger, assuming nothing, hoping for nothing, assuring her that he is a friend and no madman. He stays with the old man almost until dawn, and as he returns to the stable to begin the day's work he thinks he sees the fox halfway up a hill, smiling to himself with Lukassa's locket glinting between his dreaming fingers. When he stops for a better look, though, he loses sight of the fox in the dazzle of the sunrise.

Lal's narration returns us to the river, and she has determined that no one lives upstream and that there are no rapids in that direction. Nyateneri/Soukyan has allowed his woman's form to dissolve, showing himself lean and gray, heavy-boned yet more graceful than he should be for his size. His hair is as ragged as ever, chopped from time to time in the same scorched-earth monastery cut, and his eyes are as slowly changeable as twilight skies. His mouth is still gentle, in a hard, tired face.

Soukyan suggests that they only speak in Dirvic, a nasty tongue that hurts the mouth and coats the throat with a thick bitterness, and that has been dead for five centuries, betting their lives that no one else alive speaks it. Lal suggests making a raft, but Soukyan knows that the only trees around are so dense that any raft made of them would sink before they could get aboard. They will depend on the murderer following them, who, although not a wizard, will be well prepared for the unexpected. They play a scene for his sake, speaking in a language he cannot possibly understand and trying to make him think that they will set off downriver. Lal admires Soukyan's skill; however he may end, he was born to travel with a troupe of players such as those sleeping in Karsh's stables.

They decide to stage a fight between them, ending with Lal going off upriver and Soukyan creating a makeshift trash raft, made of driftwood, dead branches, and whatever litter he can find. They agree on the details, all the while slapping and knocking each other up and down the shore, and Lal spits in his eye and storms away. As his parting shot, Soukyan informs her that he cannot swim, and urges her to remember that she has never in her life met anyone as dangerous as the one who follows them.

At this point the narration reverts to the fox, who in response to his question tells Tikat—and us—that he is both fox and man, side by side, but below is *nothing*, such an old nothing that long ago it turned into something. Even nothing wants, sometimes even grows hungry to hear voices, songs, smell morning earth, drink water, munch on a pigeon. He is merely a finger of nothing, a toe; he does what he wants, but when old nothing calls, he goes. And old nothing is stirring, telling him to find out about the magician and his student, power groping for power.

Nyateneri is far away, and man-shape sits in the taproom telling stupid stories while listening and learning. Rosseth is too sad to talk, and Marinesha is too busy, while Tikat simply keeps away from him. Karsh looks hard at him every time he passes. Old nothing inside tells him to seek the girl, Lukassa. As the fox he does so, and she falls asleep each night asking questions about Lal and Nyateneri and holding him close.

Meanwhile things are coming to a head; the struggle for power is affecting the world and everyone in it. The magician must hide and keep the other from finding him. Old nothing continues to urge him toward Lukassa, and he meets her in man-shape and invites her for a walk. Seeking news of Lal and Nyateneri, he discovers they are in great danger. They have gone out to fight a magician, whom Lukassa knows cannot be killed because she herself was dead once. Everything she knew before the river has been taken from her, and in the emptiness death sits and talks to her, telling her different things. Arshadin is like her; there is no one to kill. They are interrupted by Karsh, looking for Rosseth but not finding him. Old nothing has what he wants, and goes back to sleep.

Lal had been following the river as closely as she could, but the further she traveled the more impassible the bank became for a rider. She never sensed her follower, but her horse did, and when its behavior told her she was no longer being followed she dismounted and unsaddled and sent the horses away. Her friend had taught her to do this whenever she was forced to abandon horses, and she had always done so, although she could not say what use it was to the horses. She makes it back to the river and begins running to catch up to Soukyan and his follower. She reaches the spot where she left him and stops running, but there is no one there. The signs show that Soukyan has both completed and launched his raft, and further signs of a struggle, but nothing to tell even Lal the Great Tracker how it had been when Soukyan had turned in the twilight to meet the man coming out of the trees.

She smells the man first, drawing her sword, but he is behind her. She should have been dead by then, and in a way she did die, right there, all that time ago, and it is a ghost who tells these stories and drinks this wine. The man

> "was small, like the other two, smaller than I—a long-faced, crook-necked, thin-built man in loose dark clothing, strolling toward me out of a particular clump of reeds where there had been no one when I scanned it a minute before. I stepped backward, with the sword steady on his heart. 'Stand,' I said. 'Stand. I don't want to kill you yet. Stand.'"

But the man walks toward her, hands held out to show he has no weapon. He tells Lal his work is done, and that he has no quarrel with her. When she demands to know what he has done with her companion, he smiles. When she demands to know what he has done with Soukyan's body, he tells her he bundled it aboard the raft and set it all adrift and alight. At that Lal tries a swift thrust, one that no one would have seen, but it touches only the man's tunic. The man congratulates her on her skill, and tells her it will be an honor for him to kill her. During the time he takes to say so she strikes at him three more times, and each time she misses badly and barely slips his counter-stroke. She responds with an attack it nearly cost her life to learn, and did cost four years to learn right, but he seems hardly to notice. After tricking her into looking past him for a moment, he lands a blow that somehow breaks only one rib, and again congratulates her on her skill. The words and the voice are those of a lover, which is the worst thing of all.

The fight continues, with him pursuing and her dodging, at times hitting him with her knee or elbow when she misses with the swordcane, which is always. All that she can say of her own skill is that she stays alive. He again congratulates her, and she again attacks, as the long dusk fades and the moonlight flattens the sheltering shadows. Each wonders if it is to be the other who is the one who will finally defeat them, but in reality it is all over. It is not because of her broken rib, and it is not because she was past her best, as she has known for some time. It was as her friend said; a master knows his master very quickly indeed. This one would have been her master on the very best day she ever knew, and yet she still had to kill him.

Finally a piece of driftwood turns under her heel, and she falls. She is up on the instant, but not before he catches her with both bare feet, high on the right thigh and again on the right shoulder. He could have killed her then, but instead asks for the story of her swordcane. Lal obliges, although she can barely stay erect to face him, and hands him her swordcane, telling him it is not passed on from generation to generation but must be stolen. She then recites the tale of the inscription on the swordcane: "Steal me, marry me," through which the cane stays in the family, until the time of her grandmother, who became the greatest swordsman in the world. She knows how to tell a story so it enraptures all hearers, and the murderer is no exception.

At the end she feigns the collapse of her right leg, as he might expect, and as she goes down she reaches into her boot for the dagger that she plunges deep into his throat. The swordcane is not stolen; she bought it from a peddler. And her grandmother never touched so much as a carving knife in her life. The person who taught her the sword was a vicious, drunken old soldier who would tell her before each lesson what his payment would be this time, and let her think about it as they fought. As he dies she apologizes for cheating him, but he was too good for her to defeat honestly. She wishes him sunlight on his road, but does not know if he hears.

Soukyan, who has not been killed and launched on a funeral pyre, is meanwhile blind in one eye and floating on the rapidly-disintegrating raft. He gives the good ship *Soukyan's Coffin* a conservative ten minutes, and himself an optimistic five. He cannot recall what has happened to him, except that he has been ambushed as easily as Tikat or Rosseth would have been, not so much as glimpsing his attacker. As he searches what remains of the raft for something to paddle with, his hand comes across a tube which he eventually recognizes. He just manages to throw it, and it bursts into flame while still in the air. He then sees Lal, launching a boat smaller than his raft but with a sail and rudder and flying down the river after him. When she sees him, she waves.

The raft completes its disintegration and Soukyan goes down, but Lal fishes him out and pounds on his back with her feet while sailing the boat with her hands. Her feet are small but memorable, especially the heels. In response to his question about the extent of her injuries, Lal tells him that she has one broken rib, perhaps two. Now that he is safely aboard the coolly invulnerable Sailor Lal allows herself to feel her own pain, but she is able nonetheless to show him how to control the boat before collapsing. Her lips are blue, her heartbeat too quick, her breathing too slow and torn, but at least there are no signs of a punctured lung. Soukyan hates boats, but is able to wedge its pointed prow into a tangle of overhanging tree roots and carry

Lal ashore.

A quick examination finds only one broken rib, and he rips a spare sail into strips and sets and bandages her rib as best he can. They both sleep, huddled naked under the sail, and in the morning Soukyan goes back down to the water to find food. He tickles two fish, uses Lal's swordcane to clean them, and cooks them on a fire he builds. The smell of food awakens her; she eats and drinks some water and sleeps again. He finds some *fasska*, a grey lichen that smells and tastes disgusting but has the virtue of healing the mind and the body. He improvises something in which to heat water from a broken *tharakki* egg, and uses the hot water to prepare the *fasska*. The magician made it for him on the day they met and again when he was nearly bitten in two by a rock-*targ*. Lal says nothing, and obediently swallows the swill with only an occasional cough. When it is gone she closes her eyes again and does not stir for the rest of the day.

A day later, the drink having done its work and having passed through the worst of it, Lal is herself again, upbraiding Soukyan for using her swordcane for gutting fish. She remembers nothing of what happened, which she does not like, but thanks Soukyan when he tells her. She intends for them to take up their journey immediately, despite her weakness, but Soukyan convinces her to wait one more day. Unknown to them, though, they are under observation all day as they plan their utterly futile assault on Arshadin. They both know there is no hope, but while Soukyan takes the pessimistic view that the best they can hope for is that Arshadin may laugh so hard that he hurts himself, Lal is more optimistic. She believes that all they need do is annoy him, and her friend, known to Soukyan as The Man Who Laughs, will do the rest.

The next morning they embark on Lal's boat, but Soukyan never becomes comfortable on it for the three days it is all his existence. He is useless baggage on board, a new and not enjoyable experience. When they camp ashore at night, however, they talk almost all night about the past, especially their childhoods. Soukyan's sister was sold into slavery by their parents, for which he will hate them forever, and Lal herself was sold and stolen. She kept her sanity by telling herself that her parents would come and find her, that they were following and would never rest until she was safe and home and avenged. But they never found her, and that fact continues to infuriate her. In order to calm her fury Soukyan kisses her, and she bites him hard for his pains. They make love very gently, because Lal's body cannot bear his weight and her arms and legs cannot hold him as she desires. When it is over Lal says, "Bad water tomorrow," and she falls asleep on top of him with her nose in his left ear.

They indeed run into rough water the next day. Lal says she knew because of the fish, which taste differently from what they had been eating, but she admits that is not true and she said there would be bad water for luck, because she had been happy with him. Soukyan is about to tell her that he had been happy with her as well, when it gets interesting on the river. The little boat rocks and pitches ceaselessly, gathering speed as it races down a long foaming gullet towards an unknown belly at the end of the run. Sailor Lal eases the boat through the wilderness like a needle through folds of silk.

They very nearly miss Arshadin's house altgother, seeing it only because of the congregation of *dharises*, birds which signify ill luck, disaster, and horror in every known land, which was roosting on Arshadin's windowsills. True to their reputation, the *dharises* bring near disaster to Lal and Soukyan; their tiny craft capsizes and they are tossed into the racing river. Without no hope of saving himself, Soukyan prepares for death, but the river instead of drowning them both retreats. They are terrified by the wrongness of it, for no river acts like this and no wizard you ever knew of could make a river do such a thing. They dare not turn toward the wattle-and-daub cottage of Arshadin behind them, even when the laughter begins.

Lal takes up the tale at this point. She tells us she will remember the dreadful *smallness* of Arshadin's laughter all her life. For it is of course Arshadin—or that which was Arshadin—who laughs, and it had been he who stopped the river. He is between them in height, thickly made in a brown tunic with a pale, bald, wide-jawed but expressionless face. He resembles most an infant born far too soon to breath more than a few minutes in this world.

Lal immediately thrusts her swordcane through his thick belly, and again through his chest, but Arshadin does not sag and there is no expected burst of blood. There is no blood in him; he had given his life to the Others that night in the red tower, and they gave him back a kind of aliveness for which blood is not necessary. He admonishes her to stop wasting her time and energy; he who commands rivers is not for her nursery sword, or the carpet-tack in her boot. Simultaneously Arshadin paralyzes Soukyan, who has imperceptibly shifted his weight in preparation for a certain spinning kick, with a mere hand gesture that also encompasses Lal.

As proof of his mastery Arshadin sketches a wide circle with his foot and spits into it, whereupon a grayness shivers within the circle and her friend stands within it, captive. It is no mere image but the man himself, snatched from his bed at the inn, still in his nightgown. Paradoxically, upon seeing him Lal feels immediately dizzyingly safe. Despite avowing that they are worth nothing to him and that they deserve what thet get for ignoring his warnings about Arshadin's power, Lal's friend will never abandon them; they can depend on him for their lives, just as she knows he depends on them for their wit, their attention for more than that.

Lal reads the bitter rage and loss in Arshadin's eyes, and is frightened, but her friend continues to play with Arshadin, his voice falling into a sleepy singsong drone as it had when he was about to set her a particularly exasperating riddle or challenge. Arshadin's entire attention is focused on him, and Lal realizes with a start that she can move again. Soukyan springs first—it takes Lal with her injured arm a moment to draw her sword—but Arshadin meets their charge with rapid shape-changing to rock-*targ* to bellowing *sheknath* to something she would quite simply kill herself to keep from seeing again. Arshadin tosses

Soukyan ten yards against a rock, knocking the wind out of him, then ignores Lal as she rushes past him to help. Arshadin turns his attention to Lal's friend in the circle, and casts a vicious spell upon him before turning again to Lal and Soukyan and shouting boulders and *dharises* after them. The boulders come careening down out of the cliffside, gouging real tracks in the dirt, bringing real trees down, and threatening to crush them both, until grayness comes down upon Lal like a heavy, smothering cloth over a birdcage.

The next thing she hears is her friend, requesting a little less bustle if she doesn't mind. Arshadin, the house, the river gorge are all gone, as are the earth, the sky, and everything but the grayness which has no dimension and no ending but just dwindles off into a further grayness. Her friend is playing with time, which no magician can ever resist even though it is the first thing they are all warned not to do. They are in a far place, he tells them, neither where nor when, but what might be called elsewhen, in a bubble of time. He will take them back to the inn, but holding a time bubble in this world takes a great amount of energy. That had been Arshadin's mistake; he tried to hold it, and him, and them all under his control at the same time, and Lal's friend had told him many times that all energy has its natural limits, even his. When they had clumsily caused a diversion, Arshadin had tried to kill him in the bubble and he had been able to take control.

Arshadin had spoken of *those who are waiting*, and Soukyan asks if they are waiting for Lal's friend. They are, he replies, but they may have to wait a little longer. Speaking a few words that do not even sound like a language but instead like someone snoring or clearing his throat, he brings them home. It is afternoon, and a gray quarter-moon is rising in the west. Lal and Soukyan look at each other; the moon the night before had been full and golden, dripping ripe into the river.

Karsh is the next speaker, and as usual he returns to the humdrum and homely. He recites that they paid him well for the horses, and never offered an explanation as to what had become of them. How they could have returned seven days later with Lal limping badly and ten pounds thinner while Nyateneri looked as many years older remains a mystery. Karsh knows the old man for a wizard, of course, and had from the first day. He doesn't like wizards, but they are usually mannerly guests, generous to the help, and more careful than most to stay on the good side of the landlord. This one, though, is frail, sick, and practically dying, but here he is on his feet and mixed up with whatever the women have been at since they left the inn. Trouble follows him like a stray dog, and Karsh has no idea what shape the trouble will take. He could not turn him out, any more than he could turn out the three women.

But the trouble does not come. Summer creaks by, travelers come and go, horses get looked after, dishes get washed, rooms get more or less swept out, and a family of Narsai tinkers leave without paying their bill. All is as usual. The three women behave almost like ordinary guests. Tikat gives up running after the white one, Lukassa. Karsh could have kicked Tikat out, just to be kicking someone, but Tikat is more than earning his keep. The only real complaint Karsh can muster has to do with the boy, and he can't put it into words. Something is niggling at Rosseth, growing worse by the day, although he says not a word about it. Karsh thinks that he may have taken to hanging after the wizard as he does after the women.

Rosseth then tells us that although it has been almost twenty years since that time, he can still recall the strange, hopeless taste of those days. Part of it is the heat, of course, but it is more a feeling that someone has the inn under a lens. It gets worse when Lal and Nyateneri return; there is rarely a moment when he does not feel himself watched more and more intensely by a cold considering that has nothing to do with him or with anything he understands or loves in this world. Sometimes it seems far away, and other times so close it seems to share his bed and finger over his dreams. There is no avoiding it, and no fighting off the evil dreariness that always attends it, always keeps him frightened in a vague, dull way, and truly tired to death. "Sad to death" is the best way he can put it.

Rosseth sees no sign of suffering from the same complaint in Tikat, who has quietly taken over the nursing and guard duties that had been Rosseth's. Tikat spends most of his time with the old man upstairs, whom he calls *tafiya*. Rosseth misses him and is jealous of him as well, mostly for his closeness to the three women, but also because someone values his presence and asks for him often, which is different than being sent for.

The women stay more to themselves than ever, and when Rosseth sees them they are always together. He wants to tell Soukyan, who still looks and moves and smells like Nyateneri, that he likes him no less for the deception and is not avoiding him out of anger or shame. He wants to ask Lal why and how they returned so soon. He wants to say to Lukassa that every time Tikat hears her voice or sees her in the stair or crossing the courtyard his heart cracks in one more place. None of this ever happens, somehow; it is as though the three of them had never come riding around the bend, as though he had dreamed the trembling dimples in Lal's shoulders, dreamed that he had watched Nyateneri kill two killers singlehanded. All that is a loneliness he had never given name to before they came; that and the heat and the fear.

Marinesha tells him that the wizard marches up and down all night, every night, talking and chanting and singing to himself. Sometimes there are others, like children, and they answer him. Tikat knows nothing of any voices. Rosseth does not think that gods, spirits, demons, monsters, or any of that ilk will ever put in an appearance in Tikat's presence, although the monsters will not wait for Karsh to leave.

One day Karsh comes to Rosseth in the stable and tells him to wait outside, and thanks him for waiting. Rosseth cannot swear that was the first time Karsh thanked him, but it shocks him; and it shocks him even more when Karsh asks how he is. Rosseth sputters that he is well enough. Karsh has wished to tell him something for a long time: he wasn't a bad child. He didn't cry much, he didn't get underfoot. He was a nice little boy. Whereupon Karsh turns and tramps back inside. Rosseth stays where he is, shaking numbly with wonderment and weariness and fear, wishing he knows his own name.

The fox next relates that Nyateneri threatens him with a dozen times death if she sees him in man-shape, so he stays a fox. There is no nice red ale, nothing but hot wind in the hot weeds where the chickens sleep. But once he looks up and Lukassa is looking down at him. She picks him up and begs him to help the wizard by making the shapes that come in the night go away. The magician needs to die, but if he dies now—sick, sleepless, raging—he will become like them, only worse. She puts him down, but instead of trotting off obediently to help the magician, the fox lies down where he is. Lukassa's eyes become bright with sadness, and she turns away.

But old nothing comes at him again, urging him to find out. He does in fact trot off to help. He knows the voices, he knows the smells, but he wishes to stay outside the room. Old nothing urges him to enter, and he takes man-shape, looking through the keyhole. The room is full of them, maggots heaving in a dead thing, making it seem to breath; he never saw so many in one place. The magician sees them, but walks back and forth and never looks at them. He had been gray once, but he is white now, ash white, burned white, like Lukassa. Lines are raked down his face, clawmarks without blood, and as he marches up and down he sings a soldier's song. If he ever stops they will be upon him, not with claws and teeth but with eyes, voices, sweet slithering laughter, on him with old shames, old betrayals, old rotting secrets. They can twist your memories, wrench good dreams into shapes too wrong or to real to bear. They can also have your soul hanging in ribbons just as fast.

The fox goes in, and falsifies a bonhomie with the magician. All eyes turn toward the man-shape, who shouldn't be there and who shouldn't be able to see them. The magician continues marching and singing, although he is so tired the man-shape's slap on the shoulder almost knocks him down. The fox wants to leave, but old nothing tells him to stay and watch; there is too much wild, wrong power here. Since the fox cannot leave, and the magician cannot die, the sendings must leave, just as Lukassa begged. Man-shape slaps the magician on the shoulder again, and sings the chorus with him. He then shouts out to the sendings, greeting them by their names like night in the mouth, like broken glass, names like burning oil, dead water, like wind in bad places. They don't like being called by their names. He shouts louder, making stupid jokes of their names, even putting them into the marching song. They begin hissing and mumbling, angrier at man-shape than at the magician, and they grow brighter and brighter, all seething with the same black fire, mark of the power that set them on the old magician. The room surges with their hurtful little voices, drowning out the marching song and man-shape's bellowing. The magician buckles, his hands over his ears, and stops singing. They will be on him in a moment, the lot of them, laughing, mocking, gnawing, but he turns, still on his knees, eyes wide, blazing green as the sky just after sunset. He throws out one hand, says three words that sound like dray grass rattling, and all at once all of them are gone. Nothing remains, not an echo, not a twist of smoke, only a cold room left huge by its emptiness.

The magician thanks him, but the fox tells him no thanks are wanted; it was not done to help him. The magician knows that, but it was clever of the fox to realize their own names would hurt their ears as much as they hurt others'. When the fox asks why he did not just snap his fingers, mumble words, and send them off, the magician says he was too tired for anything but singing. He had to face them, and he thanks his old friend again before he falls asleep.

The fox is confused. He was not a friend of this, or of any, magician. Yet he had gone to him, not wanting to; and helped him, as Lukassa begged, not meaning to, meaning only to help himself. He hates it, then recognizes that some other is here in the room watching with him—not old nothing, but a deadness, a dead place, window-high, just beyond the bed. The room is not for foxes, and he departs as quickly as he can.

Tikat meanwhile knows that the wizard is ill; he was usually the first to see him in the morning, and he knows the air of a sickroom as well as any. But his *tafiya* forbids him to sleep in his room, or even to visit him after dark. Tikat cannot know that the wizard is being galloped to madness between every sundown and every cockcrow.

Tending him draws Tikat and Lukassa together in a strange way. They speak rarely, but she no longer seems to fear being in the same room with him. She bathes and shaves the wizard and changes his sweated linen, and thanks Tikat politely each time he takes the chamberpot from her hands and empties it himself. But she never speaks his name. Tikat brings his meals, sweeps the floor, takes away yesterday's platters, and listens when the mood to talk is on him. It never happened when one or more of the women were in the room, perhaps because they loved him and Tikat did not. The old man has a liking for him, perhaps because he owes him nothing and does not care so much for his good opinion. Contrary as the old man is, it may be just so.

Sometimes he speaks of his life, which has been very long. Even if half of what he tells Tikat is true, it would have taken two ordinary mortal lifetimes to crowd everything in. Wizards must be like other people, only better, but the wizard mumbles quickly over the adventurous parts and keeps returning to the plainest human sorrows and defeats, including a woman with whom he traveled for many, many years, but then she died. Tikat cannot be sure, but thinks he sees tears in the wizard's eyes at this point. He says he is sorry, but the wizard swings his eyes back with an impact Tikat can feel in his flesh. He says that all that weeping and pining for Lukassa does not fit Tikat for understanding someone else's loss, and that there is no comparison; none. And the wizard speaks no more for the rest of the day.

One day the wizard asks him if there is anything he fears. Tikat replies that there is nothing; before he was afraid of everything in the world that had the least chance of parting Lukassa and him, but now that the worst has happened there is nothing left for him to fear. It is not right that should be so, the wizard tells him, but he envies him just the same. The thing you are most afraid of is the thing that always happens; we make it happen, though he cannot say how. The worst has already happened to Tikat, and he did not die. Tikat is not sure that surviving is the same as not dying, but the wizard amusedly dismisses his comment. He has feared many, many things in different times, but seems to have outlived them all, as he has outlived loving and hating as well. The irony is that in all those years he has never feared death, being who he is and knowing what he knows, and now he does. Living in an absolute horror of dying is a great humiliation for a magician. Grasping weakly at his shoulder he tells Tikat that he dares not die yet, he must not die yet. He begs Tikat not to let him die.

When Tikat asks what he could do to help, the wizard looks beyond him to an invisible presence in the room and begins a conversation. Tikat leaves before he begins imagining hearing a response, and runs into Marinesha listening at the door. Although he says her appearance means nothing to him at all, Tikat notices that she is quite pretty, with large dark gray eyes, a generous mouth, and skin that should have been coarsened by her work but has not been at all. She asks if the wizard has been talking to another in the room, and Tikat admits that he has been but makes it into a joke. In truth he is concerned himself.

Marinesha then hesitantly and in a low voice reminds him that Lukassa is not the only woman in the world, placing her hand upon his cheek. Tikat rejects her awkwardly and some-what harshly, and is immediately sorry, for there was no need to hurt her.

As autumn approaches with days no shorter or cooler Tikat begins to feel he has spent his entire life drudging at that inn. It is all a waste, he thinks, all of it, and it is time to say so and be done. Any yet he drudges on.

When one afternoon Karsh orders Tikat and Rosseth to replace several rotted roof beams in the smokehouse, they begin the work only to see Nyateneri and the fox in the doorway. They get the first beam in place, and Rosseth begins hammering hard and wildly, never looking at Nyateneri. Tikat sees her as a handsome woman, in a soldierly way, as tall as he with changing eyes and short, thick gray-brown hair. She is not at all beautiful, or suddenly, unexpectedly pretty like Marinesha, but even in his village people would stare at her when she strode past and remember her long after the beautiful ones. He has never seen her and the fox together, and the fox looks straight at him, putting one ear back and laughing out of his bright yellow eyes. Nyateneri says she must speak to them both.

Rosseth says, almost whispering, "Soukyan," but Tikat does not know what the word means. She/he tells them that the wizard is dying, and there is nothing any of them can do; it will be the next night. Rosseth asks how she knows; he is strong, and will last out the night as he did before when they thought he would not.

Nyateneri merely tells him that the wizard knows. He wants them all there—Rosseth, Nyateneri, Lal, Lukassa, and Tikat. It is because of the new moon; wizards can only die on new-moon nights. Nyateneri seems surprised they did not know this simple fact, and annoyed with herself for assuming they did. She turns away, but the fox keeps staring at Tikat until he stretches lingeringly and saunters off behind her.

Rosseth's voice is tight and thin as he asks Tikat why the wizard is really dying, and how they can be certain he will go with the new moon the next night. Something terrible is happening, and no one tells Rosseth anything. Tikat attempts to comfort the boy, telling him it is all imagination, but Rosseth knows it is real. They agree to talk and share what information they have.

They talk for a long time while repairing the roof. Rosseth speaks of the fox also being the old man, and of his drowned Lukassa having been drawn up from the riverbed by Lal's song. Rosseth tells him about Nyateneri being no woman but a man named Soukyan, who had left two other men—fell, dire men— dead in the bathhouse. In the end they agree that they know that

Lal and Soukyan came to that place in search of their friend, their master, and that they found him the prey of another wizard named Arshadin, more powerful than he. Arshadin keeps him from resting, sends voices and visitations to plague him by night. And if Arshadin can do so much, he is likely to be at the bottom of all the other things bedeviling the inn all summer.

But then Tikat asserts that it is nothing to do with him, and that whatever happens or does not happen with the squabbling wizards he'll be off where he belongs and never know. Rosseth responds quietly that Lukassa will be here, as will Rosseth, and Marinesha who has been kind to Tikat. Will Tikat truly never want to know what becomes of them? They stare at each other, and Tikat looks down first, admitting that he will not leave until she is in a safe place, if such a place can be found. The rest can go where they like; he has no skill at loving more than one person at a time. As he turns to leave Rosseth calls after him, asserting that although he has never called it that, this place is his home and he will defend it and his friends as best he can. He thanks Tikat for teaching him, as Tikat continues walking away.

The potboy is the next narrator, with his limited point of view. He spends his free time outside the inn despite the oppressive heat, and most of the time he heads for the stables to help Rosseth with the horses. Rosseth is his friend, although years older, who never got angry with him even when he had too much work to do to talk to he potboy the way they liked to.

That day the horses lay in their straw and will not even stand up to be curried or have their feet seen to. They do what they can, then rest in an empty stall and talk for a while. The potboy asks why it is so hot all the time, even at night, and Rosseth tells him it is because two great wizards are fighting in the sky. The boy falls asleep in the middle of the story, but is awakened when Tikat comes in and tells Rosseth heat or no heat Karsh wants a cart of vegetables unloaded. The potboy never liked Tikat, but he did point to his lunch and suggest the potboy should eat it, so the boy thought maybe he wasn't so bad after all, for a southerner.

For the rest of that day the potboy dodges everywhere around the inn, hiding in the smokehouse, the buttery, the bathhouse, and even in the smelly little shrine on the hillside. The sun stops moving in the sky, growing riper and heavier every minute, and brighter too, until it is almost white on the outside, white as daisies. But on the inside it is dark—all hard, swollen dark, like a yolk gone bad in an egg. The potboy begins to hear it beating, thumping like an iron heart, and it never moves, that clanging sun.

He doesn't know what to do, but he wants to find Rosseth and show him what is wrong with the sun. But Rosseth is still busy with Tikat. The old man in the red coat comes out; everybody likes him, except fat Karsh. He tells the old man that whatever is wrong with the sun has nothing to do with him; he just wants it to stop. The old man promises to make it stop, and stumps off into the inn, the door slamming shut behind him but making no sound.

Then right away the sky begins to darken and the sun stops its awful slow clanging. Birds started making their night noises all at once. If the potboy turns his head he knows he will see the sun skidding down the sky, but he doesn't turn. He just stands there with his eyes closed, and feels the stars coming out.

Lal then tells us what happens at the wizard's deathbed. He wanders in his mind for a long time, fighting back the new moon, but the instant the sun passes from sight he snaps awake and tells the four of them (Lal, Soukyan, Lukassa, and Rosseth; Tikat is not yet there) what to do about the *griga'ath*. Of all the things that happened so soon afterward, and of all the things that have happened to her since, nothing has ever been as frightening to Lal as those few words in that calm, rasping voice.

There is no defeating or destroying a *griga'ath*, but it is possible to distract it briefly and perhaps escape. The *griga'ath* will not recoil from flowers, for example, but for perhaps an instant it may remember flowers, and remember that it was human once. It will look exactly like the wizard, and it will be hungry. If Soukyan throws the flowers at it, vase and all, and then turns and runs without meeting its eyes, they may all escape.

At that moment what appears to be the fox in man-shape enters the room. Soukyan whirls on him furiously, and Lal, without knowing why, bars his way, but the man-shape tells her to let him pass in a voice she has heard before and her friend in a soft voice tells her to let him pass. She then knows who it is, and steps aside. The man-shape then shifts, not to the fox, but instead to Arshadin, who tells the other wizard that he had told him they would meet like this at the last.

Still calm, Lal's friend reminds Arshadin that it took him a long time to pry the sun from his grasp, and that Arshadin cannot kill him until the new moon rises. Arshadin, however, replies that he can wait; it is the Others who cannot. But Lal's friend is better acquainted with the Others than Arshadin is, and there is not one of them who would try conclusions with him even as he lies there. Lal catches her breath, thinking that even then he has a plan, and that she must be ready.

As Arshadin rails at Lal's friend, Soukyan growls softly and takes a step towards him; Rosseth glances at the door, needing Tikat to come through it; and Lukassa never takes her eyes off him. Her expression is so rapt that she might be gazing at her lover, if you ignore the set of her mouth. She looks far older than she is. Arshadin does not notice her.

Lal's friend explains that Arshadin was his equal, not his student, from the start. Though they were destined to end where they were, he loved Arshadin even so. In response Arshadin screams that he was entitled to his faith, not his love, and Lal's friend agrees. But even so, he is bound to tell Arshadin that he made a bad bargain when he traded his heart's blood for his heart's desire.

Calling them all to his bed one last time, Lal's friend tells Soukyan to remember about the flowers; Lal to give up whatever she is plotting; and Lukassa and Rosseth not to come near him. He then says a name Lal does not know, and dies.

The Others gather at the windows, looking in with malice, and Arshadin tells them he has delivered their enemy into their hands for all time. He has kept his part of the bargain, and expects them the keep theirs; he wants them to give him back his blood, as they promised. There is no answer, because Lal's friend, although dead, stirs, mutters, and opens his eyes. He stands up on the bed and stretches, making a soft, thoughtful sound, steps to the floor, and walks toward Arshadin. He smiles just a little.

Arshadin shows no fear, but speaks in the language wizards speak together, asking the *griga'ath* to know him and do him honor. The *griga'ath*, however, keeps coming, shuffling through one sky-splitting spell after another from Arshadin. The four of them do not throw flowers and do not run away; the wizard had wasted his dying counsel on them. When finally backed against the wall, Arshadin whirls and threatens the malevolent Others outside; unless they give him back his blood, he will turn the *griga'ath* against them.

The Others, however, ignore him. The night steps into the room, spilling through not only the windows but every crack, separation, and nail-hole in the walls, puddling together in a corner, slowly forming a shape that is round at the top and broken into jagged, twisted shadows below. As in the tower it has become a passage to somewhere else. A wind begins to stir beneath the archway, a wind to somewhere else. The darkness speaks to them, not in words, telling them to come. Lal, Soukyan, and Rosseth attempt to obey at once, so powerful is that command, and Lal gets close enough to see, or feel, or know, what is on the other side. But it is not interested in them, only in the *griga'ath*, which it can swing like a hammer against the foundations of the world, so it stops calling them and begins calling it. The *griga'ath* turns from Arshadin and walks toward the archway.

The others look away, but Lal looks into its eyes. They are not her friend's eyes, but the eyes of what he might have done, the sum of his nature. He is all his possible self, great good or great evil, and he is nothing, nothing but destruction. The *griga'ath* pays no attention to her, but moves past her, still wearing the face and form of someone she loved. It halts a step before the darkness, looking back, and Lal hides her face.

At that moment someone pounds furiously on the door, and Karsh with Tikat close behind him crashes into the room. The *griga'ath* takes a single stride forward and passes from this world. Lal can still see it for what seems a long time, glowing steadily brighter as it grows smaller, spinning slowly down the black archway that runs between what we know and what we cannot bear to know.

Karsh of course is the next narrator, and he brings us back to the mundane. He is in the taproom when the wine bottles crash to the floor, followed by every mug and wine glass he owns, and then by the hanging lamps. The inn that has been his home for thirty years comes crashing down around him, as he had known would happen the day he let those women cross his threshold. It is not a *javak*, or twisty storm, since the windows blew out, not in, and it isn't an earthquake since there isn't as much as a twitch out of the floor. Within thirty seconds, Karsh is the only object still standing in the taproom, supported by nothing but outrage. The cause is only a short distance above his head, and he is already on his way up.

Tikat staggers through the outside door just then, yapping something and pointing upwards. Karsh knows he must be asking about his damned white Lukassa, but Karsh wants to know about the boy. Karsh scrambles past him, pushing him well out of the way before they reach the landing. No one is going to break down that door but him.

The point of view shifts to Tikat, who searches for Lukassa. On the stair there is a hot, stinking wind blowing straight down, and it threatens to prevent Tikat and Karsh from any progress upwards. But Karsh never loses heart or looks back, that fat, roaring man. He bends his fleshy neck and bows his shoulders and lumbers ahead, heaving and cursing, hacking out a way through the wind. On the landing he pauses for a moment, shaking himself heavily, and Tikat sees his face, huge with that pale rage that takes him when nothing is going as he would have it. Then he is off again, charging along a corridor choked with falling plaster and roiling dust and shrieking, half-clad guests trampling each other to reach the stairs. When Tikat reaches the *tafiya's* room Karsh is there already, hammering on the door, then beginning to heave his whole body against it, one slow muffled thump after another. Tikat is not quite up to him when the door finally bursts open and they fall through.

At the far end of the room there is nothing, an emptiness. The emptiness is a mouth; you could see its edges writhing and folding like lips, beginning to close, and the foul wind seething between them. Far away, or far in, or far down, a bright, bright spark tumbles forever, blazing bravely in the void. Tikat knows what it is.

Lukassa stands with her back to him, near the empty bed. There are others in the room, but Tikat sees only her. She does not turn at the noise of the door being broken in, but begins to walk toward that black mouth that is closing more quickly now. She is gone before he can call, and before he can reach it himself it snaps shut and vanishes, leaving nothing behind but a sagging, crumbling wall in a little wrecked room full of the sound of her name.

Lukassa then tells us that she is not Lukassa; she is no one. No one can pass through the gates of death twice, but she walked through and they waited for her. They do not want to wait, but she will make them. Someone is calling her, far behind on the edge of Lukassa. Far ahead a star is singing, promising to tell her her name if she can catch it in time, so she should hurry.

Death is a nowhere lined with lightning, she remembers. She walks swiftly because she remembers the way. There are faces now, flowing by in the dark, between her and the star. When she dies the first time she will see those same faces.

Down in the riverbed it is quiet as quiet. On the surface the water snarls and tears. In the riverbed she looks up through stillness and watches the faces flowing past, so many heavy, weary village faces that should not smile at her with such tender knowledge. Beyond them, her star. She brushes away the faces and climbs over the water, over the beanfields and thatched roofs, and she follows the singing of the star. She remembers.

This is different. Death is death, but something is different, the darkness. She can see great yellow claws smashing down from the other side, ripping down and down, and a greenish glow beyond. The faces begin to snap their jaws as they hiss by. There are so many sometimes they hide the star.

Why must she still hear him? It is so noisy here, not like the riverbed, with the faces coming at her like lances now, with the thing on the other side of the dark chuckling to itself as it strikes and strikes. Even so she hears him calling from far away, farther away than anything, calling that name he will call her, that name that is not, never was, hers.

She must listen to the star, nothing else. It has a woman's voice. She loses it often, because the darkness is thrashing and convulsing all around her but she can always hear it singing. One day she will catch up with it if it continues singing, and then it will tell her her name.

This time being dead is very different. This time death is seething, bustling with so much movement and color and earthly to-do. It might almost be another marketplace, except for who is tending the stalls, and what might be for sale there. There will not be words or thoughts for such beings, such things, but that makes no difference because they are not real. The riverbed is real.

As she passes they will come after her, those beasts of fire and filth who jabber and coo and tear at her shadow, because they have none themselves. This death is all shadow, like the hand-pictures that someone used to make for whom? This death is a false, shabby country. And even the thing outside is nothing but loud shadow when she will face it at last in the rubble of the darkness.

Is the star nothing but a shadow too? The star seems larger, nearer; it was a man, not a woman. He burns so brightly; no wonder she sees him so far away, singing and demanding. She cannot remember what she must do when she reaches him, but she knows.

Something is there that is not a shadow, something that slips away when she comes near. It wants the star, it is moving toward the star, like she is. Real as the riverbed, it sidles toward the star. She demands that it show itself, but it will not. It lets her just so close, then slinks away after the star again. This makes her angry, for although it never catches the star it will drive it forever out of her reach. She has forever, but the star does not.

Still he calls so loudly, and still she passes on. How can he keep calling, how can she hear him? She lies back down in the riverbed again just for a moment, to see the other faces again, but they are gone, too. Even so, it is hard for her to rise and walk on after the star. Although she cannot grow tired, she thinks she wishes she might grow tired, could be hot or cold or angry or afraid. But she has something to do, and only the star can tell her what it is. Why does he keep calling that name?

Is it she who has been singing, all these centuries, trudging behind her own song? It is a children's rhyme, but what children? Was the star never singing? Was it always her, singing him back toward her, as what someone will sing her up out of the riverbed? Vegetables; she sang vegetables.

She is so close now she can see that there is no star, but only the old man, falling across this old, old sky. He smiles and holds up his hands, showing her the flames oozing out from under his fingernails. He has a beautiful face, wise and eager. He speaks to her, but she can never hear his words because the fire under his tongue gets in the way. But she does not need to hear him; she knows her task now.

When she touches his hand, he will be free of the sky and the fire as well, free of whatever this pale place wants from him. They will go back together then, back to the riverbed. It is quiet there, and the water will heal his burning. She stands on tiptoe to touch his flaming hand.

And then. There. It stands between the old man and her, and

its voice is all there ever was. It says, *Mine*. She cannot see. She cannot think. The voice pierces her until she crumbles down, covering herself, trying to scream, yes, yes, he is yours, I am yours. But the words refuse to come out of her; she has something to do, and the words know it. She cannot give in; it is not permitted. She stands up.

What she sees looks almost human at first, but it is not. She says no; he belongs to me. No one belongs to her, because she is no one, but that is what her bones say. She tells it she has come to take him back to his own place, and it cannot have him. It must stand aside.

Again she reaches for him, and again it says, *Mine*. But this time it is almost puzzled, almost uncertain. It wishes to bargain for him. She tells it he made no bargain, and it has no claim on him. This time she takes his hand, which burns fiercely in hers without burning her. She feels only something alive moving softly between their palms. The old man looks at their two hands together and bends his head solemnly to kiss hers. That burns, and she tries to snatch her hand away, but he comes with it, part of her grinning. He is not what she thought at all. Yet she still has something to do, something for him. If it is not to find the quiet riverbed, what can it be?

She must act as though she knows; she must move. Any road away from nothing must be the right one. She starts to turn back the way she has come, but he stops her. She tells him he is to come home now; they are for the riverbed. At this he spreads his arms wide, putting her hands aside like a child's hands. With one more smile he explodes out of any human size, steepling up into the haze above them so fast and so high that it can barely keep him in. She tumbles as helplessly through his unending rage as he through the pale old sky.

But he cannot harm her, she who has been through the gates of death twice. She stretches up again for his bonfire hand and shouts that he is to come with her, she is to take him home. When he is back in proper human size, she tells him he does not belong here, and neither does she.

At this the not-quite-human creature follows, and she again tells it that it has no claim; they must pass. It, however, insists on their bargain. She tells it to speak of that with the other one; there was its bargain. The old man strides by her without giving it another glance, and she follows.

The Others appear all at once, rising into the darkness like star-pictures. They are everywhere, even in the riverbed, and they all insist on their bargain. The crying from all is no worse than the crying from one; they must be all one nature, one desire. This time the old man takes her hand, and they walk toward the Others, which thicken to meet them. He raises his other hand, leveling all five fingers at them, and the fire under his nails spreads out around them, blue and green, the flames having the raging heads of animals. Those waiting will not take even one step backwards, but are afraid of him. He asks their leave politely, and they part just enough to let the two of them into their midst then closing around them. But there was always room to walk, thanks to the fire animals and their hisses and snarls.

The two of them walk on, but she is tired, and she wishes to lie down in the riverbed. When he turns she is ready; they are for the riverbed, and he will need her help if he means to find peace. But at that he rears up over her, fire racing from one hand to the other to soar out behind him in a blue-white mantle, while he opens his mouth to chuckle flaming venom straight into her eyes. She throws up her arms and cries out for someone, because she is at the end of endless nights and the end of herself. But who comes when no one calls?

Surprisingly, it is the fox who is the next narrator. When the fox was revealed as Arshadin in disguise, we naturally expected to see no more of him in the narrative. Now, however, we see that Arshadin merely stole the man-shape from the fox shape changer, and the creature is not happy about it. What can he do about it? More than the foolish magician likes. Old nothing uses the fox for its comings and goings in this world, and not even old nothing ever stole the man-shape. The fox relates the events transpiring within the inn from his point of view, as an outside observer. He sees, as no one else does, Lukassa following the *griga'ath* that had been the other magician. Yet his business is only with the man-shape, and old nothing tells him to find the thief and explain it to him. Old nothing wants the one whose hunger disturbs its sleep; it urges the fox to take it to him. The fox will have back the man-shape, and old nothing will lap up his power and make him its left hand.

Yet the fox hesitates, to old nothing's amusement. The fox must choose between the human Lukassa and the man-shape, and it is not an easy choice. Every night, just before sleeping, she asked him for his name; he has no name, and she has lost hers. They were alike a little, in that way. The fox sits still and listens.

First the fox winds the *griga'ath*, but then he hears Lukassa. Time has no meaning where he is, the end is just the same as the beginning; space is not real either. But he hears Lukassa because he is listening. The place where the man-shape was hears her. He barks, and barks again, and Lukassa hears him. Before the *griga'ath* can swallow her, make her a living part of its fire, Lukassa calls out to the fox and comes to him, kneeling, reaching across all nowhere to hold him. For her sake he lets the man-shape go.

The *griga'ath*, though, is upon them, a blazing white sky of its own. Lukassa will not put him down. There is nothing to do but nip her wrist, hard. She backs away slowly and the *griga'ath* reaches to pick them both up and gulp them both down to feed his oven heart.

There is but one way left. It had been a long time since the fox had walked as his own self; the magician had not yet been born the last time. Usually the fox would do, and when the fox would not do the man-shape would do. Now there is no help for it. Old nothing would not like it, but old nothing is not there.

Lukassa's arms are around him again, but he cannot change in her arms. He looks her in the eyes and wills her to let him go, and she looks straight back at him and does so. The fox reaches down and in and down, shakes himself awake, the deep that is no borrowing, no form, no part of old nothing even.

He has no idea what he looks like, but he sees the change in Lukassa's eyes. Lukassa was not afraid of the *griga'ath* but she is afraid now, and the ancient thing that had been the fox is saddened. It would know her.

It is now the *griga'ath*'s turn to back away, holding Lukassa up between them like a lantern, and it is the ancient thing's turn to reach out with its long gray arms and hand, ridgy gray fingers bending the air. It tells the *griga'ath* to put her down.

There is a remembering in it, of a world of water and sky when it came to be, and plenty of foxes, but no humans, and therefore no *griga'aths*. There were no magicians trying to be gods, demons, ordinaries, all together. There were creatures like him, and other things, too, in the water, in the trees. The fox forgets; the man-shape forgets; but it remembers.

The *griga'ath* sets Lukassa down and she flitters behind it, unsure of where is the worse fear. It speaks to the *griga'ath* in the First Tongue, which the fox and the man-shape never knew. It tells the *griga'ath* to depart for whatever waits for it, and turns its back. It prepares to take Lukassa home to that other world.

But Lukassa will not come. It is only four steps right and around and down, but she will not come. She tries to return to the *griga'ath*, and tells the ancient thing that had been the fox that she had come for him.

It had always been like this. Any concern with humans, any feeling at all, and there you are, telling yourself you do not know what you know. Lukassa would walk through him right now, all for one wicked, lost old man. She calls desperately for, of all things, the fox.

Confused, made as stupid as she is by her love, there is no help for it. The ancient creature turns back to the *griga'ath* and tells it to come with them, despite knowing that old nothing must be hurting itself laughing. The *griga'ath* takes a single step, then another. It halts, looking at them with eyes like green cinders. Not knowing them, can it know who it is? Can it choose, this world or that? Lukassa claps her hands and sings hope, and it tells the *griga'ath* once more to come with them.

Rosseth is the next narrator, and he admits there is a hole in his memory, just there. He remembers the wind, people shrieking, and the inn shuddering violently all over. He remembers holding Lal's hand and walking with her and Soukyan toward a blackness where a wall had been, a blackness that asked them in, very sweetly, and showed them pictures. He was going there gladly.

Then there was nothing, except Karsh shaking him and shouting at the top of his voice. He is aware of Tikat shouting for Lukassa at a wall, and he is aware of the other wizard. It is like a dream, and it continues for a long time.

Soukyan stops it, moving Karsh behind Rosseth and asking if he is all right. Lal is with Tikat, trying to calm his endless, hearbreaking calling. Soukyan moves toward Arshadin, death in his face, but the wizard gestures vaguely in his direction and he falls to the floor, unable to breathe. Rosseth starts for Arshadin, but Karsh grabs his arms so hard that he carries black bruises for days. Lal flies across the room like a thrown dagger, golden eyes slitted and cold, but Arshadin glances sideways at her and she stops dead still, staring wildly in all directions. This part also seems to Rosseth to go on forever, but it is not like a dream.

Arshadin then announces that it is over; there is a new master here. Rosseth breaks free and rushes at him, only to be stopped by Lal. Arhsadin begins a warning, but is interrupted by the reappearance of Lukassa and the *griga'ath*. The come out of a fold in the air, a swift crumpling and smoothing that Rosseth glimpses only for a moment as it parts for them. Behind them in that moment is something Rosseth cannot have seen; it is gray and big, and it sees him, too, and it cannot have, and that is all he wants to say. In the next breath the gateway is shut and Soukyan's fox is leaping to the floor, where it sits coolly on its haunches and watches Arshadin turning different colors.

What happens next happens very quickly. Lukassa takes two

steps forward and collapses into Rosseth's arms. The *griga'ath* shakes itself, sneezes, and is the old wizard again. His first act is to snap two words at Soukyan, who breathes for what seems to be the first time in a hundred years. Soukyan reaches out to Lal, who pulls him to his feet and for an instant they hold each other. Then they both turn to look for Arshadin.

He is mad, of course; anyone who must be master is mad. But that does not mean his courage is all madness. He addresses the old wizard as boldly and contemptuously as ever, asking where he would like Arshadin to send him next, since he was back and they were all together again. But his lips move stiffly around the words, and his face looks like melting ice.

The old man looks immensely weary, but the smell of death and despair is gone from him. His green eyes are clearer than Rosseth has ever seen them, and bright as new leaves, and his laughter is spring water dancing up out of stone. He tells Arshadin not to mind about him, but that they should consider a far enough place to ship him as he stands there. For nothing is ever over, and those whom Arshadin has failed do not understand failure.

Rosseth quietly hands Lukassa over to Tikat, whose eyes meet Rosseth's for a moment before he bends his head and touches her hair. Rosseth looks away. Arshadin denies any problem; he kept his end of the bargain, and if the others could not keep the *griga'ath* it was not his fault.

Karsh simply wishes to kill the fox, who continues sitting up, observing everything with its tongue lolling and its expression serenely scornful. The old wizard continues trying to persuade Arshadin with some urgency, but the younger wizard merely laughs. Whether it was laughter in the comfort of arrogance, in certainty that his dear-bought new power would shelter him from any revenge, human or Other, or laughter of someone with nothing to lose and no possible escape to debate Rosseth does not know. There are, he thinks, worse ways to remember a bad man.

The air crumples again, close beside Arshadin. A ripple

appears, turning into a blue mouth; Arshdin turns and strikes at it, crying out words that sound like trees snapping in a windstorm, one after another. The round mouth pushes forward, as though for a dreadful kiss, puckers around him, draws him in, and is gone.

In the silence Rosseth hears Tikat singing. He has never looked up, but is rocking Lukassa in his arms. Rosseth knows the song; it is the lullabye about Brynarik Bay. Tikat has the words all wrong, or perhaps Rosseth does.

Tikat goes on, beginning the narration of the denouement. Lukassa sleeps for not quite three days, with the *tafiya* watching through the nights. When she awakens on the third day he restores the inn, putting the roof back where it should be; setting whole windows neatly into new frames in remade walls; and making the floors and chimneys level and straight. The inn in fact is better than it has ever been.

The fox has been asleep on her bed, and the *tafiya* appears to have fallen asleep as well. She comes awake all at once, and immediately recognizes Tikat, who tells her she has saved them all. Lukassa tells him that when she was there she heard him calling her. She still does not remember him from before the river, but she does know he is her friend and cares truly for her. And she knows that she has hurt him. Her hand turns over in his to close on his fingers.

She strokes the fox with her free hand, and he wriggles against it without waking up. Tikat tells her that the fox was also the man in the red coat, and she tells him that there is something else he is, something not like anything. Lukassa wishes to tell him about being in that place, but she cannot. The person who could have told him how it was is dead; she died on the other side of that black gate, as surely as the girl he knew died in the river. And yet here she is, talking to him, and who is she? Is she dead or alive? And if she is alive, who is she?

Tikat tells her she is as alive as he is, and she is herself. If she is not the Lukassa he followed here, maybe there never was any such person. He cannot himself be the person he was, and he is well content with that, as long as they recognize each other. He asks her what they are to do now; he had thought they could go home, back to those two other people, but they never can.

Lukassa knows she could go with Lal if she asked, but it would only be because she asked. She could go with Soukyan if Lal asked, but it would only be because Lal asked. Tikat jokingly suggests that they could stay at the inn and grow old along with Karsh, but the wizard has a better suggestion. He will take them with him. He looks at Lukassa with changed eyes, and tells her that while he has passed the gates of death, he was worse than dead. If not for her he would have been worse than dead throughout all eternity. She has a claim on him that he will never outlive.

When she protests that she had no choice, that she did what she did without any idea of what it all meant, and that she has no claim on anyone, he stops her. Apparently his need to be forever teaching somebody something has survived the black gate as well as himself. He may in a while remember a way to let this Lukassa and that Lukassa—the one still there in the riverbed— visit each other, talk together, perhaps even live together. The roof doesn't leak, the food is generally quite good, and the house is a restful one, if a little disquieting from time to time. Tikat recalls the fox's words: *bones full of darkness, blood thick and cold with ancient mysteries.*

Lukassa insists that Tikat must come, too. After staring at the fox for a while, the wizard says in a melancholy voice, that Tikat is as welcome as Lukassa, but that he should think carefully about it because he might learn more than he meant to learn. There are gifts and dreams and voices in him that may wake in the wizard's house, as they would nowhere else.

The wizard also tells Lukassa that the ring which Lal gave her is made to comfort and quiet certain sorrows, nothing more. Her life belongs to her, not to the ring. Lukassa's heart and soul and spirit are what keep Lukassa alive, not a dead green stone in a piece of dead metal, regardless of what Lal may have told her when she raised her from the riverbed. Lukassa agrees to return the ring to Lal when they leave with the wizard, and she can then return it to him if that is her wish.

Karsh continues, complaining years later that the inn has never been right since, even if everything works. The next two weeks are chaotic. Marinesha and Rosseth run the inn while Karsh spends time groveling and begging pardon before angry, injured, and frightened guests. The clientele never was built back up to what it was, and no wizard ever offered to help with that.

Lal lets him know that she and her companions will be leaving at last, as soon as the wizard and Lukassa are fit to travel. She also expresses regrets for all the troubles, as if she understands half of what her lot has done to his life. Nyateneri never bothers with any apology, which is just as well; Karsh can't handle any more shocks.

Rosseth stays out of his way to a remarkable degree, although Karsh doesn't exactly seek him out either, even though he had charged up a collapsing staircase and broken down a perfectly good door all because he could not stand the thought of training another stableboy. Or so he says.

Karsh is certain Rosseth is planning to run off with the women and the wizard, and doesn't want to face him because he knew Karsh would read him at first glance. He decides, after consulting with two bottles of the formented harness polish they make east of the mountains, called by the locals *Sheknath's* Kidneys, that if he wants to leave so badly, let him leave and be damned. But before Rosseth shows Karsh his heels, Karsh has a thing or two to show him.

Karsh seeks Rosseth out the next morning, and finds him rubbing a vile-smelling ointment that he makes into the flanks of a bay gelding while murmuring to it gently. Karsh watches in silence, studying Rosseth, whom he thinks will not ever be as big as he is but might turn out stronger. He tells the boy that if he wants to go with the old wizard and the rest of them, he doesn't have to sneak away. He should just take what is his and go.

But Karsh also tells Rosseth that a long time ago, on a journey, he had come across a village with all the inhabitants slaughtered, except for one baby. Karsh heard him, and tried to find him, when he was attacked from behind. It seemed like there were a dozen of them, killing him, and the blood streaming from a wound on his head blinded him. He struck out, blindly, with his staff, and killed them. They were Rosseth's mother and father. He did not mean to, but he did not know. They must have thought he was one of the killers coming back. He buried them, and would take Rosseth to the place if he ever wanted to see it; he could find that horrible place again if the sea had rolled over it. He took Rosseth with him; what else could he do? He bought a goat in the next town, and dipped bread in the warm milk to feed him. Taking Rosseth with him may have been the stupidest thing he had ever done, but it might be the only good thing, too. One or two others, just maybe, but the chances are Rosseth will be all he's got to show when his time comes.

Rosseth tells him that he is not going with Lal and Soukyan, but he is leaving. Not today, but soon. As Karsh turns to leave the stable, Rosseth stops him with a single word: his name. Karsh could not remember the last time Rosseth had said his name. He asks about a song someone used to sing to him, a song about going to play all day on Byrnarik Bay. He wonders if his parents ever used to sing that song to him. Karsh responds that only parents could sing a song like that, and leaves.

To himself Karsh remarks that Rosseth will no doubt sing that song to his own brats soon enough, and always grow damp around the eyes and soft around the chin when he does. The song is as idiotic as any of that sort, but it's the only one he knows. He sang it to Rosseth all the way through that bandit country where he found him, over and over, all the way home to his country, to the inn.

Lal briefly takes up the tale, reciting how Soukyan tells her he has to go back; there really is no other choice. They are alone in the travelers' shrine, Soukyan wanting to make a departure prayer since they will be leaving the next day. Lal had assumed they could journey pleasantly together as far as Arakli, where many roads meet, but Soukyan is tired of running. He is also getting a bit old for it. If he is not to spend the last years of a short life trying to deal with new teams of assassins as they keep coming after him, then he must return to the place they all come from, the place where he comes from.

Lal does not understand; to her it is good as commiting suicide, since they do not forgive and will not rest until he is dead. But Soukyan shakes his head slowly and explains he does not want them to forgive him; he just wants them to stop following him. He wants it done with, one way or the other.

Lal is angry; it will be done with, no doubt. He will fight them all at once. A hero's death. But Soukyan laughs then; he did not say he would fight them all at once. He has a plan, and he even has an ally or two back there, and some old sleights and confidences to bargain with. He will be as safe there as he was with her on the river—but not so happy, likely never again.

When Lal wishes to hear the plan, though, Soukyan declines; it is too long a story. It has nothing to do with her; it is his life, his past, his own small destiny. He is finished with waiting for it to bring him to bay one more time. He will go and meet it, for a change—and not in a bathhouse or on a river shore, but on a field of his choosing.

She tells him gently that he cannot cross the barrens in winter, but he knows that and thinks he will make for the coast and turn south at Leishai. It is a longer road, but a safer one, for some way at least.

In response to his question she tells him she will make for Arakli; she has wintered there before. Beyond that, she is Lal; that is where she is. As Soukyan leaves the shrine they both hear Lukassa laughing nearby, a sound neither of them had ever imagined hearing.

The final word is given to Rosseth. He rides with them as far as the turning where he had first seen them. The wizard leads the way, Tikat and Lukassa ride beside him, and he rides in the rear between Lal and Soukyan. He must remember it just as it was, because he never will never see any of them again. Once they had passed out of sight of the inn, Soukyan had let his women's guise rise from him like mist dissolving in the morning sun. His hair was growing out of the convent cut, but the twilight eyes and the reluctantly gentle mouth were still Nyateneri's.

Rosseth tells them he will be gone from that place in the spring, so he will not see the richness that is sure to follow. It is too short a ride to the tree and the spring and the bend in the road, but nothing he can do or say or think about can make it last any longer. All that is left is to concentrate on remembering everything, and he did remember it all and falls asleep to it still.

Just beyond the turn the path divides, one fork skirting toward the mountains toward Arakli, the other slanting eastward to meet the main road that runs to Derridow, Leishei, and the sea. The wizard announces that they part there, and that they will not meet again. He makes it sound joyous—hopeful even. He, Tikat, and Lukassa will travel west together, and Lal and Soukyan decide to travel together to the sea; Lal needs to be aboard again. The fox then sticks its nose out of Soukyan's saddle bag, and Soukyan remarks that it has chosen Lukassa; he thought it might. He gives it his blessing to go with her. She knows, though, that the fox is not likely to go with her and the wizard as well; she kisses it quickly and says it only wanted to say goodbye.

All of them say goodbye. Lukassa kisses Rosseth as she did the fox, with a sweet clumsiness, and what she remembers or does not remember he will never know. Lal kisses him differently, telling him that wherever he is, whatever happens to him, somebody loves him. Soukyan gives him a silver medallion from around his own neck, and when he protests he has nothing for Soukyan shows Rosseth a shabby cloth spattered with rust-brown stains. Does Rosseth think that many people have shed their blood in his defense? He treasures the cloth as much as anything he owns. And Soukyan kisses him, too; so there were his three.

Just before leaving, Lukassa gives her emerald ring back to

Lal, who looks it over with some longing before she gives it to the wizard. He shoves it unceremoniously into a pocket, then turns to Rosseth. He tells Rosseth his name is Vand, and that he is to remember them.

As he returns to the inn Karsh meets him at the crossroad. Rosseth tells him that his true name is Vand, but that Karsh can go on calling him Rosseth until he leaves. Karsh says, though, that if his name is Vand, his name is Vand.

The Innkeeper's Song is a significant achievement in fantasy. Even the minor characters are sharply etched, and the major characters are memorable and very clearly defined. The shifting narrative point of view maintains the reader's interest in the characters, and seeing them from differing points of view increases their complexity. The idea that the story is being told by the characters from some point far in the future is also fascinating.

As always in Beagle, place is important, and he takes great care in description and geography. The magical elements have great depth, and a reader gets the feeling that there are more details left untold than told. Perhaps most surprising is the fact that the main wizard is never named; most of the time he is called simply Lal's friend, or for a while the *griga'ath*, or sometimes Tikat's *tafiya*. Or at least it would be surprising if he were the main character. This is Lal and Soukyan's novel, though, from the beginning. It is their story that is told, or at least, as we learn later, begun. Perhaps it is only a coincidence that the wizard has green eyes, as did Schmendrick, and perhaps it is a further coincidence that the wizard traveled around with a woman for a long time, as Schmendrick did with Molly Grue. Perhaps it is a coincidence that both Lal's friend and Schmendrick are described as the greatest magician who ever lived. Or perhaps it is not.

Beagle's sometimes almost overpowering sense of humor is under more control here, but it is ultimately irrepressible. Just as in *The Last Unicorn* the main mode is ironic, and the text quivers with word-play and puns. The humor is carefully calibrated to the character, as well; unlike in *The Last Unicorn* there is no omniscient third person narrator except in the prologue. Each character makes the jokes appropriate to his or her own station, and the reader gains insight into the characters through both their modes of speech and their modes of humor.

Once again Beagle shows us the redemptive power of love, in the face of evil, in the face of hatred, in the face of power. He gives us hope instead of fear. Lal and Soukyan's love, Lukassa's love, Tikat's love, and even Karsh's love, transcend time and overcome all obstacles. If it was the magician's misguided love for Arshadin that led to all the problems, it was the love of the other characters for him, and his for them, coupled with Arshadin's lack of love for any living creature, that lead to Arshadin's defeat. As the bards of another place and time might sing, *all you need is love*.

Although in his Foreword to *Giant Bones* Beagle asserts, "I don't write sequels," and later repeats, "I really don't do sequels," in his novella "Lal and Soukyan," published in that volume, he does exactly that, continuing the adventures of the title characters he introduced in *The Innkeeper's Song*. He further asserts that if in the future he returns to the world of *The Innkeeper's Song*, "there will be other folk telling" the tales that he sets there. Just to hedge his bets, though, he also tells us, "Then again, maybe it'll yet turn out, even this late in the game, that I actually do sequels. What do I know?"

"Lal and Soukyan" picks up the title characters some forty years later, journeying together to atone for an act of cruelty many years earlier. The novella builds on the characters created in *The Innkeeper's Song* and expands them by using the more usual convention of the third-person omniscient narrator rather than switching first-person narrators. In this way Beagle is able to give the reader more information about the characters in less space.

There lived in the desert an old woman, albeit with still youthful hands, in a one-room whitewashed hut with a little girl, Chousi-wai, for a servant who calls her *inbarati*. One day she saw a man coming a long way and a long time off, and she knew him before the girl could even discern movement. She was small, completely white-haired, with a cat's triangular face and smoky golden eyes. She was teaching the girl to be a story-teller, as she was herself.

When late that night the old woman walked out to meet her visitor, she spoke first, telling him he is thinner than he was. He was a tall, old man, with a weathered hide not many shades lighter than her own black skin. He carried a bow over his right shoulder, and the bowstring pulling his vest open revealed several thin white scars up and down his ribs and one great jagged cicatrice just above the waist running halfway around his body. They greet each other by name: Lal and Soukyan.

When asked what he wanted, he replied that a cup of tea would be nice, a night's lodging, and a kind word. She told him he could have the tea and the lodging, but that in the morning she wanted him gone. Whatever he wanted, the answer was no. He came seeking Sailor Lal, Swordcane Lal, Lal Alone, and he had found a folktale crone, withered and forbidding, living out her time by telling stories to a barbaric desert tribe which is not her own but will do well enough. She was at last what she was always meant to be; all the rest had been one of her bad old dreams.

He agreed to leave in the morning, but first he wanted to sit with her that night and speak of Lal; he had a message for her, and perhaps this woman would see that it reached her. He wondered where her swordcane was; he owed his life to it three times over. She still had it, but she used it only to knock down fruit and draw pictures in the sand. The child had no notion of what it contained, and soon neither would she. That would suit her, but Soukyan's question was whether it would suit the swordcane.

Lal's only response was that his bow had saved her life three times, so they were long quits, as he knew. In the morning they would say their goodbyes—again. She had lost track of the number of times they had done so before. In Arakli, there had been a fire, and he had known for three years that she was dead. She had searched for him, and left word everywhere he might possibly have sought her. And it was no different when she watched him ride off at Bitava, knowing where he was bound but not knowing if she would ever see him alive again. How different were the partings at Cheth na'Bata; at Rhyak? She thought they were never meant to be friends, comrades, companions, whatever word he would. Neither could ever be certain of what they were entitled to ask the other, so they wore each other out. Enough goodbyes were enough after forty years, and they did not want the same things from what was left of their lives.

And yet she shrugged, imperceptively to anyone but him, and admitted that she was not going to get any sleep that night. They agreed not to speak of Lal's home, where she was stolen and sold, and sold again, and no one cared enough to follow and find her. They spoke instead of Kulpai, where they met in the cells. They escaped on the third night, Lal remembered, when the guard fell asleep. Soukyan hooked the keys out of the guard's belt and unlocked all the cells. Except, Soukyan reminded her, the guard did not fall asleep. Lal told him a story that had him so mesmerized that he did not see Soukyan at all until Soukyan had his hands on the guard's throat.

Lal remembered also that there had been a boy, a small boy: the guard's son. He had been asleep there in the scullery, and woke up just after they took his father prisoner. The boy came charging to the rescue. Lal stopped him, but did not hurt him. They only hurt his father, and he saw. They did not kill the father, but they humiliated him before his son. As the inmates were freed, each ran past where Soukyan held the guard and spat in his face. The boy saw it all.

This guard had been decent to them, as decent as he could be. He spoke politely to them. He actually tried to be kind, and Soukyan had no idea why. There may be no innocent guards, but the boy was innocent. What was between them, that boy and his father, was that innocence. It plagued Soukyan to that day. He never used to have bad dreams, but he dreamed about that.

Lal offered him a song to chase away such dreams, but he did not want the dream gone. He needed to remember. He needed to go back there, to apologize.

When she finished cursing, proving beyond doubt that she was indeed still Lal, she opened a bottle of Dragon's Daughter from the inn near Corcorua and they both drank. When he asked if she were coming with him, Lal told him to keep drinking. Most likely the guard would be dead, and the boy most likely would have forgotten the whole business by then, like everyone else. Everyone except the ancient mercenary with a crimp in his conscience. Even though there would be no one to say it to except himself, and no forgiveness but his own, Soukyan had to do it. One of his odd, meaningless loyalties was to his idea of himself, which was hard to come by and a weary time coming, as Lal knew well.

The next morning Chousi-wai arrived as usual to find them both gone, a pair of tracks leading across the desert. She was a tracker born, like all her people; it took no conscious thought for her to know that one of the trails was some hours fresher than the other. If asked, she could have predicted the exact place and moment when Lal would catch up to him. But there was no one to ask her, and she settled in to wait patiently until Lal should return.

When, some time later, Soukyan told Lal that they would need horses, he was told for his pains that she was still not speaking to him. Since there would be no horses, they must find *churfas* instead, evil-tempered, utterly untrustworthy, stinking, and a pure bloody nuisance to steal though they may be.

Lal continued not speaking to him until late in the afternoon. She had decided that she was traveling with him precisely to prove that this was not her life any more. For the most part they traveled by night, scooping out hollows in the sand to sleep in by day and moistening their lips and tongues every few hours to mumble a bit of dried meat or dried fruit. They hardly spoke after the first day, until one late evening when the breeze brought at least a memory of coolness and the smell of what might almost have been a cooking fire. Soukyan told her that that would be Doule, a small place but big enough to have a few *churfas*. The next day they would be riding on their way like gentry. When Lal protested that she remembered nothing about riding horses, let alone stealing them, Soukyan cheerfully replied that that did not matter, because nothing that works with horses will work with *churfas*. The way to handle a *churfa* is to stick your arm in its mouth. It must, of course, be all the way in the back, where there are no grinders. No matter how angry they are, something about having a nice arm to chew on always calms them down right away. If at the same time you cover the beast's nostrils with your free hand and squeeze very tightly, it will fall to its knees so that you can mount. It practically always works.

The next morning they were close enough to Doule to hear Nounouri devotees at their prayers. Doule remained a thorn-walled enclave of dirty white huts, differentiated from the desert only by a whimsical rainy season and an increasingly put-upon underground spring. They entered through a side gate in the barricade, barely noticed by the porter. Lal pointed out the common stable in the center of town, but Soukyan vetoed that choice on the grounds that it was much too public. He suggested instead one of the wealthier-looking homes.

The inn looked a decided step down from the public stables, but neither was of a mind to be finicky. They washed and dined and then slept until close on midnight. After sneaking out of the inn, Lal followed Soukyan's lead as they stole two *churfas* from a private stable, Lal methodically cursing Soukyan, the prison guard, the guard's son, and the entire population of Doule the entire time in three languages. How Soukyan conducted them back through the town without raising any alarm, and how he discovered the unattended gap in the thorn barrier, she never knew nor cared. She thought only that she was too old to be doing this, over and over.

Soukyan kept them traveling hard south and west, with the half-moon behind them, until dawn. They were not followed from Doule. Soukyan had doubted they would be, yet he rode with wide arcs across their backtrail for the next two nights, to be certain. They continued into the foothills that kept climbing yet never quite became real mountains.

They spoke very little of Kulpai. Both Lal and Soukyan found themselves falling easily into past ways of speaking and moving, as well as taking on, with no discussion, the camp tasks each had assumed so long ago. But for his grayness and the new scars, Lal would have seen no difference in Soukyan from twenty years before. He cooked what they killed quickly and inventively, talked too much or not at all, and complained as ever about the long, tuneless epic ballads of her own people, which she habitually chanted to herself as they rode.

As the weather was slanting gracefully into autumn and their way began its descent toward the flatlands, Soukyan revealed that if she had not agreed to accompany him on his undoubtedly ridiculous journey, he doubted that he would have gone any further than that white desert hut of hers. She did say no, and he did leave alone, but he knew she would follow, because he knew her. As she knew him. As no one living knew either of them. He was even glad of Kulpai, in a way, because they would never have had that time together otherwise. Whatever happened there would have been worth it, as all the rest was, all those years. Lal's only response was that they should try not to lose each other this time, and nothing more.

That same day they heard breathing, followed by voices. The breathing was from a boy, wearing the dirty, patched half-smock and breeks of a southern farmer. His face was bloody, his nose was obviously broken, and he could not have been more than seventeen. The voices were coming up fast, and there were hounds. The boy fell down before them, hopeless, fearless; Soukyan spoke to him in two languages but got no reply. He tried a third, gesturing to the boy to take refuge behind the *churfas*. The boy did so, so slowly that he had not quite reached them when his pursuers came crashing out of the woods. The hounds were in the lead, followed by half a dozen men, all but two clad much as the boy was. The other pair carried double-edged shortswords, wore studded leather and grand long boots, and carried themselves with the insolent vigor of the backland lords they obviously were. They had thick black beards and thick red faces.

Soukyan convinced one of the hounds to give up the chase by the simple expedient of kicking his *churfa* with one heel until it erupted instantly into a spitting, bucking mass of indignation, kicking the hound with one clawed hind foot into a thorn bush from which it seemed in no immediate hurry to emerge. The second hound sat down to reconsider, looking around for instructions. The boy clung to Lal's boot.

The larger of the two armed men strode forward and planted himself before Lal and Soukyan. He bid them good day in the second language Soukyan had tried, but stepped back quickly when the *churfa* shot its head out and Soukyan admonished it with a slap on the neck. The second man wasted no time on such civilities but moving faster than expected lunged between the beasts and actually had his hands on the boy before a long, thin blade nuzzled coldly at the back of his neck. He whirled to see the white-haired black woman smiling thoughtfully at him, telling him to treat the boy gently, because he was quite young.

Swatting the swordcane's point away, free to deny its reality because of the age of the hands that held it, he responded:

> "Young, is it, hag? Aye, well, he was old enough to say *no* to his appointed master—he was old enough to come between his betters and their lawful desires. Old enough to defy those whom the gods have set over you is enough to die, by my count. On your way, ancient ones—don't trouble your venerable heads on his base account. My lord takes care of his own."

Soukyan asked the boy's name and was told it is Cajli's Ri-aan. Soukyan thought that Cajli would be the boy's father; he had once been called Jamurak's Soukyan, long ago. But Cajli was the grandfather, and the first of the armed men. He asserted that it was his right to dispose of the boy as he would; no doubt Soukyan was from a civilized land, and would understand such things.

Cajli had planned to mate the boy with his friend's yellow-haired girl, just to see what would come of it. She was primed and willing, but the boy refused and walked away, as if he had any say in the matter.

The boy's voice was clearer when he spoke again. The girl was not willing, but even if she had been he still would not have touched her. The gods made them Cajli's servants, not his beasts.

At this Cajli lost speech entirely, along with anything resembling prudence, and started for Riaan. Lal blocked him with a subtle move of the *churfa*, and from the ground Cajlli ordered the attack. The other swordsman and the four bondmen moved forward grimly, and Soukyan apologized to Lal for the inconvenience; he had forgotten about this country. She merely reminded him that he was always slower on the left side.

Soukyan's bow was out more quickly than she could see, and when the first warning shot went purposefully wide the second armed man laughed. The second arrow took his right leg from under him. Blood welled but did not fountain, and Lal noted that Soukyan could still miss the artery when he wanted to. At this Cajli sprang forward savagely at Lal, pulling her from her mount. Although once she could have kicked him off, now she merely landed tumbling and was on her feet before he was, her swordcane trained on his heart. He kept coming at her, despite her constant admonitions to him to let be, until finally when he swung his shortsword in a stroke that would have shattered her blade she killed him, slide, stamp, lunge, and away to the next before he knows he's dead. The body remembers. But she could not pull the swordcane out of his chest, and Cajli took it from her as he fell. Two of the bondmen were on her then, and as she let herself go down and roll, fumbling for the dagger in her boot, the boy hit one of the men in the temple with a stone. Riaan exhorted the men to stop; the two old ones had never harmed them, and the other two had hurt them all their lives.

The men, however, could not overcome a lifetime of conditioning, and continued their assault on Lal and Soukyan. Standing considerably aside from herself, Lal watched in distant fascination as a lean old woman she almost recognized kicked one of her attackers in the groin and killed a second with the dagger. At that the remaining men gave up, and Soukyan took the arrow from the armed man's leg before Lal cleaned the wound as best she could. The men declined their offer to bury the dead; the nobleman was due rights that none but his family could perform, and the dead bondman could not be buried at all, having failed his lord. They carried the injured lord away, never looking back at Riaan.

Lal and Soukyan, with the help of Riaan, buried the dead anyway; they may have been old, but they still cleaned up after themselves. Soukyan, who had lost a side tooth and had one eye all but closed, did his best to fix the boy's broken nose, and Lal petulantly complained about her bruises. When the boy brusquely thanked them and apologized for their hurts in saving his life before turning to march away, he got about ten yards before he crumpled down in small sections. They agreed that the boy was now theirs, and Lal took him to ride with her on her *churfa*, an act that amazed Soukyan since he had never known a *churfa* to carry two before.

The next day the boy had built a fire and was already cooking three small fish over it when they woke up. Although he had no self-esteem, and once he saw them knew that he knew nothing, not even what he did not know, they told him he had courage and could cook and was welcome to come with them.

Even down in the open country, most nights had by then turned frosty, and there was not always enough wood to keep a fire alive until morning. Soukyan disappeared for a day and returned with a cured *guangsu* skin for the boy, and he slept warmer than they that night, as Lal pointed out repeatedly. Soukyan pushed their mounts along briskly, hardly looking to left or right, remarking that they could still reach Kulpai before it snowed if they didn't have to stop and bury anyone else.

Riaan was easier with Lal than with Soukyan, despite the hide. Mostly silent during the day, he plagued her with ceaseless questions about the world beyond when they had bedded down at night. Lal expected that; what surprised her was how many of the questions concerned her family, or Soukyan's. She repeated over and over that she did not know, or that they did not discuss things like that. His curiosity stemmed from the fact he and his kind were bred like animals, and he thought it a miracle that they could know their families; it was all he could do to imagine such a thing. Soukyan thought that the boy might have been better off as he was; at least he had never learned to love anyone who was to be snatched away from him forever between one minute and the next, as had been his sister, and for that matter as had been Lal herself.

Two nights later they camped at the edge of an orchard. Soukyan told them that they were a day's journey from the Churush road, and three from Jahmanyar. In ten days, at most, they would be smelling Kulpai. Riaan could not sleep, so Lal told him a marvelous story, Choushi-wai's favorite. When she was done he sighed wistfully and said he wished it were true; he wished all stories were true. Lal smiled in the darkness, and told him:

> "All stories are lies, just because they *are* stories. But they are true even so, every one of them, and sometimes the biggest lie turns out the truest of all. And don't ask me why that is, Riaan, because I could never tell you. But it is so with stories."

The boy was silent for a long time, and then said he was glad that ghosts were true, because he could meet a ghost who could tell him about his father. He thought his father was dead, but that his father cared about his mother. Maybe he couldn't protect her, maybe he couldn't be with his son, but he did care about them. Sometimes the boy made it up in his head that his father died trying to save them, but he had to know. Lal told him that he might be sadder for the knowing, and that he had to know that, too.

Lal spoke with Soukyan about their conversation that night, and he immediately assumed, rightly, that she wanted to call the boy's father back from the dead, using the one bit of magic they had ever managed to learn, even though they had also learned why even great wizards fear to summon the dead. Her attitude was that in a just cause, and with respect, there was no harm. The harm, Soukyan told her, was to the tissue of things—the things that exist beyond their desires. It was not a wall that separated their world from those others that they knew so little of, it was a dam. Open the way, with the best of intentions, for one perfectly harmless spirit, and neither of them could possibly guess what might come spilling through. They were never supposed to be here, ever; the universe hated it. She should leave it alone.

Lal, however, was never one to leave it alone. She felt she was Riaan; because she knew what had been done to him better than he did, and because she knew what such a life could make of a child. As the prison guard and his son still haunted Soukyan, so it would haunt her for all the time she had left not to do the little she could for him. Because she knew. After Kulpai, she proposed, but Soukyan did not know where he would go after Kulpai, or why.

In the city of Jahmanyar they stayed at an inn on a side street, but rather than eat in their room as Lal wished, Riaan begged earnestly to have it served to them in a real taproom. As they went downstairs, Soukyan remarked to Lal that this was what it was to be grandparents, and that he hated it already. Lal's response was that she thought they must have had a nice daughter.

In the taproom they were entertained by a magician. Riaan was mesmerized by his parlor ticks, but Soukyan dismissed him as third-rate when he began by snapping his fingers to make fire shoot out of his fingertips, and followed by conjuring up something with yellow eyes, long yellow teeth, and blooded wings that flashed high across the taproom and vanished up the chimney with a thunderous fart. When the magician produced beer far better than the inn had ever served, however, Soukyan revised his estimate to second-rate. The magician then called up a ghost with words Soukyan and Lal could not hear above the crowd. It grew just as a pearl would grow, or a child, accumulating itself around a single fiery spark where its heart should have been. But it was dead; it had been dead for a very long time, and it had not died peacefully or found any grace beyond the grave. Someone threw a bottle through it, and when a general melee broke out Soukyan and Lal rushed Riaan from the room. The magician mopped his forehead and absently flicked a finger at the creature to banish it. Riaan asked if it was indeed a real ghost, and although Lal admitted it was she also told him that not all ghosts are like those in stories.

Riaan continued unusually quiet over the next few days on the Churush road, and his companions found his silence distracting. It was a thoughtful silence, and there was no penetrating it. Lal said privately to Soukyan that real grandparents would know what to say to him, but Soukyan responded that real grandparents would not have started him thinking about ghosts and calling his father back.

Lal watched the boy carefully, never letting him out of her sight. Soukyan did the same. Three days from Kulpai, Lal asked Soukyan what would happen when they got there, and he admitted he did not know. He would start looking at the cells, of course, and if the guard or his son is not there then he would ask for his family, or anyone who might have known him. What she wanted to know was, find him or not, when would it be over for Soukyan? She had no desire to winter in Kulpai. One single day, no more, was all he asked. If there is anyone in Kulpai for him to speak to, to say what he must say, he will know it by then. If not—so be it, then not. Neither of them knew what they might do with Riaan.

That night neither of them slept well. Soukyan found no comfortable way to arrange his big body on the damp ground, and Lal was troubled with such dreams as had not found her in many years' hungry searching. She woke violently, running from a man long dead, who laughed sweetly as he followed. It was Shavak, she told Soukyan who held her when he awoke instantly to her small cry, he was always the worst one and she didn't even kill him.

They missed Riaan immediately, and saw lights bobbing and dancing far away, moving slowly closer. They heard his voice, although they could not make out the words he was chanting, but Soukyan knew he was summoning. Lal, running after him, shouted that he could not know the words; she had never uttered them while he was near. Soukyan replied that the magician did; they had not heard him in the taproom, but the boy did. There are many spells to call a ghost.

As they approached Riaan they saw a figure taking form, growing out of the lights they had seen, around the light, and the boy's voice leaping up in exultation, itself turning into light. Lal tripped and fell, and as she got up she heard Riaan's victory chant splinter into a cry of horror.

There was only one light then. The shape was all but complete, and although the face was yet indistinct Riaan and Lal already knew that it was Cajli. It walked toward Riaan, reaching out for him with its powerful arms, smiling with its shining face. The ghost called to him, telling him that in his world or its, he belonged to it, and nothing would ever change that. Not while he lived, not after he died. He called to Cajli's Riaan to come to him, and warned Soukyan not to come between them, for peril of his soul. Then Lal was there, a very old woman who had run too far on old legs, stumbling between Riaan and the white figure to gasp defiantly and draw her swordcane. Be it ghost or demon or walking heap of putrid meat, she would kill it a second time if it did not back from him. Soukyan was at her side in an instant, arrow at the string.

When after additional provocation and an attempt by the spirit once again to draw Riaan to itself Soukyan loosed the arrow, it not only passed through the ghost as the bottle had passed through the other ghost in the taproom but also provided a pathway for a sickly yellow-green fire to backtrack straight to Soukyan's hands. He opened his mouth and fell, curling on his side almost at Riaan's feet.

Lal had started to strike as soon as the arrow took fire, and had no chance to turn the swordcane's point aside. She felt its contact with the ghost as an instant of agony so cold that her flesh barely had time to recognize it as pain before she too was down, face hard against the mucky grass, body flopping like a landed fish.

Out of the side of her eye she could see that Riaan had shaken free of his paralysis and was edging away, sliding one foot after the other only by force of will. The ghost followed, unhurried, but its grimly benign chuckle had turned threatening. It told Riaan that he was born to serve it for eternity, and that he would serve him better in that world than in this or have eternity to regret it. It commanded Riaan to take its hand, now.

In the moonlight the boy's face looked as white as that other face, and seemed on the edge of flying completely apart. For all that, when his answer came it held a trembling unassailable high: "I was not calling you. I would die and be a hundred times more rotten than you before I would ever say your name again. I was calling for my father. I call him now."

Nothing happened. The ghost's laughter rose to a howl:

"Why, there's you answer, boy, there's your father indeed. Son of nothing, child of no one, there's not even a ghost that knows your name. Ash, ember, vile little cinder, you've no one in any world to belong to, save only me. Welcome then, welcome twice over, Cajli's Riaan."

Riaan never gave in, never surrendered to a loneliness more fearful than Lal ever knew. He sang back at it that he didn't believe it; alive or dead, he did not believe it. And he called to his father once again, called with stolen words he did not understand to someone he did not know, someone so hopelessly far away in the endless dark. And someone came.

There were no lights this time, only a rather small, nondescript figure taking shape before them so slowly that it seemed to be trudging across a black desert far wider than the one Soukyan had crossed to Lal's door. Nor was there any sound. Soukyan fumbled blindly for Lal's hand, already seeking his.

Tired to death in life, the new ghost was nowhere near the end of its weariness; it had merely come one more journey to answer one more command. It said simply, in a flat country voice, "Well, here I am." Riaan gave a curious little sigh that Lal remembered all her days, and whispered his simple question: "You. You, please. Is it you?"

It did not speak again for a very long time, but when it did it whispered, "Riaan?" The boy wept, and the ghost went on. "I named you.... Is that crying? Why do you cry? Here I am." Lal held on hard to Soukyan's hand.

And so they might well have stayed until dawn, but for the ghost of Cajli. It approached the other ghost, and recognized it as a former field hand. But the other's strange attention was bent all on Riaan. It said, "Eliath. My name is Eliath." The boy managed to stop crying, and responded that he was then Eliath's Riaan. He repeated the name over and over, and that too might have gone on until morning and long past, but for Cajli's ghost. It approached Riaan, closed a bloodless hand on his forearm, and said, "Now."

Soukyan and Lal never agreed on what happened next. To Lal it seemed that the weary little phantom that called itself Eliath instantly seized the hand of Cajli's ghost, breaking its grip on Riaan in a motion as swift and burning as a shooting star. Soukyan remembered a light as well, but what he saw moving against it were figures ripped from the night itself: inhuman silhouettes, all but shapeless, all but joined, swaying back and forth, dancers ringed by a white fire. There was no distinguishing Eliath's ghost from Cajli's, nor any way of knowing which would prevail, or what prevailing meant. The struggling figures were beginning to come undone, raddling and unraveling like worn silk. He could not see Riaan at all, but he heard the boy cry out again, not in pain this time but in desperate fear, and not for himself.

When they talked about it later, Soukyan told Lal that it was all wrong; those two should never have been there, and they should not have been fighting. The more they fought the more wrong it became, until the tension was too much for someone— for something.

Lal saw only the hands. But what she did see at the last, and what Soukyan never mentioned, was a third hand, small and dim against the light, yet preserved in outline. The hand appeared to seek out and grip one of the other hands fiercely, beginning to tug it toward the edge of the circle. Only for a moment Lal glimpsed this; then the whiteness ate up the sky and she heard, or thought she heard, a sound like the banging of the windblown door of a great empty house.

Until she heard the boy calling she did not realize that her eyes were tightly shut. When she opened them she saw Riaan standing before her with the ghost of a bondsman glimmering shyly at his shoulder. Of Cajli's ghost there was no trace, no least echo, not even in the boy's eyes. "Here is Eliath, my father," Riaan said.

Lal bowed awkwardly, but Soukyan pushed abruptly past her to examine the boy's hand. There were four parallel marks on the palm, the exact color of the moonlight, and the single fat sear crossing the back, where a thumb would have clenched. It was as if it had been frozen, but Riaan claimed it did not hurt, and that he could use it, although his eyes closed for an instant as he demonstrated movement. He explained that he had to do it; he had to make Cajli let go, or Cajli would have taken Eliath with him. It was his father who saved him, and simultaneously he had saved his own father. He was glad he had the strange scars on his hand.

Riaan's father or not, the ghost of Eliath was still a ghost, and Riaan must not touch him. Morning was coming, and with it the ghost would have to depart. Lal and Soukyan waited aside, and Soukyan reminded her that as he had said, things were better as they were. But Lal disagreed; not for this one. This one had to *know*. Like Soukyan.

At that, Soukyan looked back at the boy and the ghost of his father. If he had never come to find her; if they had never come to Kulpai; or if they had sailed there, as they did another time; if the boy had kept his mouth shut and bred whomever they put him to; or if *they* had kept their mouths shut.... But Lal stopped him with a hand on his arm, reminding him that the real reason was that they had not, after all those years, disowned their own hearts.

The ghost of Eliath became more tenuous and filmy by the moment, and soon all that was left of it was Riaan, and a soft, raw gasp of bereavement that could have come from either of them, or from Lal herself. Riaan came to them in his own time, and told them that his father would come to him again if he had need, but that he would not.

Kulpai was exactly as unpleasant a place as Lal remembered. Soukyan left Lal and Riaan sleeping in the least dangerous inn on the morning following their arrival, and strode toward the lockup under the city wall. When Lal awoke, Riaan was also gone. After tidying herself and her gear and menacing the cook into producing something that came quite close to being a meal, she made her leisurely way down to the harbor. Riaan was where she thought to find him, sitting on a stanchion at the end of the wharf. He admitted it was too much for him; too much world beyond his village, too much sky, too much sea. He did not know what would become of him; where was he to go from Kulpai? Lal's only answer was, where were any of them to go from Kulpai? Should she return to telling stories in the desert? Was Soukyan to go on wandering like dust in the wind, with no more cause than seeing what happens next? Riaan could go with either of them, but if she were he, she would wait right there for the sea to speak to her.

Riaan gave a short laugh that was too old for him, and said:

"You are Sailor Lal, born on the water—the sea will always speak to you. Why should it bother with someone who never saw it until this morning?" She could only respond that she never knows its reasons, but the sea was looking at him. If it chooses, it will speak soon enough, if he would sit still and listen.

When night came and Soukyan had not returned, they walked silently back to the inn and had their dinner. The meal was long over and the taproom empty except for the two of them when Soukyan walked through the door. He looked as though he had been in the rain a long time. He sat at their table, drank the fierce, oily Kulpai brandy that the barmaid brought him without being asked, and told them that the man's name was Haruk. He died twenty-three years ago. Some thought the son had married a woman from Arakli and moved there, some thought he had gone to sea. The trail was not only cold, there was no trail at all. Lal had been right, of course.

Lal found herself savoring the defiant absurdity of his mission. The journey itself was his apology; he knew that, and the journey knew that, and nothing else mattered.

The odd thing, Soukyan told her, was that no one at all seemed to recall their escape. As long as that time had lived with him, Haruk himself probably forgot to mention the whole wretched affair.

The barmaid, though, had overheard him. She wanted to know if that was their doing—a black woman and a tall brown man. No, she was no relative of Haruk, though she did know him a little when she was a girl. Her great-uncle Gauvarda was one of those set free that day, and he spoke of it often, as well he might have, as an innocent man. Among the Nounouri it is a great shame to be imprisoned, innocent or not. Her great-uncle never forgot the two of them, and he would wish her to offer her gratitude.

Soukyan began to laugh, sounding as young as Riaan. He had come from a far country, dragging these two good friends along with him, all to ask forgiveness of a man he dishonored half his life ago. He wanted to ask him, or his son, or a grandchild, but the only person who halfway understood his idiot quest was the great-niece of another prisoner.

She agreed; atonement mattered greatly to them as well. We all die unforgiven by someone, but that cannot be helped. But penance at least is in themselves. It was too bad it had not been her family he had offended. What with her son married and gone, and her husband short a hand at the tiller and the nets, even a grandsir like himself would have come in useful. Even a child with a bad hand. She turned away abruptly, dismissing the notion and apologizing; her troubles were her troubles.

Riaan watched her leave, and Soukyan wiped his mouth and stared at them both as Lal said an odd thing: "I think perhaps the sea just made up its mind."

Riaan saw them off the next morning, coming out from behind the bar where he would be helping the barmaid until her husband's fishing boat returned. He said shakily that he hated saying goodbye like this. Soukyan replied that there isn't any good way; Lal and he would have known by then if there were. Riaan kissed them both solemnly and tenderly, as one would kiss one's grandparents. They knew, he told them, that he would never be done thanking them. Lal snorted; it sounded remarkably dull to her. If he ever got over it he should send to them and they would come and see him. She added that he should be careful on that bloody boat; they try to kill you. Things swing around and hit you on the head; he should never trust a bloody boat. When he cried out sadly, asking them how he should know where they are, Lal and Soukyan looked at each other before Lal replied that he should ask the sailors; some of them will always know where they are. She then bid farewell to Eliath's Riaan.

They were clear of dreary Kulpai before Soukyan remarked to Lal that she could have told Riaan that she was going back to her desert, to her little house and her stories. But Lal surprised him by saying she was not going back there; she was going instead to the place where she was born. It continued to plague her. There were ghosts and ghosts; she had told Riaan that. It was time, long past time, for her to turn and face hers.

Soukyan reached out to grip her forearm tightly as they rode. What if the same thing were to happen to her? What if there were no one left to know her, no one left to rejoice with, to remember with, no one who still wondered what became of little Lal. What then?

Then there were other places she always meant to see, and perhaps one or two more things that were always meant to happen to her. There was so much forgotten, and so much of herself laid by until he beguiled her into their very foolish journey. She thought she would take a ship, and then it would be less than two days' ride; and then she thought of Choushi-wai. She would spend the rest of her life in that little hut, waiting for Lal to return. She had forgotten about Choushi-wai.

Soukyan had a solution for that problem, too. He could go back and tell Choushi-wai, and rest there for perhaps rather a while. Lal had roaming to do still, while he seemed to be at last coming to a stop inside himself. He needed stillness. She continued to stare until he slapped her shoulder, not lightly, and told her to keep moving because it was too cold to stand there.

In half a day they came to a tributary of the Queen's Road, at which they had separated once before. Breaking a long silence, Soukyan asked if she thought they would mind, in the village. Lal did not think so; he had tales of his own to tell them, and that would certainly be a change from her old warhorses. Choushi-wai would certainly not mind; she was a little in love with him, and would feed him until he looked like a *jejbhai* being fattened for Thieve's Day. He summed it up: at the small end of their lives they were trading places. She agreed; it seemed the most natural thing in the world.

If it was, he wanted to know why she was so angry. She burst out that she was angry because they would never see each other again. He knew it, and she knew it, and there was no help for it. Forty years' worth of farewells is enough for anyone—she had told him that when he first came to her—and still she let herself in for one more. She was angry at herself, and he should just let it be.

They came close to missing the inland road because of the weather, and it was Lal who noticed the wagon ruts half-covered in snow. They halted the *churfas* and looked at each other across the wind for a long time. Soukyan told her that the boy may turn out to be no fisherman, and they may have to go back there and rescue him again. She merely told him goodbye, and asked him to help Choushi-wai with her reading before tugging on the beast's ear and turning back toward the coast road.

There was an outraged silence, then a bellow: "And that is *it*. That is *all*? After forty years?" Without turning her head, she replied that she had told him; it was just one goodbye too many. She kept a vow to herself not to look back, and had even begun singing to herself as a distraction. Consequently, she almost fell off the *churfa* when Soukyan came striding up on foot and shoved his arm in the animal's mouth to forestall a scream of alarm. He told her to get down, the effect being spoiled only slightly by his being out of breath, and after a moment he said her name, more softly. At that she slid to the ground, and they held each other tightly for a long time.

Lal said she felt like Riaan, finding his father, losing his father, seeing the ocean for the first time. It was too much for her. He let he go then, remarking that they might yet find themselves together in the same lockup one more time. You never know. But this time she did know, and she said so. She kissed him with the innocent ferocity of a young girl, and then was up on the *churfa* again, saying to him over her shoulder, "Sunlight on your road," as though they had shared together nothing more than a meal, a stretch of road, or a single night. "And on yours," he replied. "At least you know where to find me. If you should need me."

"Oh, I will always need you.... There's the plain bloody aggravation of it." Soukyan did not stare after her, having made his own private vow. Lal began her tuneless singing, and he remarked yet again that only a *churfa* could like it. His *churfa* stumbled forward, and the mists closed around them.

Repentence, atonement, and forgiveness are important in Lal

and Soukyan's world. Ghosts may be run from for a long time, but not forever. Beagle even flirts again with the metafictional idea he developed more fully in *The Last Unicorn*: all stories are lies because they are stories, but all stories are also true. More important than the destination, though, is the journey; and more important than forgiveness is love. Beagle shows us more clearly than before what motivates his favorite characters, and we would do well to emulate them in our own lives.

With "Lal and Soukyan" Beagle left two important stories about his title characters untold. At the end of *The Innkeeper's Song* Soukyan is off to return to his origin, and face his pursuers. He has clearly already done so by the time of "Lal and Soukyan," forty years later. That story was finally told in "Return," in 2010. But at the end of "Lal and Soukyan," the story of Lal's return to her place of birth remains to be told, and perhaps with it the end of this love story. There are many other stories to be told of Lal and Soukyan as well, as Beagle has hinted in "Lal and Soukyan," but only these two are necessary. I believe that once more before he puts aside his pen Beagle will return to this world, and tell us what happens to Lal at the end, just as he told us of Soukyan in "Return."

In 2003 Beagle produced the story "Quarry," in which he explains how Soukyan and the fox first met. It is not the necessary story of Lal's return to her place of birth, but it is interesting nonetheless.

"Quarry" is told in first person, and the narrator is Soukyan, many years before. He tells of the place he escaped from, giving us a tantalizing glimpse of life behind the monastry walls—the twilight room with its tall chairs; the cold, stone table; the tiny green birds outside; those smiling, kind, gentle eyes on him— and tells us that he wakes up screaming every time he dreams of it. If he left they would hunt him down; one unpunished deserter was more than they could tolerate. But leave he did.

He knew the Hunters would be after him, and that they never gave up. He would have to kill them. He had killed once before, but was not skilled. Nor was he skilled in covering his tracks;

it was a miracle he was not taken the first night. He would have been, except that he slipped on a frond, fell down a slope he did not see, hit his head, and crawled into a sort of shallow half burrow, scraping every last bit of rotting vegetation he could reach over himself in hopes of covering his scent before he passed out. He awoke in the late afternoon of the next day, hungry and weak and sick. There was no sign of his pursuers, so he drank a little and crawled back in to sleep until nightfall.

He covered more distance than he expected that night, and holed up in what may have been a *sheknath's* cave. There was still no sign of pursuit. He was not fool enough to believe he was free, but he began to hope, which was just as bad. On the fourth day he came close to the Queen's Road, and hid under a leech-bush until moonset. When he went on, he saw them.

Each of them stood away at an angle, making him the third point of a murderous triangle. They simply appeared; both were weaponless, one was smiling, and one was not. In the dimness he saw laughter in their eyes, and a weariness such as he had never imagined, and death. But they let him by. They were playing with him, letting him know that he was theirs whenever they wanted him.

There was nothing else to do; he went forward. Ragged, scabbed, and filthy as he was, not one traveler turned his head as he slipped onto the Queen's Road. The road at that time had a curious sort of elbow, a last untamed remnant of the original wagon-road, beginning just before the first tollgate he would reach. Since he had nothing for the toll, he made up his mind to dodge onto the old road, with no idea of where to go, but with the mad fancy of eluding both the killers and the collectors. Had he carried his plan through his life would have been different, most likely, and shorter, surely.

As he prepared to turn off he edged closer to a wagon on the road, which was carrying *jejebbai* manure. His legs were tensing for the first desperate stride when he heard a voice in his ear saying the single word, "No." He whirled, saw nothing on the manure cart, and determined he must have misheard a driver's grunt. He prepared to leave again, and this time heard very clearly, "No, fool." It was not the driver; the driver never looked at him. He was being addressed—commanded—by the manure pile. Then he saw the eyes, gray and very bright, with a suggestion of pale yellow far below the grayness. The man—he was certain it was a man's face—beckoned to him to join him.

Soukyan stopped where he was, letting the cart jolt past him. The sharp voice from the manure was both clearer and more annoyed when it said, "Boy, if you have any visions of life beyond the next five minutes, you will do as I tell you. *Now.*" The last word was no louder than the others, but it was enough to bring him scrambling into the cartload of muck quicker than he has since lunged into a warm bed, with a woman waiting. The voice told him that if he stayed still they would ride past the toll collectors like royalty, and those who followed him would pass and never take his scent.

The man saved his life, most likely, for they rolled past several tollbooths and the driver paid the toll each time, never knowing they were there. With the last barrier safely past they slid from the cart, tumbled to the roadside in such cover as there was, and rose to face each other in the daylight. They stank beyond anything but laughter, and laugh is what they did then, until they could barely breathe.

The man was old. His hair and brows were as white as his mustache, and the gray eyes were streaked with rheum, yet his cheeks were absurdly pink, like a young girl's cheeks although he carried himself as straight as any young man. When Soukyan first looked into his eyes he knew already not to trust him, and yet he wanted to, anyway. He can do that.

Soukyan introduced himself, the first time the reader has heard his name, and the man, who clearly knew the area, led him to a spring where they cleaned themselves. Afterwards they talked, and Soukyan told the man most of his story. The man lied so much about everything it was impossible for Soukyan to sort out whatever truth there might have been, but it did not matter. The man was there for him when he needed a friend, and it has happened so since.

The man told him what he already knew: that his followers would run behind him until he died. They would never return to their masters without him, or what was left of him. Soukyan acknowledged that without the man, he would have been dead, and the man admitted that he had his own purposes and small annoyances with which he had to deal, so it suited him to share roads with Soukyan for a little. He told him they might yet prove of some use to each other.

Having no goal and no vision of a life beyond flight, Soukyan had no real choice but to go where the man led. The man's wood-craft was sufficient for them both, and as they traveled he made sure the area was safe every night. They never slackened their pace, and never grew careless in covering their tracks. The man ridiculed Soukyan constantly about how little he knew of the world; what education he had received was worthless to them. When Soukyan defensively told him that his father had taught him how to shoot a bow, the man derisively said that he would be sure to stand behind him when he did so. Soukyan found it tedious, and sometimes hurtful, but the man began to teach him things.

One thing Soukyan did understand from the first was that the man was also a fugitive. Cunning and knowing though he was, even he could detect no sign of the Hunters. One night Soukyan, though, caught a glimpse of the thing pursuing the man; it had three bird-like legs, the third of which was more like a tail, although it had its own claws. The head and upper body were more human-like, but it disappeared before he could get a good look. The old man leaped up out of a doze, teeth bared, and crouched to launch himself in any direction. And then he turned into a fox. Soukyan could not say he actually saw the change; he never did, really. It was nothing more than a sway in the air, not even a ripple, and there he was. The fox gave one wild glare before he sprang away into the mist, and Soukyan did not see him again for a day and another night. Nor did he see the great bird-legged thing; it was obviously seeking the old man, not Soukyan. It was no Hunter.

The old man came back in human form, and Soukyan did not see that change, either. He did see later, though, the sets of footprints that showed exactly where the change happened. Plainly, the man did not care if he saw it or not. When Soukyan asked him what he was, he replied that he was what he needed to be. Now this, now that, as necessary. As are we all.

Soukyan, though, was not so easily mollified. Not everyone turned into a fox and abandoned his friends, leaving them to face monsters alone. Nor did everyone lie from sunup to sundown. He had no more use for him, and they had no future together. From then on Soukyan would travel alone.

The old man promised that he would tell Soukyan everything he needed to know, but of course he did not. What he did tell him was that the creature he had seen was a Goro—one of the bravest, fiercest folk who walk the earth. To be killed by a Goro is considered a great honor, for they deign to slay only the bravest and fiercest of their enemies. Merely to make an enemy of a Goro is also an honor, and that was what the old man had inadvertently done. He made a mistake; he stole a Goro's dream.

The dream of a Goro was as real and substantial as was Soukyan, and each one took solid shape in our world. It would manifest itself in whatever form it chose. Once when he was traveling among the Goro in his fox shape, a dream took the form of a shiny stone, and the fox likes shiny things. So it took it.

A stolen dream cries out to its begetter. No Goro will ever rest until its dream is safe at home again, and the thief gathered to his ancestors in very small pieces. A Goro will keep all of his dreams, although they may amount to nothing more than a heap of dead twigs and dried flower petals, because he must present the whole unsightly clutter to his gods, when he goes to them. If even one is missing, the Goro will suffer bitterly after death. The fox had lost interest in that particular stone long ago, but such a sin against a Goro required vengeance. It was a true sacrament among them, much more than a matter of settling tribal scores.

As Soukyan saw it, that meant they had two sets of assassins following them, both unstoppable. So they packed and Soukyan again followed the old man; there was no more choice in the matter than there had ever been.

The old man led him from the high desert to the Mihanachakalai, a wide wasteland which had once been a rich river valley until the course of the river changed. There, he told Soukyan, they would turn and make their stand. Those which followed them would never stop; the best they could hope for was to meet them on ground of their own choosing. He chose the Mihanachakalai.

But the old man kept muttering to himself as he wandered about, searching for the perfect location. When finally he found it, he urged Soukyan not to think, but to try and remember something he did not learn at that asylum of his, something his mother may have taught him, something old people used to say, something that children used to whisper in their beds to frighten each other. Soukyan did remember, vaguely, something about houses that were not there all the time, house-things blooming now and then from haunted soil, springing up like mushrooms in moonlight. He remembered stories about people going into such houses and never being seen again, but those were mere fables. The house that they saw in the place where they were had been once improved by a fire, but it had no magical qualities.

The old man explained that his plan depended upon their followers coming upon them simultaneously, and being forced into the house. Once inside, neither the Hunters nor the Goro would ever trouble them again. Soukyan was skeptical, but had no better plan of his own to offer. The old man disappeared toward the house himself, urging Soukyan if attacked to run toward the house, but on no account to go into it.

When the half-moon rose that evening, he saw the pair of Hunters, coming at him from different directions. The sight of them froze his tongue in his mouth, and he could no more have shouted a warning than he could have flown up to the moon by flapping his arms. When he lost sight of them it was even worse, and he ran toward the house as he had been instructed.

When the first hand clutched at Soukyan's neck, he did turn to fight them, although he shrieked in terror. It was not a Hunter who held him, though; it was the Goro, who gave him three *daks* (Soukyan did not know what a *dak* was, but he didn't think it was very long) to tell it where the fox was. When he honestly told it he did not know, the Goro only gripped him the tighter. It wanted the shapeshifter's life, not his, but it made no difference to the wrath of that clench.

Then the Hunters hit the Goro from both sides. It hurled Soukyan into a ditch and turned on them. As each side took the measure of the other, the Hunters told the Goro they had no quarrel with it; they merely wanted Soukyan. It told them that it wanted him, too; or more precisely, that it wanted what he knew. Neither side could back down, and an epic battle followed while Soukyan looked on.

The Goro knocked one of the Hunters with one of its legs so far the Hunter was dazed when it got up, and although the other Hunter attacked from the rear the Goro followed and kicked the first again so hard that it broke its neck. It did not sound like a dry twig snapping, as some say. The second Hunter let out a howl of purest grief and fury and attacked again, but the Goro moved with amazing speed and the attack fell short. Soukyan tried to slip away unnoticed but slipped and fell in a rut; the Hunter gave a sudden short laugh more terrifying than the Goro's roar and came running for him.

Soukyan found himself in a defensive position, curled into a ball with his arms and legs flailing, trying to prevent the one blow that the Hunter needed to end it all. He found a cook's paring knife that the old man had insisted he carry, and lunged blindly upward, slashing the blade along the Hunter's rib cage which turned it like a melting candle. Soukyan managed to roll free, and the Hunter told him there was no escape. Soukyan knew this to be true, but nonetheless urged the Hunter to come and get him. The Goro stood off a little way, apparently waiting for them to destroy each other. The Hunter advanced sideways, showing as little a target for Soukyan's knife as possible. Soukyan summoned all his strength and courage for one final attack, and launched himself at the Hunter. They both went down in a heap, the Hunter's laughter ringing in his ears, and the Hunter took away the knife, broke it in two, and made a mistake. The Hunter threw the shards in Soukyan's face, shifting his weight as he did so. His right knee slipped in some blood, and Soukyan's arm was free for an instant. He could not stab with the fraction of knife that remained; he meant only to mark the Hunter, to make sure he remembered he had killed a man full grown and not a mere child. One last time Soukyan slashed wildly at the Hunter's face, and at the exact wrong time the Hunter turned his head. The knife sliced the artery in the neck, and there was nothing the Hunter could do but widen his eyes and die in Soukyan's ams.

The body was immediately snatched away and the Goro hauled him to his feet. Soukyan again told it he did not know where the old man was, but the Goro again did not believe him. The Goro raised no paw, but it commanded Soukyan to take it to him. He felt the command, and the implacable will behind it, and to disobey was not possible. He turned and headed toward the house, the Goro following.

Close to the house they stopped, and the Goro lost all interest in Soukyan. It spoke to itself, saying, "He is in there. I have run him to earth at last." To his own astonishment Soukyan found himself explaining that it was a trap. The fox had no honor, and would never face him directly, even in such a house.

At that the fox emerged from the shadows that the house made in this world, running toward them with a small stone held in its jaws. The Goro went mad, accelerating toward the fox with a roar that seemed to come from the tortured earth itself. The fox wheeled and raced away, and the Goro went after him. Soukyan shouted for it to stop, but there was no stopping it now. The shadow of the farmhouse-thing reared up as they neared it, spreading out to shapelessness and reaching for them. It seemed to Soukyan that the fox swerved in an attempt to escape at the last moment, but that the attempt failed. The fox with a little yelp and the Goro with no sound at all both vanished into the shadow's grasp.

Pitying them both, Soukyan plunged both his arms in after them, trying to save either or both. His hands closed on something he could not feel for the cold of the gulfs between the stars. He screamed, and the shadow fought him. It wanted whatever he had, but he could not let that happen. When his hands came back to him, they held the fox.

The house creature collapsed before his eyes, leaving only a small hole, similar to the hole left when you pull a weed up by its roots. Or think you have. There was no sign of the Goro. The fox turned into the old man, who told him things had gone exactly as he had planned them.

Soukyan began to walk away, and the old man followed. Soukyan made it clear that wherever the old man went, he would go elsewhere, even if it meant crawling into a manure wagon again. There must be a human life for him to live somewhere, and he would find it.

The old man explained that the house was not exactly an animal; calling it a vegetable would be closer to the mark. They come and go, always where they were before, and there are never too many. He could not say where they are from, or what becomes of their victims. They have a very short blooming season, and if they take no prey they rot and die back before your eyes, as that one did. He had made use of that particular one before. The Goro was not to its taste; perhaps the Goro gave it a belly-ache.

The Goro had not listened when Soukyan tried to tell it the house was a trap; that's its nature, just as not wanting to know things is the nature of humans. In response to Soukyan's question the old man revealed that the nature of whatever he was was deceptive, misleading, ureliable. Illusory was as good as any.

Soukyan decided he could have had worse counselors.

In "Quarry" Beagle leaves as much unanswered about Soukyan and the fox as he answers. Readers of *The Innkeeper's Song* know that there is always a third Hunter, more deadly than the first two. Beneath the fox and the old man is what the fox calls "old nothing," and beneath that is something older still. Readers will expect to hear more about both than Beagle gives them. Yet Beagle gives us more about Soukyan than perhaps we bargained for. This is not just an encounter with Hunters, it is his first encounter; he has just escaped from the monastery. This is Soukyan before his tutelage by *the Man Who Laughs*. We know where he is going because of the stories told in *The Innkeeper's Song* and "Lal and Soukyan." We see where he has been in "The Quarry." All that is left for Soukyan is the tale of his return and redemption.

Beagle clearly had the story of Soukyan's return to his monastery to face his pursuers in mind at the end of *The Innkeeper's Song*, and he finally told it in "Return," published in September, 2010. Lest there be any misunderstanding, Beagle subtitled the novella "An Innkeeper's World Story."

Soukyan again narrates the tale, but this is an older, more experienced Soukyan, fully trained by *the Man Who Laughs*, lover of Lal, fresh from the adventure of *The Innkeeper's Song*. The narration is retrospective; that is, the speaker is many years in the future, presumably at or after the time the various narrators of *The Innkeeper's Song* are making their reports. Soukyan makes a point of telling the reader that after so many years it is difficult to remember all the details.

He was being sought, yet again, by Hunters, and knew that he could not shake them for very long. He expected an attack at any moment, and regretted yet again that he never learned to throw a dagger from his boot as Lal does. The first Hunter approached him empty-handed and asked if he could help; Soukyan explained that there is no beast that will not turn at bay at the last. At the end of his explanation he sprang forward, whipping the unstrung bow at his side and causing the lead he had squeezed around the end of his bowstring to curl around and around the Hunter's neck and catch. Soukyan pulled him forward and broke his neck before the Hunter could get the bowstring loose.

At the sound of his horse's frightened whinny Soukyan whirled to face the second Hunter, but instead saw the second and third struggling with each other. He would have been less surprised by a black sunrise. As Soukyan explained in *The Innkeeper's Song*, there are always three Hunters, the first two working together and the third, more dangerous than the first two, staying apart. None will quit until all are dead, and then there are always three more. The first time he faced them (in "Quarry") he thought there were only two, and he carries a still-tender spot on his skull from that encounter, a reminder that the gods have a certain fond indulgence for ignorant children.

Here the third was restraining the second, who broke free and came for him in a blind rage. Soukyan met him with an arrow in each hand, and the Hunter was dead before he hit the ground. He looked the third Hunter in the eyes, but the third held his gaze for a long moment, backed three steps into the trees, turned, and was gone.

Soukyan went after him, which was more foolish than anything he had done since he was old and experienced enough to know better. He followed the trail easily, although he was not as good a tracker as Lal. Soon he came upon what appeared to be the body of the Hunter, until it sat up and smiled at him. Nothing seemed wrong except a small scratch on its arm, but within minutes it was truly dead, its last words being the cryptic, "The Tree fails."

It took quite a while to carry him back to the clearing, and even longer to bury all three of them, but Soukyan always cleaned up after himself. Found remains mean more trouble than they are worth. Soukyan finally said, "Sunlight on your road," and then he was done.

He sat and thought for a long time. He had never been overly comfortable with unpredictability. Lal expected it in most circumstances, and the fox positively reveled in it, but like a cat Soukyan preferred to know the ground before he put foot to it, to find people how he left them, and for them to behave as he was accustomed to them behaving. The notion that a Hunter might go mad and struggle with another, let alone that the other should die at his feet rather than at his hand, did not connect; none of it made any sort of sense. He needed things to make sense.

All that he had experienced must surely signify something, and the only way to find out was to return to *that place*, as he called it. Only those who had long ago been his masters and his companions, and later his spurned and murderous enemies, would be able to tell him. He was simply going to have to persuade them to tell him without dying in the process.

And he would have to go alone. Lal had made him promise that he would never return to *that place* without her, but she and her swordcane were otherwise employed. He had not seen her for more than three years. The fox, who came and went as he chose, was off on some devious enterprise of his own.

Soukyan had called *that place* a monastery for lack of a better word. They did indeed have monks sworn to certain oaths and obediences, and there is a distant, unchanging hierarchy of masters, but secrets are the stock in trade of the establishment. There was literally nothing that kings sought to hide, that queens prayed to forget, or that the wiliest of officials, church powers, and businessmen worked to disguise, that was not known in *that place*.

Soukyan had been a boy of eleven when he first came there (although in *The Innkeeper's Song* he had said he was nine), and when almost twenty years later they offered him entrance into that hierarchy, he somehow had the good sense to run from the proffered power. The Hunters followed.

To return would be a long journey, and he was grateful for once to have enough money to bargain for a good young mare rather than the usual *churfa*. As for provisioning, he needed no more than his bow, his flint and steel, a little dried meat, and the sharp little dagger taken from a lady who took rejection poorly. He thought the dagger might come in handy, at least for cooking. He had no plan; no strategy at all. He reasoned that two decades of plotting and speculating and reasoning had brought him no closer to ridding himself of the Hunters, nor of *that place's* lingering hold on him. He would see what proximity would do, aided by the disguise taught to him by *the Man Who Laughs*, whom Lal refered to as *my friend*. His idea was to approach boldly and innocently in the guise of a benighted traveler, a tall brown woman whom he had not been since he left the Gaff and Slasher.

He continued traveling in the general direction of the monastery, and when he judged the moon and stars to be just right Soukyan said the spell as he remembered it. He let the woman shape drift down over him, like a cobweb, letting it happen slowly so as not to frighten his mare. Her name in the old days had been Nyateneri [spelled **Nyatenari** for some unknown reason in the text of "Return"], but that would no longer do. He needed to choose another.

It was tedious journeying, not because of anxiety over his destination but because of steadily intensifying recollections of a boy running in the darkness, his chest splitting with pain, his heart hammering with triumph and terror, weeping for his sister and listening for the dogs. He remembered too well.

He also remembered the cook who took him in, wet with tears and soaked through with sweat and a dead man's blood. She also hid him again twenty years later, when it was worth her life to do so. He never forgot her, either.

A mile or so from his goal he dismounted and walked the mare the rest of the way. He intended to ride away as he had come, and his life and death might very well hang upon the mare's good health. *That place* was oddly elegant, even attractive, with its two single wings, two soapbubble roofs, and a single spire. It was a little like the house he once knew that was not really a house, and ate things. He stabled his mare, walked around to the great double front door, and pulled the bell rope. He called out, saying he had lost his way and was seeking lodging for the night; could they help him?

As he had expected, it was Brother Laska who opened the door to him. Brother Laska had been doddering in Soukyan's youth, and he was doddering and palsied then, hanging on to the great door to stay erect, and seemingly barely capable of speaking a single sentence of challenge or welcome. Nevertheless he remained as ominous and chillingly senile a figure as Soukyan remembered, and he would have wagered whatever he possessed that Brother Laska continued in *that place's* highest council. Soukyan greeted him as Jalsa, the name he had settled on, believing that if Brother Laska did not know him in his woman's guise then no one would.

Nor did the old man seem to; he merely turned and tottered upstairs to deliver Soukyan's message. Soukyan, seeing no reason to remain outside, followed him in. Nothing, and too much, had changed. As far as he could tell not a single item in the grand entrance hall had been moved or replaced, cleaned or repaired. But now, grown, traveled, and far more questioning, he noted the worn weariness of chairs and benches, carpets and curtains and such ornamentation as there was. The stone elegance of the exterior was matched nowhere within.

The man who came downstairs to greet him was Brother Caldrea, but by his bearing and air of confidence Soukyan could see that he had been promoted. And there was only one rank above "Brother" in *that place*. He raised an eyebrow at the sight of Soukyan's bow, but addressed the woman he seemed to be pleasantly enough and led her to a cell where she could spend the night. As a woman she would not be permitted to dine in the refectory, but he would provide food for her in his own quarters. This worried Soukyan, who doubted that his small enchantments would survive Brother Caldrea's probing for an entire evening, and further needed time to explore himself. He slept most of the rest of the day, rising about an hour before dinner time to clean himself up as best he could, and to dig a few remotely passable clothes out of his saddlebag. He then set out for Brother Caldrea's quarters.

He passed half a dozen brothers on the stairs as he began, some of whom nodded silently to him as he passed and some of whom averted their faces, as if he were being shunned. It was clear *that place* was still being used as a clearinghouse or meeting ground for every kind of treacherous plot and betrayal. He was surprised that Brother Caldrea's quarters did not occupy the entire top floor, as had those of the prior Masters, but instead shared the second floor with the bare cells of other senior Brothers, for whom Soukyan had carried messages in the old days. He went out of his way to lose his way, and made sure he required an escort in the end. Soukyan arrived appropriately late, and Brother Caldrea apologized for not having thought to send a servant.

The food was delicious beyond description, lending credence to the servants' old belief that certain people in that house dined differently than the rest of them. After dinner, however, the Master asked Soukyan why it was that he felt there was something he should know about her, indeed did know about her although he could not quite put his finger on it. Soukyan confessed that he had not come there by mistake, but instead was looking for—Soukyan. He pretended to be the sister of the man Soukyan had killed all those years before, when he first went to *that place.* When the family found out where Soukyan had gone for sanctuary, naturally they gave up all hope of revenge or justice, and trusted to the well-known mystical wisdom to be found there. Their mother was dead within a month, and Jalsa's marriage did not survive, so unsympathetic was her husband to the loss. All of them could tell similar stories. They all struggled to survive without her brother, and they struggled still. She had come to ask the Master if he would give the murderer to them.

After studying her for a few moments, Brother Caldrea informed Madame Jalsa that Soukyan had left them. In response to her request to know where he had gone, he clarified: she had misunderstood. Soukyan was dead. In very nearly genuine astonishment, Soukyan asked for how long, and was told for quite a few years. There was some trouble, of a sort the lady need not be concerned with, and he left. There was really no other choice.

"The Hunters," said Soukyan. "You sent the Hunters after him." That time it was Brother Caldrea's turn to attempt to conceal surprise. Soukyan laughed briefly, and explained that everyone knew of the Hunters. Who they are, what they are, what services they perform, what they are to him and his companions—all that was a mystery. But they do not walk in the world and leave no trace of themselves. Tongues wag.

He rose to leave, but Brother Caldrea sat him down again with little more than a wave of his finger. That was the first time Soukyan realized how fully he had become the Master. Brother Caldrea explained that the Hunters were not mere hired killers; they were as much a part of the establishment as he was. Not everyone was monkish there, all were not devoted to the contemplation of the Infinite. Some took part in the affairs of the world, and that was why Soukyan was dead.

Brother Caldrea offered a servant to accompany Jalsa to her quarters, but Soukyan declined. The Master assured her there would be a good breakfast awaiting her in the morning, and that her horse would be groomed and fed as well.

Back in his cell Soukyan lay down on the rope mattress and forced his eyes to close, but after an hour's contemplation he realized he was not strong enough for what had to come next. He rose and went down the stairs, only to be waylaid by the ancient Brother Laska. The old man told him he knew why he had come, that he knew what he sought, and that he could take him where he wanted to go. Soukyan maintained his identity as Jalsa and declined, but Brother Laska caught his attention by saying, "The Tree."

Caught off guard, Soukyan froze, but when he regained his composure he again denied what the old man said. Brother Laska's face lit up with a terrible triumphant smile, but he agreed to take Jalsa to the stable.

They were good, not just for monks but for professionals of

any sort. They waited until Soukyan was almost to the stable before they rose silently up all around him, even dropping from the rafters like spiders. They brought him back to the mansion quite courteously, even allowing him to walk on his own, but with his arms bound. He passed the rest of the night in the same cell he had been assigned the previous day, sleeping surprisingly well until a young novice brought him an excellent breakfast. He ate slowly, paced the little room for a time, and even exercised as he could. He was sitting on the bed attempting to meditate when Brother Caldrea appeared. The Master called him Soukyan, and all pretense disappeared. The house itself knew him from the first, and told Brother Caldrea.

As the woman shape slipped from him, Brother Caldrea noted that the years had been hard for him. It was the eyes; man or woman, the eyes betray the life. Had Soukyan remained with them....

Soukyan interrupted the Master. Had he remained with them, he would have been just like them. He'd have spent his life dealing in pathetic secrets and fears, blackmail and lies and meaningless mysteries. It was not for him.

The Master's smile hardened. What was not for Soukyan was power. Not because he did not want it, but because he wanted it too much, and he knew he did. In that sense, he was quite wise to run off. What puzzled Brother Caldrea was why he returned, and in such a manner.

Soukyan explained that he came back to destroy the Hunters. He was tired of them, and it was time for them all to be gone. The Master considered, and shook his head in apparent agreement. It was very fortunate that he had chosen just that moment to return to them. The Hunters were extremely eager to rid themselves of him. They were quite literally born with that desire burning in their veins. He was grateful that Soukyan would be able to gratify them in their yearning, their hunger. It had been a long frustration.

Since bluster was all he had left, Soukyan blustered. The Hunter had not been born, he told Brother Caldrea, that could kill him. The Master agreed, and suggested they would wait together just a little longer for that birth. Then, after warning Soukyan not to try to escape again and knowing that he wasted his words, he was gone.

There was no lock on his door, only a young guard, proud to have been chosen for so important a task and outfitted with all manner of sharp objects dangling from his belt. Soukyan was reasonably sure he could silence the guard well before he could get any of his toys free and pointed at him, but he saw himself in the young guard and had no wish to harm him. Besides, there were more guards beyond. Soukyan went back into his cell and closed the door.

There he stayed, for days he grew too bored to bother counting. He invented ways to entertain himself, including remembering old songs and trying his hand at poetry. He wrote four ballads during that time, all of them drawn from heroic legends of long ago and all of them quite bad. He also meditated a good deal on what Brother Laska and the dying Hunter had meant.

Brother Caldrea visited him often, bringing delicacies to eat that far surpassed what he had been given as a novice. The Master told him he was quite important, the only one who had ever gotten away, the one who defied the Hunters. He had an important part to play. A moment was approaching, Brother Caldrea told him, one that concerned him greatly.

Soukyan made his first attempt to escape in broad daylight. He always believed that an air of authority was everything, so he knocked out the first guard and simply strolled down the hall as if he belonged there. It got him past three more guards and almost to the double doors before a dozen monks fell on him from all sides, putting paid to that particular getaway.

Maintaining form, he made two more straightforward attempts to escape, both of which failed resoundingly. He was moved to a more secure cell, and Brother Caldrea both praised his inventiveness and regretted that they would have so little time together, but the moon was the moon. It had not occurred to Soukyan that the Master, and obviously the Hunters, were waiting for a certain phase of the moon.

The third Hunter came before the moon. He was dead; Soukyan had buried him. He had said, "Sunlight on your road," to him. Yet there he stood, holding a candle and addressing Soukyan by name. Soukyan had been fooled the entire time; not a mark on him but a forearm scratch, and yet he took the Hunter for dead just because there was no breath and no heartbeat. Obviously the Hunter did not need these things in the usual fashion or degree. Soukyan had been tricked into going there from the beginning, and his disguise deceived no one. The Hunter told him it wasn't fair; he had killed so many of the Hunter's brothers, and he was allowed to kill Soukyan only once. He even seemed a bit depressed as he set to his work.

Torture is often thought of as a matter of instruments, but the Hunters take great pride in their skill. This one used only a small silver knife, with the tip daintily divided as if for skinning fruit. It was not quite so efficient on flesh, and after a while the Hunter threw it away and began going at him like an insane masseuse, like a butcher tenderizing a tough piece of meat. Soukyan could feel in his bones how badly the Hunter wanted to kill him, and he would grin his bloody grin in the Hunter's face, because he knew it would not be allowed. Then the Hunter would hit him harder, because he knew it too, and Soukyan would go away again, world without end.

There are a few ways of dealing with even the worst agony, of *absenting* oneself from it, that *the Man Who Laughs* had taught him long ago. Soukyan employed them to the fullest extent, as he had prepared to do when he first looked into the Hunter's mad blue eyes. He had to stay present so he could pay attention to three different purposes. The Masters clearly wanted something from him, something that he would give them to stop the beating at some time. But first he had to focus more clearly on what they were saying as the Hunter took out his fury on him. Soukyan wanted something, too. If he could hold onto consciousness long enough, what he was enduring could yet turn out to be worthwhile.

Finally the Hunter hit him hard enough that he skidded across the floor on his back, coming to rest with his head between two Masters. Brother Caldrea told the Hunter that was enough, and he would question him when he came to. Soukyan kept his eyes tightly closed, and then heard the Masters discuss the subject he wanted most to know about: the Tree. It was dying, but now there was hope.

The questioning began with a feint; they asked how he gained the skills that allowed him to kill so many Hunters. When he rejected the question they got down to cases: what did he know about the Tree? With more bravado than he felt, he told them he had come to destroy it and tear out the roots, so no one would ever know where it had been. They concluded he knew nothing about the Tree, and left him with a promise of more interrogation to come. The Hunter, however, told him: "Nothing you do ever harm the Tree, never. No axe you swing ever touch the Tree, no spade of you ever dig into, no poison you put to the Tree ever bite—no fire, no fire you set...." They would meet at the tree soon.

Soukyan was left alone for the next several days, during which he mainly slept. Brother Caldrea came every day to be sure he was recovering from his ordeal. Soukyan knew that it was time for him to go, using the way taught to him by *the Man Who Laughs*. It was a way he had known all along, but did not want to take. He still did not want to take it; he knew the cost. But he had no choice. He said certain incantations and other spells, but alone in the dark he could not tell if it had worked and he had become invisible. When he stepped out of his cell, though, and approached the guard, it must have worked because he was able to lay him gently down to sleep.

The spell endures no more than a quarter of an hour, or seventeen minutes at the outside, so there was no time to waste. He would pay for it with three years off of his life span, or perhaps five. *The Man Who Laughs* had told him he had used it many times, but wizards live a very long time. He could only hope that he was losing years during which he would just as soon have been dead anyway.

Soukyan was able to get out of the building and into the marshes where he had run when he escaped the first time before he became visible again. He slept, and awaited the new moon. His targets were the Hunter, and the Tree.

He had seen no Hunters since his arrival, other than the one that tortured him. Surely they would have been alerted because of his escape. As a boy he had seen them on rare occasions: small to medium in height, lithely built, with light eyes, pale skin, and distinctly quick, agile movements. He never spoke to one. He spent much of that last day roaming the entire area, wondering where they were.

Dusk had always been a bad time for Soukyan, although he had never known why that should be. He was desperate enough to determine on a completely insane gamble in order to obtain a weapon, since his were thoroughly hidden. He stalked one of the younger guards, determined to catch him by the neck, strangle him silent, and drag him into the woods to finish him. He was good at this; if he were not, he would have been long dead himself. As he crouched and prepared to spring, though, he heard Brother Laska behind him rasp quietly in a wheezing old voice, "Stir an inch and die, traitor Soukyan!"

When he turned around he saw the old man, grinning his splintery brown grin and holding Soukyan's bow by the end, like a spear. Brother Laska did nothing when Soukyan took the bow from him, only muttering that he had the arrows and that Soukyan was to come for them two hours after sunset, when the Masters had gone. He turned away, standing straighter and more tall than Soukyan ever remembered seeing him. He added, over his shoulder, that he would then take Soukyan to the Tree.

Brother Laska did not lie. After sunset the Masters left, one by one, with Brother Caldrea last. Soukyan entered *that place* for what he knew would be the last time, and Brother Laska handed him his arrows and quiver, his pack, and his dagger. He even had Soukyan's flint and steel, and gave that to him as well. He told Soukyan that he knew he would come for them, and

Soukyan mistakenly thought he meant his weapons. Brother Laska corrected him: he knew Soukyan would come for the Hunters. He did not like the Hunters, and never had. It was the fault of a previous Master, from before Soukyan's time. He woke up the Hunter's Tree. Brother Laska would take Soukyan there.

Responding to Soukyan's request that he tell him about the Tree, Brother Laska explained:

> "Power. *Power.* Who says no to having power, great power? Invincible assassins when you need? Master Caldrea wants somebody dead, the Tree drops three Hunters right into his lap—finished, they go right back in—...Tree *draws* them in. With target dead, Tree draws the Hunters back inside itself, gets nourished both ways. Everybody *feeds*—Tree, Masters, every-body, right? Well, so, maybe not target, not exactly, but target has his part to play, too. Because each death, each killing, *something* goes into the Tree, something the Tree needs—*I* don't know what to call it."

Soukyan understood that the Masters planned to—*had to*—feed him to the Tree. Brother Laska explained further:

> "Because the Tree serves one task at a time—only one, only one killing at a time. And you survive and survive and survive like nobody else, ever. So the Tree goes hungry, hungry. The Tree dies.... Your doing. You live, the Tree fails. Live much longer, kill too many more of its Hunters, the Tree dies."

Brother Laska then told him that the bow was not enough; he also needed a sword. When Brother Laska offered Soukyan his own antique sword, however, he declined, checking to make sure that his dagger was still properly sharp and well-balanced, while hoping he would never have to throw it.

Brother Laska began to lead him to the Tree. After a lengthy march, Soukyan heard several voices, but it was a murmur, not the rumble of a large crowd. And there was firelight, and one song rising out of the murmur and above it, high and clear and quite distinct, although the words were in no language Soukyan knew. He recognized the voice of Brother Caldrea, and Brother Laska told him the Master was calling the Tree.

The Tree stood in a clearing, not as tall as he had vaguely imagined it, but seeming as massive as a cathedral, its many broad, low branches decked prominently with long, wicked black thorns. Its bark and leaves were of the same deep, deep red, but its roots, bulking up out of the ground like a countryman's great swollen knuckles, were as black as those thorns, and looked somehow as dangerous. A group of eight to ten monks stood in a ring around the Tree, but only Brother Caldrea continued chanting. On Brother Laska's prompting, Soukyan looked at the branches, and saw what seemed to be nine chrysalises or cocoons dangling down, all an unpleasant greeninsh-yellow, all mansized, each suspended from a black thorn, and each beginning to ripple and shudder as something inside each one fought to break free. Their struggles grew more intense, and one was just starting to split at the top.

The Tree made Hunters in response to the Master's request, bore them like fruit. There were nine for him this time, which Brother Laska claimed was a great honor. Nine Hunters called for only one man. But Soukyan corrected him: "Eight," he said, and fired an arrow into the one starting to open. A Hunter fell, dead before he was born, at Brother Caldrea's feet, and the singing stopped.

Soukyan had three more arrows in the air as the monks turned and saw him and Brother Laska, who promptly ducked into a hollow. Master Caldrea called them off; Soukyan was to be left to him. He turned back to the Tree, chanted several phrases it would have broken Soukyan's throat to repeat, and every one of the remaining chrysalides cracked wide open at once. Five more Hunters dropped to the ground, all landing as lightly as cats, but the other three remained, dead or dying from Soukyan's arrows. One of the five, apparently the destined partner of the first killed, lunged at Soukyan in rage, but the arrow aimed for his heart caught him in the throat instead and he died choking on his own blood.

The rest were then on him, and Soukyan fully expected to die on the spot at their hands, but Master Caldrea called them off. They bundled him off to the Master, standing by the Tree, who welcomed him to his great destiny.

Yet Soukyan noticed, close up, that there was a strange air of instability about the Tree. The Hunters, too, were not quite right. He did not know exactly what the difference was, but he knew Master Caldrea knew it, too. The Master told Soukyan that he had hurt the Tree; the more Hunters he killed, the more the Tree had to produce. From the crowd of monks emerged the third Hunter who had tortured Soukyan, and he told him it would be soon, all was well, and then he gripped the back of Soukyan's neck, first lightly and then harder.

At that Master Caldrea strode forward, pulled out a small silver knife, and tore open the front of Soukyan's shirt to the navel. There was no divided tip as there had been with the previous knife; this one came to a single point, with a channel on both sides of the blade to lead the blood away. Master Caldrea employed it as an artist does his brush, or a seamstress does her needle. It was fine, delicate work, centered over his heart, and it took a long time. None of the cuts were deep, but the third Hunter poured a thin gray-green liquid into them, which vanished as it touched the skin over his chest. As the Hunter did this, the Master began to sing, and it was as if as each line left his lips something left Soukyan and vanished into the wind. He cried out, but the Master told him to hush; he was just giving back what never belonged to him—the energy, the spirit, of the Hunters he had killed. But the Tree welcomed him, the Master said; it forgave.

The Master then took Soukyan's dagger, and with his other hand he took some of the blood from Soukyan's chest and smeared it on the face of the third Hunter, who kneeled nearby.

He then told Soukyan that it was over now. Not for the Hunter; not just yet. He could not sacrifice himself until Soukyan's blood had soaked into the roots of the Tree. Then the Hunter would die, on the same dagger, to seal the bargain. The Tree would die, too, to be reborn mightier than ever, with the Hunter's blood to guard it and with Soukyan's soul, his self, imprisoned within it. The Hunters to be born of such a Tree would be sufficient to return power and influence to the House, and Soukyan would know it better than anyone.

Soukyan struggled, but it did no good. His head was held by the third Hunter, exposing his neck for Master Caldrea's blow, when a scream like a rock-*targ* being raped by a lightning bolt pierced the air. They turned to see Brother Laska bearing down upon them, brandishing with both hands the antique sword that Soukyan had doubted he could even swing. He was almost upon the Hunters by the time Soukyan pulled free, and his face was a mask of insane fury. Monks and Hunters alike scattered in all directions to be out of range of that blade.

Soukyan picked up his dagger from where Master Caldrea had dropped it, and then found his bow and quiver. The remaining four Hunters were spread out to come at him from different directions. Depending on range and other things, Soukyan could often have a third and even a fourth arrow in the air before the first had found its mark, but the distance was too short and his assailants far too adept to let themselves become easy targets, popinjays for his convenience. He did bring down one with a lucky shot, but he had to get rid of the bow as quickly as possible to avoid being tripped up by it.

It was the dagger that gave him a chance. The Hunters kill with their hands, but Soukyan was able to keep them at arm's length. It was all in and out, dodging and lunging, sideways leaps and rolls and back somersaults. He was not as swift as they were, but he had knowledge of their favored tactics that they did not have of his. Even so, he should have been dead. His one providence lay in the fact that these Hunters were not quite what the others had been. There were changed by a shadow's depth from almost invincible to almost vulnerable. The Tree's growing exhaustion had made that much difference.

The dagger accounted for another, surprisingly quickly, and the remaining two consulted silently as Hunters do. Soukyan seized the moment to scramble after his bow and quiver and loose off two arrows, both of which struck home with a satisfying certainty, leaving him in command of a field grotesquely strewn with near-identical bodies.

Only Master Caldrea remained, standing before the Tree with his arms outstretched. "There will be others," he told Soukyan. "There will always be others." "Not from this tree," Soukyan replied, and took his flint and steel from his pouch and kneeled in the grass.

But Soukyan remembered the words of the third Hunter: "No fire you set." He put his flint away, and picked up a brand from the monks' own dying fire. The scrubby grass was so parched that it went up with one touch of the brand. Master Caldrea screamed, and when Soukyan turned he saw him stumbling toward the Tree. Soukyan sprang after him, but something came down on the back of his skull, just above the neck, so hard that he lost consciousness. When he awoke the third Hunter was sitting on his chest, pinning both his arms. Soukyan saw the trunk of the tree already encased in rippling fire, along with something darker that could only have been Master Caldrea. The Hunter smiled down at him, said, "All my brothers," and slowly raised his hand and turned it, just so. He never completed the killing blow, though, since at that moment Brother Laska separated the Hunter's head from his body with his antique sword.

Brother Laska nodded happily. "No Tree, no more Hunters. The House will grow strong again.... Best be gone, you. The brothers will talk."

There is a battlefield prayer to be said when there is no time to bury the slain properly. Soukyan said it. He and Brother Laska then returned to *that place*, and Soukyan thanked him for his help. Brother Laska insisted on accompanying him to the stable. As he was kneeling to examine his mare's off hind foot, some instinct or sound or something else sent him dropping and rolling and scrambling to the side as the blade ripped into a truss of hay just above his head.

It took Brother Laska a moment to free his sword, giving Soukyan time to scramble to his feet and put some distance and a full bale of hay between them. Soukyan was as dumbfounded and speechless as the old man must have known he would be. How could he, Brother Laska asked Soukyan, pass up the opportunity to bring back the head of the monster, the destroyer, the defiler of the very heart of their House? The other Brothers would surely make him the new Master. Soukyan did not doubt it, but he did not want to kill the old man, or even to fight him; Brother Laska had saved his life. When the old man replied with a swing of his sword, though, Soukyan reconsidered and made a twisting leap from the top of an overturned barrel to the top of a stall door, which he quickly rode into Brother Laska, knocking him down and jarring the sword from his hands. Soukyan was on it, and then on him, pressing the flat of the blade into his throat with one hand while patting his wrinkled cheek with the other. "But not tonight, Brother, not tonight. Tonight this head stays on these shoulders," he said, as his own dagger came up from the floor in Brother Laska's left hand, missing his neck but gouging the flesh above his collarbone. There was that much fight still in the old man, and yet Soukyan did not want to kill him. But his left hand was on the sword on Brother Laska's throat, and he felt something go, collapsing under the pressure. It was fast, and quiet.

Soukyan took the body outside and buried it, remarking that Brother Laska had not always been a doorkeeper, and wishing him sunlight on his road. When he turned toward the stable again, he saw the remaining monks. They did not impede him, but when he moved around them the oldest of them fell to his knees.

"We have come to offer you all that your passage has left us.... Caldrea is dead. The Hunters are ended with the Tree. If this house is to survive, it must do so, not only under a new Master, but under a new *sort* of Master."

Soukyan had to face the truth of what Master Caldrea said of him. He fled from power because he desired it so much, because he feared his own ambition. He faced it now in the eyes of the monks who had offered him their leadership—a mighty matter once again, with the Tree no longer draining the secret strength of *that place*. He told them no, and moved to his mare. It could be different they, they replied; they could be different. But he knew they could never be different. He rode away without a backward glance.

He rode randomly north, and why not? Northward lay the little kings, the smaller dukes, and the clan warlords, and one or other of them was bound to require a bodyguard, a caravan guide, or a settlor of their petty grudges. All those were things he knew how to do. From then on for some little while to come, all directions, all pathways, and all employments were going to feel very much the same.

The published version of "Return" comes with cover art and four interior illustrations by Maurizio Manzieri. While the illustrations are closely based on the text, to my mind they add nothing and in fact detract from the images formed by a reader's imagination. This is particularly true of the portrait of Soukyan with his bow, the third internal illustration. However a reader may conceive Soukyan, it certainly would not be like that.

In "Return" we see Soukyan at his best, and are given a glimpse of what he could have been at his worst. In the Innkeeper's World, as in our own, power corrupts, and those who seek power are the least worthy to receive it. There is magic in this world, as we have seen, and power, and both magic and power can be used for good or for ill. Each of us in our time must make our choice.

Beagle published *The Innkeeper's Song* in 1993, and "Lal and Soukyan" in 1997. "Quarry" appeared in 2004, and "Return" in

2010. While there are many stories in the Innkeeper's World to tell, including many about Lal and Soukyan, the story of Lal's return to the land of her birth, anticipated at the end of "Lal and Soukyan," must be told for the cycle to be complete. At the present rate, we can expect it in about 2016, if Beagle maintains his momentum. He does not require a suggestion from me, but I would like to see it titled: "Homecoming."

Beagle has announced that he will publish a new edition of *Giant Bones*, under the alternative title *The Magician of Karakosk*, and that he will also publish a new volume of stories set in the Innkeeper's World, most likely in 2013. Presumably this new volume will contain "Return," and we can hope that it will also contain other stories featuring Lal and Soukyan, including "Homecoming" or its equivalent.

CHAPTER FIVE:
THE UNICORN SONATA

Unlike *The Last Unicorn*, which is a fairy tale for adults that also appeals to children, *The Unicorn Sonata* was conceived and marketed specifically for older children, known in the publishing trade as "young adults." The main character is a thirteen-year-old Hispanic girl, Josephine (Joey) Rivera, who discovers a parallel world called Shei'rah, one of "many and many that slip by each other among the stars." Shei'rah has almost nothing in common with the world of *The Last Unicorn*, except that it contains unicorns and other magical creatures such as satyrs, water nymphs, six-inch dragons, two-headed serpents, and phoenixes. It most resembles C. S. Lewis's Narnia, without the Christian allegory. As is the case with most juvenile fantasy, *The Unicorn Sonata* is a straightforward parable of growing up, but with Beagle's deftness of touch. While ultimately the least successful of Beagle's novels, *The Unicorn Sonata* is well worth reading if somewhat dated by its many popular culture references that ground it too firmly in its time.

The title of the book comes from the fact that unicorns in Shei'rah create the music which is its soul. Joey hears the music and has the sensitivity necessary to communicate it to the rest of us through the writing of her Unicorn Sonata. She works in a musical instrument sale and repair shop for the gruff Greek musician John Papas (naturally enough, a father figure) in exchange for music lessons. It is there that she meets the boy Indigo who wishes Papas to buy his horn, and upon hearing the haunting music Indigo coaxes out of it Papas is anxious to do so, even at the exorbitant price in gold the boy asks. It turns out that Indigo is one of the seemingly immortal unicorns from Shei'rah, some of which pass from their world into ours. It is while following Indigo to discover more about his music that Joey first passes into Shei'rah.

The major movement of the novel involves Joey's relationship with her grandmother, Abuelita ("Little Grandmother" in Spanish), who is in a nursing home. Joey visits her every Sunday, and eventually takes her to Shei'rah. It is Abuelita who provides the solution for the disease that affects the unicorns, derived from her memories and wisdom, with the assistance of Indigo's willing sacrifice. She ultimately decides not to return to the nursing home but to remain in Shei'rah, even though she understands that she is dying. Joey respects and supports her choice.

By far the most interesting aspect of *The Unicorn Sonata* is the ten full-color illustrations created by Robert Rodríguez. He shows us Indigo with his horn; Joey when she first sees Shei'rah; four unicorns at night; the water nymph who befriends Joey; the unicorns fighting the perytons; a view of Joey contemplating Shei'rah; another view of Indigo playing his horn; Joey and Abuelita riding a unicorn in our world on their way to the Border; Abuelita curing the unicorns; and Abuelita watching Joey ride a unicorn through the water back to the Border between Shei'rah and our world. These illustrations represent Rodríguez's understanding of the most important moments in the novel, and they have a twofold affect. First, of course, they assist the reader in visualizing the action. The illustrations are charming, idealized but relatively realistic, and they demonstrate the mood as well as the action. But they also limit the imagination of the reader; it is hard to visualize Joey, Abuelita, Indigo, or the unicorns other than as Rodríguez has painted them. Unlike a picture book for very young children who cannot yet read, where the story must be conveyed entirely through the pictures, *The Unicorn Sonata* is aimed at pre-teens and young teens who don't need illustrations to understand a book. There is probably a good reason why novels for adults aren't accompanied by such illustrations, and it is surprising that the editor of a novel for young adults would think that such a novel does. Beagle, in his Acknowledgments, praises editor Stephen Roxburgh but surprisingly does not mention Rodríguez or the illustrations.

The popular culture references are scattered in narration and dialogue throughout the novel, mostly about Joey, and they serve to ground her in her time (the novel was published in 1996) and place (Los Angeles). Joey at various times refers to "the deep blue gone the deeper black of interstellar space on *Star Trek*"; wears "an oversized *Northern Exposure* T-shirt"; teaches a water nymph to sing "Yellow Submarine"; observes a homeless man pushing a PayLess Drugs cart present a slice of pizza and a diet Fresca to his girlfriend, a homeless woman who is also a unicorn in Shei'rah; and hears that they were showing *Harold and Maude* at the nursing home. None of these references are particularly integral to plot or character, other than to demonstrate Joey's television and movie viewing and music listening habits. She is a regular young teen-aged girl, with whom the presumed reader (who would be the same, or who aspires to be the same) can identify. The problem comes with the time that has passed since publication—a reference that might have seemed hip and fresh in 1996 now seems dated at best and unfathomable at worst. Unlike *The Last Unicorn*, *The Unicorn Sonata* will not continue to be read and enjoyed by future generations.

Joey has a bad home life and a bad self-image. Within the first few pages of the novel, she tells Papas that if he calls her home, he had better do so real late, since her parents aren't in very much. She also tells him that she did badly on a science test, as usual. "I can't do anything right. Nothing. You name it, I screw it up. Tests, homework, gym class—I'm going to fail *volleyball*, for God's sake." She doesn't fit in anywhere—she doesn't like baseball, she doesn't have a boyfriend, and she dances "all wrong, everybody says so." Papas, her surrogate father, reminds her that she helps him very well at the store, and she makes up music.

The reader sees—or perhaps hears—Joey singing wordlessly to herself as she goes about her chores. She "thought of it as her dishwashing song, when she thought about it at all." When she first heard Indigo play his horn, "it made her throat lock up and her eyes sting; and yet she was amazed to feel herself smiling." When Indigo gave her the horn and asked her to play for Papas, "the music was simply there, and had always been there, dancing through her on its way." The music stayed with her, even after Indigo left.

Nor is Papas the only one who appreciates Joey's music. When Joey asks her if there is anything she can bring when she visits on Sunday, Abuelita tells her to "Bring me a song.... One of those songs you make up. I would like that." Abuelita, who loves all music and who smells better than anyone else in the world, calls her "'Fina,'" which the narrator tells us was her childhood name and that Abuelita is the only one who still uses it.

It is Indigo's music that leads Joey to Shei'rah. She thinks of it as *"The music I hear in my head, always, all my life, the music I can never name."* She knows she has crossed the Border because it is night on her side, but dawn on the other side, and the suburban streets she knows have vanished completely. There are no houses, no people, no roads; everything is wild. It is only the music that keeps her from being frightened; it is everywhere.

Joey first meets a rather conceited satyr (half man, half goat) named Ko, who calls her "Daughter" because he is 187 years old and it pleases him to do so. He first tells her where she is. Ko suggests they go to see "The Eldest," who will certainly know what to do. Joey cannot simply go back, because the moon, which restricts entry to and exit from Shei'rah, is already gone. Trying to comfort her, but achieving quite the opposite affect, Ko tells Joey, "All will be well, daughter. I am very nearly sure of it. All is quite often well in Shei'rah."

Ko explains to Joey that the Eldest do not *make* the music, the Eldest *are* the music. There are three different kinds of Eldest: one like the sky, one like fire, and one like the earth. All things change in Shei'rah but the Eldest, but they are beset. The Eldest are unicorns, and they are becoming blind.

The Lord Sinti, an ancient black unicorn who smells like oranges and who is the Eldest of the Eldest, tells Joey that although there are many worlds, Shei'rah is bound to our world, and it is something in our world that is causing the blindness. Not even he knows what it is. Anyone who wants to can pass from our world to Shei'rah and back again; all that is needed is a deep desire, the music, and the moon. Time is different in Shei'rah; a person from our world can spend as much time as she likes there, and when she returns she will not have been missed. The Eldest can change shapes to look like us, and some have passed into our world, although it kills them sooner or later if they do not return. Their horns separate when they change, which is why Indigo was able to attempt to sell his to Papas. Without his horn, he would have been unable to return to Shei'rah.

It turns out that Papas also knows about Shei'rah; he has seen the Border himself, but has not crossed over. He met Indigo there. He does not hear the music himself, as Joey does. Abuelita, on the other hand, also hears the music in her dreams. When Joey describes Shei'rah to her, she wonders if it might be heaven; she looks forward to being reunited with her long-dead husband Ricardo. She even asks Joey if she has seen him there. Nonetheless, Abuelita remains a skeptic until she sees Indigo transform into a unicorn to carry her across the Border.

Unicorns like Indigo pass into our world despite its problems because they do not accept what Indigo calls "the lies" of Lord Sinti and the other Eldest; like rebellious teenagers everywhere, they want a life free from lies and hypocrisy. They want a choice about who they are and what they do. Indigo asks Joey,

"And do you think that is such a wonderful thing?
To be eternally magical, angelic, pure, with no choice

at all? No say ever in who you are because of *what* you are? I tell you, you stupid, stupid, ignorant, miserable little mortal object, I would rather be you than to be the Lord Sinti himself. And none of the Eldest has ever said such a thing to any creature."

He later acknowledges that without his horn he will die, but before he dies he will have lived.

One of the unicorns crossed over into our world, Valadyi, is a homeless woman whom Joey meets; there are others whom Indigo tells her she has seen. Indigo seeks to sell his horn for gold so that he may live better in our world than the other unicorns who retain their horns; ironically, he ends up selling his horn to provide the gold which Abuelita requires for her cure for the blinding disease that afflicts the unicorns of Shei'rah. Joey promises to assist him, and it is clear at the end of the novel that she has become mature enough to do so.

When Joey fails to understand Indigo's passion for freedom of choice, Papas explains: "His business.... His choice." It is also Papas who tells Joey what she must do:

> "Okay, main thing, you got to learn to write the music down real fast now, you got to learn how to weave the voices together, how to paint with the voices, you understand me? You got to make it so people *see* that place you go to, Shei'rah, so they *feel* it, not just hear. Lots of hard work ahead, Josephine Angela Rivera."

She does so, and the results are magnificent. Her Unicorn Sonata moves all who hear it, and communicates perfectly the joy and sadness that is Shei'rah. Joey has found her place in the world.

Prior to gaining the self-confidence she needs, Joey is like many another teenager: afraid to try because if she tries and fails she would have no excuse. This attitude is expressed in her reluctance to attempt to return to Shei'rah. She tells

Papas, "Because what if I walked down that street and nothing happened? No music, no Border, no Shei'rah, just nothing. I couldn't stand that, Mr. Papas. I'd rather not know, you know?" Papas again has the encouraging reply: "Yah, I know, Josephine Angela Rivera. But all your life that's just when you got to find out. Better, believe me. That too I know." The very next night she returns to Shei'rah for the first time.

It is during her second visit that Joey comes upon the bones of a dead unicorn. When she confronts him, Indigo tells her that unicorns are not immortal, just ancient. Every once in a while, one does not return from deep meditation with the Lord Sinti. Rather than admitting that one of them has died, the Eldest say that the missing unicorn has simply left them and withdrawn into the Great Solitude. It is a very old lie, and old lies become truth in enough time. When they become old enough, all unicorns join in the lie. It is that joining that Indigo and others like him refuse.

Joey hates the nursing home where Abuelita lives—she hates the food, she hates the smell. She wants Abuelita to come and live with her and her family again. But Abuelita knows it would never work. She is too old and stubborn to live with anyone again, and she cannot live alone because of her arthritis, and because she falls down sometimes. The nursing home is as good as anyplace else.

Established customs and routine matter a great deal to Abuelita. "They are all I have left now, 'Fina," she said to Joey. For people her age, the children are gone, the friends are gone, the body is going; the only thing that stays is the way she likes to do things. Her "foolish old habits" help her remember who she is. So they walk around the park at the nursing home three times every visit. During one of the circuits, Abuelita gives Joey a golden bracelet inset with ivory. When Joey protests, Abuelita tells her, "Now don't you start carrying on like your brother. It's only a bracelet, it's only a grandmother, it's only life. No worse, no better, like I told you—only life, that's good enough for anybody." In exchange, Abuelita suggests that Joey can give her the dream music, which leads directly to their joint visit to Shei'rah.

Their trip is exhausting to Abuelita; the Border has shifted. Without the help of Indigo they would have been forced to go back to the nursing home. Once there, however, Abuelita is rejuvenated by what she experiences. Seeing the Lord Sinti for the first time, she exclaims, "I dreamed this. I dreamed you." With utmost courtesy, the Lord Sinti replies, "We dreamed each other.... Welcome, Alicia Ifigenia Sandoval y Rivera.... Once in a great while it happens that a dream in your world touches a dream in Shei'rah. It is a rare thing, but it does happen." When the Lord Sinti explains that he at first mistook Joey for Abuelita, the grandmother corrects him; her full name is Alicia Ifigenia Josefina. "My 'Fina *is* me, only better. The new improved model."

Abuelita is concerned that the Eldest are blind. She has a vague recollection of a folk remedy from her youth, and attempts to remember it while she tours Shei'rah. Along the way she charms the water nymph who is Joey's special friend; dances with the younger cousins of the satyr, Ko; and becomes friends with the tiny dragons whom Joey has never been able to tame. Joey worries about what will happen when it is time to take Abuelita home, but Abuelita seems to have no worries at all. The Lord Sinti tells them that a major shift in Shei'rah's position relative to our world is coming, and it might be necessary to leave quickly. Afterwards it may not be possible to return.

Joey continues to write down snatches of the music she hears, and when asked by the water nymph what she will do with it replies: "Well, I'll give it to people.... I mean, back where I come from there are all kinds of people who'd love to play the music of the Eldest. They can learn it from what I'm writing right now, and then they'll play it all over the world. My world, on the other side of the Border."

Joey finally confronts the Lord Sinti about what Indigo calls his lies about the unicorns' immortality, but it is Abuelita who answers her. "Child, no one lives forever.... That is not allowed.

I could have told you that." Although she is speaking for herself, the Lord Sinti immediately affirms her insight.

> "Perhaps that is what binds us together,...your people and mine, your world and ours. Our lives are so much longer than yours,...so long that we truly forget at times that we are not immortal. And yet we fear death just as deeply as you do—more, surely, because Shei'rah is so much kinder to us than I think your world is to you. It shames us, this knowledge that we die, and if we keep it from our young ones we keep it from ourselves too, as best we can. I do believe we were different once, but that was before even my time, and this is the truth now."

Abuelita breaks the solemn mood by declaring, "*Ay*, you should come to the Silver Pines Guest and Rest Home.... If you want to see what comes of lying to your children."

Abuelita thanks Joey for bringing her there, wherever it is. It is a relief to be able to just *be*; to sit and think about nothing, to smell flowers, to tell stories, to go dancing and drinking, with nothing to explain to anyone. "When you are old like me, 'Fina, you will understand what a good thing it is to have nothing to explain."

Abuelita eventually remembers the cure for blindness they used in her village when she was a child. It involves gold, melted down with things added to it to make an ointment that is rubbed in the eyes. People who could not see at all had their sight restored by the treatment. Abuelita tells Joey to find some gold while she remembers the other ingredients. Joey tells Indigo of her need, and its purpose, and Indigo agrees to sell his horn to Papas and give the gold to Joey in exchange for her promise to help him in her world. To persuade him, Joey tells him that he should do it

"Because it's what you want.... Because you know my world a lot better than I'll ever know yours, and you know what it's like, and you still want to live there just *because* it's like that. I mean, you're scared of it, that's why you keep almost selling Mr. Papas your horn, and then not. And you ought to be scared, because it's a really, really scary world where I live. But that's why you want to be there, because it's not Shei'rah. And I don't think the gold ever mattered to you, not really. The gold's just an excuse for not *moving*. I do that all the time."

When selling his horn to Papas, Indigo admits, "Oh, I always wanted.... *Sure*—no, perhaps never—but I must act as if I were sure. Isn't that the first lesson of living in this world?"

Indigo asks Joey to tell him something good about her world, something she likes that they do not have in Shei'rah. She responds thoughtfully, "That man.... Under the freeway. The one who was taking care of your friend? Who brought her pizza?...You were right, that's as good as we get. That's the best we have." Love, even among the homeless who live under the freeway, is the essence of humanity.

Indigo sends Joey off with the gold to Abuelita, telling her: "Go. Save my people's sight, or leave them with sticky, useless ointment filling their eyes. It does not matter. We do what we must." Joey responds, through her tears: "Mr. Papas will help you.... And I'll be back, and I'll help. It'll be all *right*." "It is all right now," Indigo replies. "Why do you suppose the Eldest became blind in the first place? Ask your grandmother.... She will know, your Abuelita."

With the gold Abuelita prepares the ointment, and the Eldest of Shei'rah come to be healed. Joey had never seen so many, of every color and every age. After two days and a night, during which time Abuelita refuses to let Joey take over because somehow it is better if she does it, the process is complete, with the Lord Sinti last of all. The ointment works its magic, and the unicorns can see again.

Shortly thereafter it is time to leave Shei'rah, but Abuelita decides she is not going back. She tells Joey she has to go back: "You have your family, your school starting, your whole life, everything waiting back there for you. And Indigo, you must find Indigo. But there is nothing waiting for me except Silver Pines and death. No, I like it much better here." When Joey asks her what she can tell her folks, Abuelita replies,

> "Tell them that I went back to Las Perlas. I have been threatening to do that for years.... And do you know what, 'Fina? It is almost true.... I will miss you, my 'Fina.... The way I miss your grandfather. I will miss you. Except that you will come back to see me here, somehow, just like every Sunday at Silver Pines, and he never can. The rest...the rest, not so much."

When Joey presses her as to why the unicorns went blind, as Indigo told her to, Abuelita responds: "*Ay*, that boy.... It was that he has been trying so long to sell the horn for money. They can't do that, that's not what they are, what this place is. Things just start getting disordered, pulling apart, *comprendes*, 'Fina?" When Joey reminds her that he did sell it, that he was the only Eldest who ever sold his horn, Abuelita corrects her: "But not for *himself*.... It is as I told you, the worth is the reason."

As she prepares to leave, she hears the Lord Sinti telling her: "Tell Indigo that we understand what he has done. If his great hunger to belong fully to your world brought on our blindness, his sacrifice has set us free, and perhaps himself as well. We will remember him. Tell him that, Josephina Angelina Rivera."

After returning to our world for the last time, Joey does not go home first; instead, she goes to the music shop to see Papas. She no longer hears the music, but when she sits at the piano,

> "The music of Shei'rah came winging up under her hands, welcoming her home. In the little shop the little

piano sounded like a full orchestra, exultantly embroidering strains born on the other side of the Border that cascaded through Joey, spilling through her so exultantly that she could not consider or contain them."

The music calls up her experiences in Shei'rah, and allows others to share them. Papas tells her:

"Oh, yeah, you got something, all right, something like nothing else ever. Don't know what happens from here—we show it to a few people, maybe somebody plays it, records it, maybe yes, maybe not—but you got your Unicorn Sonata for keeps, kid. This doesn't leave you. This stays.... Thank you."

When Joey expresses regret that she can no longer return to Shei'rah, Papas reminds her,

"That place, it's still there, right? Ain't like it stopped being—it's still *somewhere*, right? Okay, so it moved, so what? So you move too. So you look around for that other place everywhere you go, starting now. There's unicorns all over everywhere, even Woodmont. You know that, I know that, maybe nobody else does. You look for them, you listen for the music, you listen for Shei'rah. It's somewhere, you'll find it, you want to find it enough. You got time."

"I guess," Joey responded. "Abuelita said I'd find it again." "Right now I'm sort of keeping an eye out for a skinny kid with really pretty eyes and an attitude. He's around here somewhere."

Beagle has remained consistent in his attitudes and themes. In *The Unicorn Sonata* he emphasizes freedom of choice and he shows us the reasons not to fear death. The worth of life is itself the reason for living, and love is the most important thing we have. Communication is the key, whether through music as in Shei'rah and as Joey learns, or any other form. Caring for each other and doing things for the greater good make life worth living and death not worth fearing.

Beagle has announced plans to expand *The Unicorn Sonata* into a four-book series, the first two of which are tentatively titled *Shei'rah* and *Indigo*. He has said that he plans "major literary surgery" on the novel. They are to be published by Conlan Press as part of a projected "box set" of definitive editions.

CHAPTER SIX: *TAMSIN*

In *Tamsin*, an adolescent novel published thirty-nine years after he published *A Fine and Private Place*, his first ghost story, Beagle writes in first person, using an eighteen-year-old young woman struggling to recall her experiences at the age of twelve as his narrator, rather than the omniscient third person narrator. The title character is in fact a ghost, a woman who had been dead for 313 years when the narrator, Jennifer Gluckstein, met her. The novel is full of supernatural creatures from English mythology, including a boggart, the Wild Hunt, the Black Dog who always appears as a warning, the Pooka, the billy-blind, Oakmen, and even the all-powerful Old Lady of the Elder Tree, but the ghosts form the centerpiece. They are in some ways different from the ghosts of *A Fine and Private Place*, but in significant ways they are similar.

Jenny first meets the ghost of a cat—or rather, her cat meets the ghost of a cat, and Jenny sees them lying together on her bed in the moonlight.

> "It was another cat. A long-haired, short-legged, blue-gray cat with deep-green eyes and a wide, pushed-in sort of face—a Persian, for God's sake. I don't like Persian cats much, but that wasn't the problem. The problem was that I could see through it.
>
> Okay, not quite *through*—it wasn't really transparent, but almost. Its outlines were a little fuzzy, but Persians look like that anyway. It looked darker beside

Mister Cat, lighter when it moved and had my blanket behind it; and when it sat down for a moment to scratch, I lost it altogether in the moonlight shining on the white wall. When Mister Cat nudged it with his shoulder, it opened its mouth and this tiny, tiny faraway meow came out. Not a real meow. More like an old yellowing memory of a meow."

The boggart—a comic creation which would also be right at home in the world of *The Last Unicorn*—warns Jenny: "'For yer ma's sake, a single word of advice, like. A warning.' He pointed at the Persian, shaking his finger the same way he'd done at me. 'Ware t'servant, ware t'mistress—and ware T'Other Oone most of all.' And you could hear the capital letters on T'Other Oone. Believe it." With the stage thus set Jenny meets "t'mistress" immediately, and "T'Other Oone" in due course. All are ghosts, but the boggart is mistaken; Jenny need beware only T'Other Oone.

The mistress is Tamsin Willoughby. When Jenny first sees her, she is sitting in a chair with the ghost Persian, clearly "t'servant", on her lap.

"I remember wondering crazily if a ghost could feel the ghost-weight of a ghost-cat, since I hadn't felt a thing when the Persian jumped up on my bed. Because there wasn't any more question about the woman than the cat—I could see the window through her, and the chestnut tree through the window; and when she put the cat down and stood up to face me, I saw that her hair and skin and gown were all the same color, a kind of pearl-gray, but with a light in it, the way the rain clouds can look when the sky's almost purple behind them. She said, 'Jennifer. Aye, I thought it would be you to find me.'"

Jenny tells us that time didn't mean anything to Tamsin. "There was so much loneliness in that smile, but there was amusement, too, and understanding. She wasn't anything more than understanding; she was held together by memories of understanding, memories of laughter." The color of her eyes keeps changing, as though she couldn't quite remember the color they had been. Tamsin told Jenny,

> "You must remind me when I forget—and I will forget, because that is what I do, that is all I am. You would think—would you not—that after so many, many years, surely there would be naught left me to forget, who'd seen but twenty summers when I...when I *stopped*."

When Jenny wonders whether her cat and the Persian ghost, with whom he has obviously fallen in love, have any sort of future, Tamsin passes her concerns off with, "La, what odds makes that to a cat?... Cats have no cares for who's quick, who's...stopped. Shall we be like them?"

Tamsin can look practically solid when she gets excited or "worked up" about something. She and Jenny had a conversation, and she

> "listened, and laughed, and grew more and more visible—more *present*—until her hair and the flows of her gown swayed with her laughter, and I couldn't see through her at all, although maybe that was because the room was getting darker. And I actually forgot what she was, just for that little time."

Without something to stimulate her, Tamsin merely sits in her chair, the Persian on her lap, "moonrise on moonrise, year on year, age on age—until the forgetting shall have me altogether. But that must not happen, must not...." When Jenny asks her about the boggart's T'Other Oone, though, she comes close to turning pale, and tells Jenny, "Child, Jenny, never ask me that again. Never ask again, nor of me nor of any—nor of *yourself*, do you understand me? Promise me that, as we stand here, Jenny, you *must* promise, if we are to be friends." Jenny promises, but knows that she'll break the promise even as she makes it.

Tamsin is free to go where she chooses, so long as she remains within the bounds of the family farm, where she died and where she was buried. She floats rather than walks, not quite touching the ground. The farm was and is her home, but she looks upon it as a prison. She tells Jenny,

> "But Jenny, do we not every one leave home when it comes time to find another? A father's home for a husband's—is that not so? And that in turn for a third, for the long home where all will meet again at last. All, all...except such as are bound, ensnared, barred away forever from such joy."

The term "long home", meaning grave, incidentally, comes into modern English from Middle English and Old English, or Anglo-Saxon, and was used by J. R. R. Tolkien in *The Lord of the Rings*, usages with which Beagle was intimately familiar.

According to the Pooka, a ghost who has once left the earth never returns. But Tamsin is so barred, bound to the earth and ensnared within the bounds of her farm, and the reader under-stands that the movement of the novel is Jenny's quest to find out why and to remove the impediment. It will undoubtedly involve T'Other Oone, and so it does.

Tamsin never exactly slept, but she did doze. She explained to Jenny:

> "Jenny, have you known it ever, that zone between aware and asleep when dreams float through you—or you through them—as though you and they were of the same substance? Beyond control, beyond words to

name them, yet there's an exchange, a penetration, for all one knows them to be baseless phantoms. So with me, often, as I wait by my window. And is what I see truly what is? Or are these visions of what might have been? What might be? I can never tell."

The Pooka tells Jenny that it was not wise for Tamsin to speak to her. "Wisdom is no concern of mine—but for the dead to linger so long that they come to have speech with the living... this is not *right*. The least of boggarts would know that." When asked where she should be, the Pooka responds:

> "Not here. It is dangerous, it makes a wrongness, and in time other wrongness follows. Somewhere a single stream runs backward—one tree flowers in deep winter—in one nest a hatchling devours its parent. A door meant to close behind Tamsin Willoughby bides open.... This concerns me."

When Jenny chides him about doing nothing to help Tamsin, the Pooka explains:

> "That is not in my power.... If I could have been of help to Tamsin Willoughby, I might well have done so long ago, but I cannot. It is forbidden, which is only to say impossible. She is not of my world.... [She] belongs no more to the world she reveals than do those who trudge behind her. Quick or dead, Tamsin Willoughby remains human, and even I cannot guide her in her turn. I might as well be the Black Dog, silently foreboding, or I might be the billy-blind, forever offering the right advice at the wrong time. Quick or dead, there's no helping a human, but if anyone is to succor Tamsin Willoughby, it must be you.... Only you. And no chance of that unless you come rightly to understand her plight—which you do not, no more than she.

Listen to the Wild Hunt. The Wild Hunt will tell you what you must know."

In Tamsin's world ghosts can choose to be seen by whom they like, and Tamsin has chosen Jenny to talk to. That, Jenny's best friend tells her, should tell her something about herself, but Jenny can't see it. Ghosts are not seen in mirrors, Jenny tells us, nor do they have a sense of smell. As Tamsin explains, "I have no sense of smell, but an imagination of smell—can you comprehend such a thing, Jenny?...Besides, there's comfort in a kitchen, always, for me as much as any other."

Tamsin eventually tells Jenny, and so the reader, of Edric Davies, her lost love. He was a Welsh musician, engaged by her father to play while she sat for her portrait. The narrator tells us that when she spoke of Edric, Tamsin

> "was absolutely clear, perfectly distinct, as solid and real and *alive* that moment as Mister Cat snoring between us. What it was was a light, that faint, faint ghost-light all around her, growing bright enough to throw my shadow on the bed. I don't believe in angels and halos, and I've never seen anyone's aura, but Tamsin looked like all that stuff when she talked about Edric Davies."

In her despair, though, Tamsin's appearance began to change. Jenny tells us,

> "She was *tattered*, as though dogs had been tearing at her, ripping away her memories of herself. There were *holes* between shoulder and breast, I remember, and another one gaping below her waist...and you couldn't see through them—there was *nothing* on the other side. I read about black holes now, where comets and planets and all the light in the universe gets sucked in forever, and I think of those holes in Tamsin."

After speaking with Jenny for a while,

> "very, very slowly—she came back. It's hard to describe now. It isn't that she became clear and whole and solid, recognizing me, because she didn't. What happened was that the old transparency returned, little by little, until you could see irrigation pipes and skinny young cornstalks through her; and I was as overjoyed as if she'd come back to me in the flesh. The holes— or whatever they really were—faded as her memories knitted themselves back together; when she looked at me again, her eyes took me in, and she smiled."

The depth of Tamsin's love was beyond Jenny's experience at twelve, although the narrator at eighteen knows enough about it to tell us. Tamsin's face changed, a little, and Jenny could see Edric. She explains, "That can happen with ghosts, when they're thinking of a person who meant as much in their living days as they did to themselves." Later Jenny tells us that

> "ghosts *change* when they remember something that intensely—but I'll swear forever it was more than that. Her eyes were brighter than I'd ever seen them, bright as flowers in moonlight, and she was *there* in them, three hundred years before—she was on the stairs in this same house, so frightened she could hardly stand up, and so wildly happy, and so brave. It was still there, that moment, in her own eyes."

Later Jenny tells us, "Feelings like that don't die; memories like Tamsin's memory of Edric and her lost sister don't die. That's why you have ghosts."

T'Other Oone is the ghost of George Jeffreys, a/k/a Baron Jeffreys, a/k/a Lord Chief Justice Jeffreys of Wem. He was sent by King James II to make an example of Dorset after the failed rebellion. Guilt or innocence did not matter to him, and he once convicted an eight-year-old girl of treason, raving at her in the courtroom until she collapsed and died. He kept a journal, which remained in the County Museum, and it contained several entries pertaining to Tamsin's family. His portrait hangs in the Judge Jeffries Restaurant in Dorchester, where he resided during the Bloody Assizes. Jenny went to see it, and this mad, evil man

> "was out and out pretty.... It was almost a woman's face: delicate, calm, even thoughtful, with big heavy-lidded eyes and a woman's soft mouth. You can't possibly imagine that face screaming and raging and foaming—which is what everybody says he did—sentencing people by the hundreds to be hacked into pieces, stuck up on poles all over Dorset. There's no way you can see that face doing those things."

And yet he did. And over dinner at her parents' farm, the mad and evil Judge Jeffreys fell in love with Tamsin.

Tamsin tells Jenny:

> "Pretty eyes. So they were—nor did he ever take them from me in all that time, not for two minutes together. Edric would be playing, and the portraitist daubing and scratching, my father snoring—and those *pretty* eyes so softly on me.... He saw everything.... Aye, and he knew the truth of us, I think before *we* did. He never spoke word to Edric, but whiles that gentle gaze would rise to take the two of us in—never more than a moment, a single breath—and Jenny, the *pit*, the fiery, filthy cavern just below that gentleness! Afterward—him having taken his leave at last—I'd weep and shiver all night, and bite my fingers with fear, and no way Edric could ever come to comfort me. And one still night—once only, somewhere in the house—I heard my mother weeping as well.... And no hope, for

all knew he would surely ask for me when his horrible Assizes was done, and who in Dorset would say Judge Jeffreys nay? Who would dare?... Do you wonder I fear him still, Jenny, even to speak of? Do you wonder I forget?"

Yet Edric dared to say him nay, through the power of his love. Edric and Tamsin made plans to run away together, as young couples in love have done from the beginning of time. The Black Dog appeared to Tamsin, to warn her, but she paid him no mind. As she went to meet Edric, she met Judge Jeffreys instead. The Judge spoke to her of marriage, and told her that he knew how Edric harbored a rebel. In reality, one of Edric's students had joined Monmouth's Rebellion, and Edric went after him. He found his body in a ditch and brought it home. Tamsin describes the scene to Jenny:

> "He went on, on, half raving, half singing—now swearing eternal adoration, now threatening horror to my entire family if I were denied him. After a time I but half heard him, Jenny, so hard was I listening for my father's returning—and for Edric as well, come at last to carry me safely away. But there was no one, and the rain fell harder."

Tamsin ran away through the rain, but when she reached the spot they had agreed to meet Edric was not there. She ran on, shrieking through the storm, to be found by the Pooka disguised as her brother. She was taken home, but sickened and died from exposure in the storm. Just before she died, Judge Jeffreys whispered to her what he had done.

Jenny found Edric's portrait of Tamsin in the same restaurant where the judge's portrait was hanging. Much to her surprise, she found a tiny portrait of Judge Jeffreys in Tamsin's portrait, reflected in a copper-colored beaker. His presence in the painting connected them in some way, and may have been the reason why he could hang on, or come back. Or perhaps the fact that Tamsin didn't leave when she was meant to left a door open for him to come through.

The ghost of Judge Jeffreys appeared to Jenny at last, saying merely, "I am here. Tell her." He reappeared from time to time, but wasn't as easy moving about the farm as Tamsin was. He stayed close to the Manor, perhaps because he was afraid of getting lost, perhaps because he knew Tamsin would have to return there sooner or later. Jenny admitted she still didn't "know how it really works with ghosts." But Mister Cat knew, and he kept leading her to Judge Jeffreys. He looked more like a real person than Tamsin did, perhaps because of the robe and wig he always wore, or perhaps, as Jenny speculates, "it was that he knew what he wanted, dead or alive, so being dead didn't make any difference to him, the way it did to Tamsin. Meena thought he didn't know he was dead." No one but Jenny saw him, and he saw no one but Jenny. Over and over he would tell Jenny, "I have come for her. Tell her."

Jenny describes him like this:

> "The best way I can put it is that the presence of him rustled like his voice, like an attic full of old dead bugs: the empty husks of flies in ragged spiderwebs, still bobbing against the window—the beetles and grasshoppers that froze to death winters ago—the dusty rinds of little nameless things stirring on the floor in a draft, crunching underfoot wherever you step. Judge Jeffreys didn't just *sound* like that. He *was* that."

Jenny gathered her courage and told him that he would not find her, but his response was cool.

> "She will come to me.... She belongs to me. Since first I spoke her name and bowed over her hand—since first our eyes kissed across her father's table.... From

that moment, she was mine. She knew then—she knows now. She will come."

Jenny tells Judge Jeffreys that Tamsin hated him, and loved Edric Davies. His response was out of control:

"That damned Welsh villain! That canting, cozening, rebel-loving rogue! Jesus God, to see him—to sit watching, day on day, as he plied his vile sorcery against her susceptible innocence. A hundred times—a thousand!—oh, but I was hard put not to leap from my chair and strangle him where he sat, twangling at the jacks and looking sideways, looking, *looking* at her...."

Judge Jeffreys then tells Jenny that he had told Tamsin just before he died that Edric had fled from him "as a demon flees from the face of the risen Christ." He explains:

"A great power was granted to me when last we met, Edric Davies and I. I was the unworthy instrument of the Almighty, humbly privileged to speed him to such a doom as all the saints together could never lift from him. There will be no return from where Edric Davies is gone."

Judge Jeffreys had given the soul of Edric Davies to the Wild Hunt.

With two 300-year-old ghosts on the place, the farm doesn't stay normal for long. Jenny experiences the appearance of ghostly landscapes, hills long ago leveled and boulders long ago removed from fields. She was seeing the farm before it was the farm, before Tamsin's father, before the Saxons, before the Romans, before there were people there at all. These visitations were the result of the presence of Judge Jeffreys. Then the people began to arrive. A group of soldiers appeared, whom only Jenny could see, they in their time, she in hers. But they could apparently see and hear her, as well. One tried to kill her with his sword, but she was as much a ghost to him as he was to her.

The Wild Hunt hounds souls through the sky. It is mostly heard in Dorset in the autumn and winter, and a lot of people would say that's because it's when the geese are traveling south. But those who know think that "more folks die in the cold months, as the year dies, and perhaps the Wild Hunt have their best pick of poor souls to hound through the sky then." There is a belief in Dorset that the Wild Hunt

> "can be *summoned*—called down and actually set to run a victim to his death—by someone who knows the proper spell, and has the required force of personality to achieve it. But it's a risky thing to attempt, as you might imagine, and in any case the pursuit only lasts for one night. So there'd be a bit of a chance to escape that way."

Jenny began searching for the Hunt, and finally found them.

> "Some of the Huntsmen were men, some women, some neither, some never. Some wore armor and helmets; some were stark naked, carrying no weapons at all, stretched along their mounts' necks like spiders. I couldn't make out any faces, not until Mrs. Fallowfield pointed with her free arm, and then I could see them all. I still see them, on bad nights.... Because I'd seen too much and not enough, both. I'd seen the tattered *human* figure flying before the Wild Hunt, and heard that desperate, hopeless screams once again, even through their clamor. I couldn't talk—I could barely breathe—and I couldn't look away."

Jenny had seen Edric Davies, chased forever through the sky by the Wild Hunt.

When Jenny next sees Tamsin, the ghosts are confronting each other in a potato field. Tamsin appears to be under his spell, and he is drawing her to him. Jenny literally throws herself between them in an attempt to save Tamsin, and even throws rocks (or maybe potatoes) at Judge Jeffreys, but of course they pass through him without touching. She finally gets his attention, but he merely speaks to her disdainfully:

> "How now, girl? I cannot touch her, say you? But I *will* touch her—here, in your sight—as the wretch Edric Davies never had power to do, not with all her guiltless connivance. For I will make her a part of myself—I will make her a *sharer* in myself, intimate equal in deed and memory, until there shall remain no singular Tamsin Willoughby, but a greater Jeffreys withal, a Jeffreys enhanced, not merely possessing the object of his desire, but *including* her. See now, how 'tis accomplished. See now."

Jenny tells us the judge had been hunting her and drawing her in "by the pure power of want, by the power of hating Edric Davies beyond death, beyond whatever waits for everyone as he had waited for Tamsin Willoughby." He has stopped eternity in its tracks.

Jenny believes him, and in her belief is inspired to do the only thing she can to save Tamsin from him. She tells her what he has done to Edric, and the judge looks at her with the look he used when condemning innocent victims in his courtroom. Jenny tells Tamsin that she was there to save Edric, and it is enough to snap her out of the judge's spell. Tamsin

> "began to remember her own real shape, the color of her hair and her skin and her clothes, her own texture in the world. I saw her growing Tamsin again around that last poor fragment of herself, until she was facing me, as solid looking as *him* with her eyes full of what

I'd just told her. She didn't speak, but she knew me. She knew us both."

It is the *knowledge* that saves Tamsin. She knows what she is supposed to do, and is prepared to fight the Wild Hunt and Judge Jeffreys, too. She vanishes from the field, leaving the judge to rant and rave:

> "Devils, devils—devils, imps, demons and cacodemons! I am God's own, and by the holy names of Jesus and His Father, I charge you—back, back to your burning cesspools, back to your stinking pits of abomination, back to your eternal filth and vileness! Tamsin Willoughby is mine to me, and not all Hell itself shall keep us from being joined as we were destined to be joined! Not all the loathsome might of Hell shall keep me from her!"

Of course he is wrong; the power of love will keep him from her.

Jenny eventually finds Tamsin once again, and discovers the real reason Edric has been pursued by the Wild Hunt for so many years. It was not merely that Judge Jeffreys called the Hunt down upon him—that would have given him to them for one night, but not for more than 300 years. It was because Tamsin herself cursed him at the moment of her death for deserting her, when he failed to arrive at their rendezvous so long ago, and she vowed he should wait forever for someone who would not come. She acted out of despair, fear, and illness, and promptly forgot what she did, but she finally remembers. As she explains,

> "The last breath of a passing soul has such power—the power of a transient angel, of a momentary demon.... And I loosed it against him. It was I sent him to his eternal torment—I, not Judge Jeffreys. My doing, my doing—three hundred years."

Having remembered what she had done, she knows what she has to do. But in what she does, there is nothing Jenny can do to help. The Wild Hunt comes, and Tamsin goes to meet the Hunstmen. Jenny follows, astride the Pooka. She can see Edric, with the Hunt close behind, and Tamsin with her arms upraised and her hair blowing in the wind. Tamsin cries out to the Hunt, and the Huntsmen hear her although Jenny cannot. They turn from Edric to pursue Tamsin. The Pooka delivers Jenny to Tamsin's feet, telling her, "Here is your friend, and here is the Wild Hunt. This is your affair, not mine. Tend to it, Jenny Gluckstein." Jenny forever remembers the smell of the Huntsmen, a smell of the sea and of fishing boats with sails drying in the sun, and is so frightened she is certain she will never be afraid of anyone else again.

Tamsin speaks to them then, saying, "I take back what belongs to me. You have no claim on him, nor did you ever. The evil was mine alone, and long will I be in atoning for it. I take Edric Davies back from you now." They do not object, and Edric walks to her side. Jenny watches them meet after three hundred years, and finally knows what love is. She tells us, "if somebody ever looks at me the way the ghost of Edric Davies looked at the ghost of Tamsin Willoughby, that'll be all right. It won't happen, but at least I'll know it if I see it." Tamsin tells the Huntsmen, "We will go. You will pursue Edric Davies no further, nor me neither. You have no power here. Go back to your home beyond the winds—go back to the bowels of the skies, and trouble us no more." It even seems to Jenny that they would obey her—until Judge Jeffreys screams.

> "*Never*! They'll not walk free of me, neither of them, *never*! The Welsh bastard fell at my hand, there in the muck of the byre, which was nothing but his vile due—and I did enjoin you by certain cantrips to harry his spirit away, which was his due as well, as it ever shall be! Obey me! Living or dead, I command you

yet!... The woman is mine, as God yet wills her to be. The Welshman is yours, as *I* mean for him."

The Hunt then take off after them all, with Tamsin helping Jenny to escape at the risk of her own soul. Judge Jeffreys, too, pursues them, for his own ends. When they can finally fly no further, and the Hunt is upon them, it is Mrs. Fallowfield, dreadful and beautiful, with her face the pale-golden color of the half-moon and just as old, who saves them.

Mrs. Fallowfield is the Old Lady of the Elder Tree, the personification of nature itself, and the Wild Hunt and all other creatures, living and dead, must obey her. When Judge Jeffreys implores her to give Tamsin and Edric to him because it is the will of Almighty God, she informs him in no uncertain terms that: "We was here when your Almighty woon't but a heap of rocks and a pool of water. We was here when we was all there was.... And you'll tell me who's to bide with me and who's to hand back? *You'll* tell *me?*" When Judge Jeffreys attacks, she stops him with a mere gesture, and gives him to the Wild Hunt until someone cares to come for him as Tamsin had come for Edric. No one ever will.

Mrs. Fallowfield wills Jenny to forget, but at the end, before vanishing with Edric to go wherever they are supposed to go, Tamsin kisses Jenny lightly on the left-hand corner of her mouth. As Jenny tells us, "nobody knows better than I that I couldn't have felt anything, because Tamsin was a ghost—but nobody but me knows what I felt. And I'll always know." It was the kiss that allowed her to remember.

The Pooka has the last word, years later, when Jenny is at Cambridge, reading English history because, for a while, she had been a part of it.

> "Jenny Gluckstein,...mystery belongs to mystery, and not to Dorset or London. You are yourself as much a riddle as any you will ever encounter, and so you will always draw riddles to you, wherever you may be. If

there should be a boggart in New York, he will find your house, I assure you, as any pooka in London will know your name. You will never be further from—what did you call it?—*old weirdness* than you are at this moment. And on that you may have my word."

If *A Fine and Private Place* is about how a person can learn to be real to himself and to someone else through the power of love, *Tamsin* is about how love can transcend time and overcome all obstacles. Beagle believes in love, even if he doesn't believe in ghosts, but ultimately it doesn't matter. He uses ghosts who love in death to show us the power of love in life. While other writers do the same thing with the natural, Beagle uses the supernatural. In Manlove's phrase, he uses a substantial and irreducible element of the supernatural—**substantial** because of the sheer amount of the impact of the supernatural upon the story, and **irreducible** because it is not possible to explain the supernatural away, as if it were a dream. The world of the novel is "of another order of reality from that in which we exist and form our notions of possibility," as Manlove put it. The supernatural elements evoke wonder in the reader, ranging from astonishment at the marvelous to a sense of meaning in the mysterious. The mere presence of the supernatural, of course, evokes wonder, but the skill of the writer in developing the mystery through the deft use of complications, reversals, and recognitions enhances it immensely.

While the overall thrust of *Tamsin* may be said to be comic, since it ends well for the good characters and badly for the bad character, though the characters be ghosts, its tone differs significantly from the comic tones of *A Fine and Private Place*, with which it shares themes, and *The Last Unicorn*. Beagle will return to escapist fantasy in *A Dance for Emilia*, dealing again with his most often used themes, but in *Tamsin* he certainly has a more serious purpose. It may be said to be imaginative fantasy in the best sense of that term.

Beagle revealed in a July, 2007, interview in *Locus* that

Tamsin began as a screenplay for Disney, and that he remains hopeful that a movie will yet be made from the novel. In the same interview he asserted that it was one of three books of his (the other two being *The Innkeeper's Song* and *Giant Bones*) "I sometimes look at when I really need a shot, that particular little shiver that says, '*Damn*, I'm good!' (It's immediately followed by fear: 'How did I do that? I bet I couldn't do that today.')"

While *Tamsin* was marketed as a Young Adult novel, as was *The Unicorn Sonata*, it certainly does not condescend to its supposed audience. As is true of all the best novels intended for a teen-aged audience, *Tamsin* fully repays adult readers as well.

CHAPTER SEVEN:
MAJOR SHORT FICTION

Beagle has published more than two dozen pieces of shorter fiction over the course of his forty-year career, but five novellas stand out as particularly important: "Come Lady Death," in 1963; "Lila the Werewolf," in 1971; "Lal and Soukyan," in *Giant Bones*, 1997; "A Dance for Emilia," in 2000; and "Return," in 2010. A complete survey of his shorter fiction is beyond the scope of this book (although I deal with the story "Two Hearts" in the chapter on *The Last Unicorn*, and with "Quarry" in the chapter on *The Innkeeper's Song*, above), and the reader is directed to the anthologies included in the List of Works Cited. The short stories are well worth reading, but these five novellas are crucial to achieving a full understanding of the leading American writer of fantasy of our time. I deal with "Lal and Soukyan" and "Return" in the chapter on *The Innkeeper's Song*, above. The other three are the subject of this chapter.

"Come Lady Death" involves a very rich and very bored old woman, Lady Neville, who gives the biggest and most spectacular parties in eighteenth-century London but who no longer finds life worth living. She decides to spice up her guest list by inviting Death to her next ball. Naturally enough, everyone thinks of Death as a man, and Lady Neville is convinced he is a nobleman, but no one knows where to deliver the invitation. Because Death spends so much time among the poor, being their only friend, a hairdresser with a sick child is given the invitation to deliver when Death comes for the child. When he returns with a reply written in what is obviously a woman's hand, Lady Neville has the hairdresser who has obviously just lost his child whipped and thrown into the street when he cannot provide any details about her.

The night of the ball brings all of her nervous guests, awaiting the arrival of Death. No one will dance, and even Lady Neville herself, who publically proclaimed that she does not fear Death, is more than a little nervous. When Death has not arrived by midnight, everyone thinks with relief that it has all been a joke, but then Death herself arrives in the person of a beautiful young woman in a white dress. No one will dance with her until Captain Compson, "gray haired and handsome in his uniform," steps forward to take her hand, knowing what is expected of a gentleman although terrified. Lady Neville says to herself, "Ah, that's what comes of having a reputation to maintain. Captain Compson too must do what is expected of him. I hope someone else will dance with her soon." No one does, however, and Captain Compson dances with her for the remainder of the evening.

The Captain had previously seen Death on the battlefield but there Death took the shape of a man, tall and powerful. When he asks her about it on the dance floor, she replies, with gay and soft laughter: "I thought that among so many beautiful people it might be better to be beautiful. I was afraid of frightening everyone and spoiling the party." Later he lifts his hand and touches Death's golden hair very lightly, and Lady Neville observing him realizes that although he seems young he is older than any of them knows. All the women are jealous of Death, and all the men are frightened of her. Yet still she dances.

At the end of the night, Death declares that it is time for her to go. Lady Neville and Captain Compson, then all of the guests, beg her to stay. Seeing through their hypocrisy, Death questions them closely: "Be sure of what you want, be very sure. Do all of you want me to stay? For if one of you says to me, no, go away, then I must leave at once and never return. Be sure. Do you all want me?" Assured that they do, because they are tired, blind, afraid, dull, and stupid, Death agrees: "Very well,...I will stay with you. I will be Death no more. I will be a woman." She then tells them what they dread to hear: that there is a price to pay. "Some one of you must become Death in my place, for there must forever be Death in the world. Will anyone choose? Will anyone here become Death of his own free will? For only thus can I become a human girl."

When no one volunteers, not even the gallant Captain Compson, Death must choose herself.:

> "Then I must choose, and that is just, for that is how I became Death. I never wanted to be Death, and it makes me so happy that you want me to become one of yourselves. I have searched a long time for people who would want me. Now I have only to choose some- one to replace me and it is done. I will choose very carefully."

She considers many of the guests, including Captain Compson, who "is too kind to become Death, and because it would be too cruel to him. He wants to die so badly." Ultimately she chooses Lady Neville, because

> "[t]here is no one quite so weary of being human, and no one who knows better how meaningless it is to be alive. And there is no one here with the power to treat life...the life of your hairdresser's child, for instance, as the meaningless thing it is. Death has a heart, but it is forever an empty heart, and I think, Lady Neville, that your heart is like a dry riverbed, like a seashell. You will be very content as Death, more so than I, for I was very young when I became Death."

Death is excited about becoming human again, for that is the way of it: Death chooses her own successor from among those humans who are suited for the job, and then trades places with a kiss. Lady Neville, however, warns her that she may not like it after a while. "Perhaps not," replies Lady Death. "I will not be as beautiful as I am, and perhaps people will not love me as much as they do now. But I will be human for a while, and at last I will die. I have done my penance." She cannot remember what she was doing penance for, and it will be the same for Lady Neville. She says, for Lady Neville's ear only as they exchange the kiss that will transform then both, "You will still be beautiful when I am ugly. Be kind to me then." Lady Neville, understanding and accepting what lies before her, promises that she will.

Immortality in Beagle's fiction is not what it is cracked up to be. This life is what counts, and by our actions shall we be judged. Concern and kindness to others is the mark of a life well lived. In "Come Lady Death" Beagle has crafted a warning comparable to that of the anonymous author of *Everyman*, or perhaps to that of J. R. R. Tolkien in "Leaf by Niggle," with more entertainment value. While the tone is restrained here, elements of Beagle's consistent good humor shine through.

In "Lila the Werewolf," on the other hand, Beagle gives his rollicking sense of humor free rein. The main character is Joe Farrell, whom Beagle apparently liked well enough to resurrect as the main character of two short stories, "Julie's Unicorn" and "Spook," and in *The Folk of the Air* some years later. Farrell, an Irish musician who works in a bookstore, has been living with Lila in New York for three weeks before finding out she is a werewolf. She comes home bloodied after a night of hunting under the full moon.

> "Farrell, whose true gift was for acceptance, especially in the morning, accepted the idea that there was a wolf in his bedroom, and lay quite still, closing his eyes as the grim, black-lipped head swung towards him. Having once worked at a zoo, he was able to recognize the beast as a Central European subspecies: smaller and lighter-boned than the northern timber

wolf variety, lacking the thick, ruffy mane at the shoulders and having a more pointed nose and ears. His own pedantry always delighted him, even at the worst moments."

Lila transforms into his naked girlfriend and slips into bed beside him saying, "Move over, baby. I came home." She had torn the throat out of a half-grown Russian wolfhound Farrell was watching while its mistress was in Europe for the summer. Farrell accepts the situation, having nothing against werewolves and never having liked the wolfhound much anyway.

The next day Farrell tells his friend Ben about Lila, but Ben's only response is to tell him that he told Farrell about girls from the Bronx and to offer to let Farrell stay at his place for a few days. Farrell declines the offer, since it is after all only Lila, and she could have killed him the night before if she wanted to. He will be safe at least until the next full moon. Farrell tells Ben,

> "The thing is, it's still only Lila, not Lon Chaney or somebody. Look, she goes to her psychiatrist three afternoons a week, and she's got her guitar lesson one night a week, and her pottery class one night, and she cooks eggplant maybe twice a week. She calls her mother every Friday night, and one night a month she turns into a wolf. You see what I'm getting at? It's still Lila, whatever she does, and I just can't get terribly shook up about it. A little bit, sure, because what the hell. But I don't know. Anyway, there's no mad rush about it. I'll talk to her when the thing comes up in conversation, just naturally. It's okay."

Ben responds as the reader least expects: "God damn. You see why nobody has any respect for liberals anymore? Farrell, I know you. You're just scared of hurting her feelings." Farrell admits there's some truth to the charge. "If I break up with her now, she'll think I'm doing it because she's a werewolf.... I wish

I hadn't found out. I don't think I've ever found out anything about people that I was the better for knowing."

Lila's psychiatrist is dealing with her rejection issues, and Farrell thinks that if he tries to protect himself it will probably set her back. "Listen," he tells Ben. "I've done some things I'm not proud of, but I don't want to mess with anyone's analysis. That's the sin against God."

There was no good casual way to bring the subject up conveniently before the next full moon, however, and Farrell fears confrontation more than he fears werewolves. He could no more talk to her about being a werewolf than he could criticize her guitar-playing, her pots, or the political arguments she got into at parties. At the next full moon he waits up for her, curled up with *The Golden Bough* while listening to Telemann laced with Django Reinhardt, a gypsy jazz guitarist. Lila's annoying mother calls several times that night, insisting that she had reason to believe that Lila was there. Farrell rather ungraciously responds, "Well, I have reason to believe you're a suffocating old bitch and a bourgeois Stalinist. How do you like them apples, Mrs. B?"

> "As though his anger had summoned her, the wolf was standing two feet away from him. Her coat was dark and lank with sweat, and yellow saliva was mixed with the blood that strung from her jaws. She looked at Farrell and growled far away in her throat."

Farrell simply tells her that her mother is on the phone. He hangs up just as the sun rises and the wolf turns back into Lila. When her mother calls back, Lila answers in her own person, and explains what has been going on:

> "Well, there was a little trouble.... See, I went to the zoo because I couldn't find—Bernice, I know, I *know*, but that was, what, three months ago. The thing is, I didn't think they'd have their horns so soon. Bernice,

I had to, that's all. There'd only been a couple of cats and a—well, sure they chased me, but I—well, Momma, Bernice, what did you want me to do? Just what did you want me to do? You're always so dramatic—why do I shout? I shout because I can't get you to listen to me any other way. You remember what Dr. Schechtman said—what? No, I told you, I just forgot to call. No, that is the reason, that's the real and only reason. Well, whose fault is that? What? Oh, Bernice. Jesus Christ, Bernice. All right, *how* is it Dad's fault?"

The reader can clearly hear the other side of the conversation, and it is one that each of us has had with his or her mother, with the exception of the werewolf business, of course.

Farrell finds out from Lila that it has been happening to her for nine years, since she hit puberty. "First day cramps; the second day, this. My introduction to womanhood," she tells him. She has never told any women, and besides Farrell and Dr. Schechtman the only man she has told is Mickey, her previous boyfriend who is an acidhead in Vancouver and will never tell anyone. It has only had a minor impact on her life, causing her to miss riding camp and playing the lead in the school play. Winter is bad, because the sun sets so early, but on the whole it has been less of a problem than her allergies.

Farrell asks her if she only kills cats and dogs and zoo animals, and Lila has a melt down. She needs someone besides Bernice and Dr. Schechtman, and she tells Farrell she loves him and begs him not to leave her.

> "She was patting his face as though she were blind. Farrell stroked her hair and kneaded the back of her neck, wishing that her mother would call again. He felt skilled and weary, and without desire. I'm doing it again, he thought. 'I love you,' Lila said. And he answered her, thinking, I'm doing it again. That's the great advantage of making the same mistake a lot of

times. You come to know it, and you can study it and get inside it, really make it yours. It's the same good old mistake, except this time the girl's hang-up is different. But it's the same thing. I'm doing it again."

Farrell's girls always cry, sooner or later, but never for him.

Farrell's building superintendent is Latvian or Lithuanian, and he speaks very little English, but he knows Lila is a werewolf the moment Farrell brings her home.

> "At the sight of her the little man jumped back, dropping the two-legged chair he was carrying. He promptly fell over it, and did not try to get up, but cowered there, clucking and gulping, trying to cross himself and make the sign of the horns at the same time. Farrell started to help him. But he screamed. They could hardly hear the sound."

Not only is the superintendent afraid of Lila, Lila is equally afraid of him. Farrell tells Ben that he doesn't know how the superintendent knows. "I guess if you believe in werewolves and vampires, you probably recognize them right away. I don't believe in them at all, and I live with one."

Farrell knows he doesn't love Lila even before he finds out she is a werewolf. Lila tells Dr. Schechtman about him, and he thinks Farrell might be good for her. Farrell believes their affair will end naturally in time, but Ben wonders. "What if it doesn't?... What'll you do if it just goes on?" "It's not that easy," says Farrell.

> "The trouble is that I know her. That was the real mistake. You shouldn't get to know people if you know you're not going to stay with them, one way or another. It's all right if you come and go in ignorance, but you shouldn't know them.... See, I know her.... She

only likes to go to color movies, because wolves can't see color. She can't stand the Modern Jazz Quartet, but that's all she plays the first couple of days afterward. Stupid things like that. Never gets high at parties, because she's afraid she'll start talking. It's hard to walk away, that's all. Taking what I know with me."

"Damn, you have to be so careful. Who wants to know what people turn into?" Farrell tells Ben. The superintendent still hates Lila, and with more cause—during one of her transformations she killed his Dalmatian. Ben advises Farrell to leave the country.

Lila's mother calls again on the night of Lila's transformation in May. She wants Farrell to convince Lila to come to a discussion of what went wrong with the Progressive Party, but he is not interested in being her messenger. When Farrell tells her that Lila is out, Bernice realizes what Lila is doing and tells Farrell, "It's such a comfort to know that you're there. Ask her if I should fix a fondue?"

The problem with this particular transformation is that Lila in werewolf form goes into heat. Farrell at first doesn't understand, but a quick call to Bernice makes it all very clear. "It hasn't happened in such a long time. Schechtman gives her pills, but she must have run out and forgotten—she's always been like that, since she was little. All the thermos bottles she used to leave on the bus, and every week her piano music—." "I wish you had told me before," says an exasperated Farrell in his understated way. "It isn't a thing you tell people!," says Bernice. "How do you think it was for me when she brought her first little boyfriend—."

Farrell drops the phone and almost makes his escape, but he is stopped by a snarl from the werewolf and the banging of the superintendent at the door, determined to shoot Lila with a silver bullet. Farrell chases Lila all night, and discovers her in several locations, always surrounded by a pack of male dogs. Each time he breaks up the orgy before it can get properly started, and each time the werewolf runs off, followed by the pack, growing ever larger. Farrell knows she must have blood before morning.

Lila's mother joins the chase:

> "Standing in broccoli, in black taffeta, with a front like a ferry-boat—yet as lean in the hips as her wolf-daughter—with her plum-colored hair all loose, one arm lifted, and her orange mouth pursed in a bellow, she was no longer Bernice but a wronged fertility goddess getting set to blast the harvest."

Once in a while Farrell crosses paths with the superintendent with his Army .45 marked with a cross and silver bullets blessed by a priest. He keeps repeating, "She kill my dog." He never sees her, but he is never very far behind her.

Farrell never finds Lila that night, but neither do Bernice or the superintendent. "Dumb broad," he says. "The hell with it. She wants to mess around, let her mess around.... A moral lesson for all of us. Don't fool with strange, eager ladies, they'll kill you."

Early in the morning he finds her, the blood lust still upon her, and before he can stop her she goes on a rampage against the little dogs being walked by their mostly gay and prostitute owners in the early morning, having for some reason spared all of her canine lovers from the long night before. She is still in heat, and the dogs are drawn to her even while seeing her kill her other suitors. The superintendent comes upon the melee and shoots at her, the silver bullet missing but breaking a nearby car window because Farrell pushes a dog-walking prostitute into him at the last minute. When he shoots again he misses again, hitting one of the little dogs anxious to mount her instead. He takes careful aim for his third shot, having only three silver bullets, and it is clear that the werewolf cannot reach him before he fires. Farrell is immobilized, with fear or some other emotion that he cannot identify, but from nowhere comes Bernice to step between her transformed daughter and the murderous superintendent. *"Don't you dare!"* she commands him, pointing her finger as if she, too, held a gun.

The superintendent, however, is too enraged to be stopped. He shoves Bernice aside and shoots the werewolf at point-blank range, wailing, "My dog, my dog!" Lila, who had been in the process of transforming when she was shot, at first appears to be dead, and Bernice mourns her:

> "Lila, Lila,...poor baby, you never had a chance. He killed you because you were different, the way they kill everything different.... Lila, Lila, poor baby, poor darling, maybe it's better, maybe you're happy now. You never had a chance, poor Lila."

Far from dead, though, Lila exclaims: "For God's sake, Bernice, would you get up off me? You don't have to stop yelling, just get off."

The narrator sums up the situation for the reader:

> "As for the people who had actually seen the wolf turn into a young girl when the sunlight touched her; most of them managed not to have seen it, though they never really forgot. There were a few who knew quite well what they had seen, and never forgot it either, but they never said anything. They did, however, chip in to pay the superintendent's fine for possessing an unlicensed handgun. Farrell gave what he could."

Lila vanishes from Farrell's life immediately, and he later hears that she has moved to Berkeley and gone back to school. He never sees her again. He tells Ben, "It had to be like that.... We got to know too much about each other. See, there's another side to knowing. She couldn't look at me." It turns out that Lila had not been attacking the gunman when she was shot; she was going straight for Bernice, and there is very little about Lila that Bernice does not know.

Bernice calls Farrell two years later and informs him that Lila is marrying a research psychologist at Stanford, and they are going to Japan for their honeymoon. He not only knows about Lila, he's proud of her; it's his field. Farrell is really happy for her, and a little wistful. Compared to Lila, the girl he is presently with has a really strange hangup.

"Lila the Werewolf" gives us the youthful Beagle's tongue-in-cheek take on male-female relationships, as well as a strong dose of the humor we see so completely in *The Last Unicorn*. It gives us our first glimpse of the youthful and puzzled Farrell, drawn so completely in maturity in *The Folk of the Air*. It is his most complete rendering of the archetypal Jewish mother, a more extreme version of Mrs. Klepper from *A Fine and Private Place*. Both were likely based loosely on Beagle's mother, Rebecca Soyer Beagle, to whom he dedicated *The Rhinoceros Who Quoted Nietzsche and Other Odd Acquaintances* in 1997 with these words:

> *for my mother,*
> *Rebecca Soyer Beagle,*
> *who told me stories,*
> *and never thought I was weird.*

Beagle published "A Dance for Emilia" in 2000, a full forty years after the publication of *A Fine and Private Place*, and dealing with some of the same themes. While hopefully not his last word on the subject of the afterlife, it is certainly his most recent. The publisher's blurb on the dust jacket tells us that it is "Based on the author's real-life struggle to cope with the loss of a friend." We can never put much stock in such a blurb—it exists merely to sell books, after all—but this time it rings true, and in fact Beagle is on record in his headnote to "A Dance for Emilia" in *The Line Between* as saying it is as autobiographical as anything he has ever written. It was born out of his mourning the death of an old friend, Joe Mazo, in 1994. Beagle dedicates the work as follows: *"For Nancy, Peter, and Jessa, and for Joe."* Other than Joe, we don't know who these people are, but we don't need to know. Beagle knows, and they know, and that's sufficient. As we all do, Beagle is growing older, and losing friends along the way is the price we pay.

It is interesting to note that the narrator of "A Dance for Emilia" is an artist at the height of his powers, as was Beagle when he wrote it. Jacob Holtz is an actor rather than a writer, but he has paid his dues and grown in his craft. He has lost his friend Sam Kagan to death, as he thinks, and is struggling to deal with the loss, along with Sam's other friend, Marianne. Marianne and Sam had been an item a number of years ago, and had remained friends after the relationship crashed and burned. Sam had been an arts critic who had wanted to be a dancer, but gave up his dream when it became clear he would never be good enough. He had a cat, a large Abyssianian female named Millamant (the name of the main female character in the best-known Restoration comedy, *The Way of the World*), and a new girlfriend named Emilia Rossi. Emilia was 26 ½ years younger than Sam, not Jewish, and a journalist. Millamant liked her, which was probably the main reason Sam liked her.

Jake went to New York after being told of Sam's death, and made the funeral arrangements. He met Emilia at the funeral. They worked together to take care of Sam's loose ends, including cleaning out his apartment. When they finished, Jake went back to the West Coast and Emilia took Millamant back home to New Jersey with her. They stayed in touch.

About two years later, Emilia came to visit Jake, and she brought Millamant with her. Millamant, it seems, had begun dancing. Emilia had seen her do it three times, and she did it for the first time for Jake the first night. When she finished, she spoke to them. It was Sam. "Jake. Clean your glasses," she/he said. And, "I love you, Emilia." When asked if he was really in there, Sam replied, "You want I should wave?...As to where I've been, it comes and goes. Talk to me.... Talk to me. Please, talk

to me. Tell me why we're all here. Tell me anything. Please."
And they do.

When Jake suggests to the Yiddish-less Emilia that it might
be a *dybbuk,* that would be just like him, Sam responds as the
Sam of old:

> "Of course, I'm not a bloody *dybbuk*! Don't you
> read Singer? A *dybbuk's* a wandering soul, demons
> chasing it all around the universe—it needs a body, a
> place to hide. Not me—nobody's chasing me. Except
> maybe you two."

Later, when eating catfood, Sam speculates on his possession of his cat's body.

> "Interesting point. It's Millamant who needs to
> eat—it's Millamant who needs the nourishment—but
> I think I'm beginning to see why she likes it. Very odd.
> Sort of the phantom of a memory of taste. A touch of
> nutmeg would help."

While Jake and Emilia try to sort out matters of custody and
visitation, Sam brings things back to basics.

> "Well, I'm back. Where I'm back *from*—where I'm
> back from doesn't go into words. I don't know what
> it really is, or where—or when. I don't know whether
> I'm a ghost, or a zombie, or just some kind of seriously
> disturbed spirit. If I were a *dybbuk*, at least I'd know
> I was a *dybbuk*, that would be something.... But here
> I am anyway, ready or not. I can talk, I can dance—
> my God, I can *dance*—and I'm reunited with the only
> two people in the world who could have summoned
> me. Or whatever it was you did.... But for how long?
> I could be gone any minute, or I could last as long as
> Millamant lasts—and *she* could go any minute herself.

What happens then? Do I go off to kitty heaven with her—or do I find myself in Jake's blender? One of Emilia's angelfish? What happens then?"

Of course, no one knows what happens then. That's the problem. Sam admits it, saying: "We don't know. We have no idea. I certainly wish somebody had read the instruction manual."
Jake gets a little disturbed, saying,

"There wasn't any manual. We didn't know we were summoning you—we didn't know we were doing anything except missing you, and trying to comfort ourselves the best we could.... Not everybody has people wishing for him so hard that they snatch him right back from death. I'm sorry if we woke you."

Sam sets him straight on that score.

"Oh, I was awake.... Or maybe not truly awake, but you can't quite get to sleep, either. Jake...Emilia...I can't tell you what it's like. I'm not even sure whether it's death—or maybe that's it, that's just it, that's really the way death is. I can't tell you."

Sam tries again to explain how it is.

"It's like the snow on a TV set, when the cable's out. People just sit watching the screen, expecting the picture to come back—they'll sit there for an hour, more, waiting for all those whirling, crackling white particles to shape themselves back into a face, a car, a box of cereal—*something*. Try to think how it might feel to be one of those particles.... It's not like that but try to imagine it anyway."

The conversation turns serious when Sam suggests, "Jake. Maybe you should send me back." Jake responds:

> "Send you? We don't even know how you got here in the first place, and you don't know where *back* is. We couldn't send you anywhere the BMT doesn't run.... Why would you want to? To leave us again?"

Sam quickly issues his denial:

> "I don't ever want to leave.... If I were in a rat's body, a cockroach's body, I'd want to stay here with you, with Emilia. But it feels strange here. Not wrong, but not—not *proper*. I don't mean me inhabiting a cat—I mean me still being me, Sam Kagan still aware that I'm Sam Kagan. However you look at it, this is a damn afterlife, Jake, and I don't believe in an afterlife. Dead or alive, I don't."

He feels obliged to clarify, though.

> "There was more. I don't know that I missed anything much, but there was more coming. And if it's an afterlife, then the word means something they never told us about. I don't think there *is* a word for it—what I was waiting for. But it wasn't this."

And with that, Sam begins to dance again, showing off for Emilia. Things continue for a few days, until finally Emilia begins to crack from the strain.

> "If he's Sam, then he shouldn't be eating on the floor, and if he's Millamant, then he shouldn't be making her dance all the time. She's old, Jake, and she's got arthritis, and Sam's dancing her like a child making his toys fly and fight. And it's so beautiful, and he's

so *happy*—and I never saw him dance, the way you did, and I can't believe how beautiful...."

She is right, in that Millamant is being consumed by Sam's dancing. Jake finally comes to agree; it is not right, and he tells Sam he thinks so. "Sam, it's no good. I don't mean for Millamant—I mean for you, for your *ka* or your karma, or whatever I'm talking to right now. This can't be what you're supposed to be...doing, I guess. Emilia makes sense." But Emilia changes her mind; she no longer cares about anything but Sam. She wants him back any way she can have him. It is disgraceful, and she knows it is disgraceful, but she no longer cares. Sam, however, agrees with Jake. "He's right, Emilia. And you were right the first time. I have to go."

Emilia cries, "Go where? You don't even know, you said so yourself. You could wind up someplace worse than your damn TV screen—you could lose yourself for good, no Sam anymore, in the whole universe, not the least bit of Sam, not ever, not ever." "Maybe that's the idea," responds Sam. "Maybe that's it—maybe you're not supposed to come back as the least bit of yourself, but to be completely scattered, diffused, starting over as someone utterly different. I almost like that." But Emilia is too far gone. "I couldn't bear to lose you twice. I'm telling you now, I have no shame, I don't care. I don't care if you show up as a—an electric can opener. Don't leave me again, Sam."

Sam is determined to leave, but first he must make her understand.

"Matter can neither be created nor destroyed. Didn't they teach you that in high school, out in frontier Metuchen? *Listen! Listen*—when I was a speck, a dot, nothing but a flicker of TV snow, I knew you. Do you understand me? By the time you and Jake got me back here, I had already forgotten my own name, I'd forgotten there was ever such an idea as Sam Kagan. But I was a speck that remembered Emilia

Rossi's birthday, remembered that Emilia Rossi loves cantaloupe and roast potatoes and bittersweet chocolate, and absolutely cannot abide football, her cousin Teddy, or Wagner. There's no way in this universe that I could be reduced to something so microscopic, so anonymous that it wouldn't know Emilia Rossi. It they give my atoms a fast shuffle and shake most of them out on some other planet, there'll still be one or two atoms madly determined to evolve into something that can carve *Emilia Rossi* on a tree. Or whatever they've got on that damn planet. I promise you, that's the truth. Are you listening to me, Emilia?"

She is listening, but all she hears is that he is going to leave her again.

And Sam/Millamant dances once again, for Emilia alone, and when he finishes dancing, he leaves. They do not know when, or how, but when she stops dancing Millamant simply crawls into Emilia's lap and lies there, not purring. Sam is gone.

Some years later Emilia marries a special-education teacher. She calls Jake when Millamant dies. Jake continues to mature in his art, not yet playing Captain Shotover or Lear but doing well enough as Falstaff, James Tyrone, and Uncle Vanya, and Emilia has a son. She thinks of Sam every day, but never wonders; she can't afford to. A little neighbor girl, Luz (*light* in Spanish), takes an interest in her son from the day he is born, and she dances—with no music, no lessons, pure and private. She doesn't dance like Millamant, but she dances for Emilia.

Jake sees the dance when he comes to visit. He tells her, "He told you, whatever became of him—his soul, his spirit, his molecules—he'd always know you. But he didn't say whether you'd know him."

"It doesn't matter," Emilia tells him, hugging his arm with her face as bright and young as that of Luz. "Jake, Jake, it doesn't matter whether I know him or not. It doesn't *matter*."

Luz dances Jake to his taxi when he leaves, and their eyes

meet. The last words of the novella are Jake's, in narrator mode, reminiscent of Tamsin's final words: "And what I think I know, I think I know, and it doesn't matter at all."

Love may not conquer death in the fantasy of Peter S. Beagle, but it is clearly the best reason for life. We live forever through the memory of those we love. Beagle skillfully uses ghosts, the fantastic, death, and the afterlife to teach us these homely lessons.

While Beagle's novels are his most important works, his major short fiction presents his attitudes and ideas compactly and completely. They would be worth reading even without the novels, but when read in context they provide additional insight into the mind of the writer.

CONCLUSION

Beagle is on record as desiring each of his novels to be as different as possible, to create an entirely new universe for each new work of fantasy. In this he has mostly succeeded, at least in his major works. While each is, in Manlove's phrase, "a fiction evoking wonder and containing a substantial and irreducible element of supernatural or impossible worlds, beings or objects with which the reader or the characters within the story become on at least partly familiar terms," the element of the supernatural or impossible contained in each is never repeated from one novel to another. It is thus possible to speak of the world of *A Fine and Private Place* as being significantly different from the worlds of *The Last Unicorn* or *The Innkeeper's Song*. And while *A Fine and Private Place*, *Tamsin*, *A Dance for Emilia*, and even to an extent *The Innkeeper's Song* and "Lal and Soukyan" all deal with ghosts and may properly be called ghost stories, they are significantly different kinds of ghost stories. Beagle has avoided repeating himself.

At the same time, all of his major works but one have the same flaw: he goes too far in each. Whether it is one too many fights with magical creatures or one too many subplots or one too many comic or ironic twists to the plot, Beagle can't seem to leave well enough alone. The one major work in which this is not true, *A Fine and Private Place*, was heavily edited before publication, and Beagle tells us that his editor required the removal of an entire mystery subplot before accepting the book. Perhaps he would have benefitted from a stronger editorial hand in his later work.

Not surprisingly, this flaw (if it is a flaw) is missing from most of his shorter fiction. Ironically, Beagle only reinvented himself as a writer of short fiction in recent years, although his output has been prodigious. Many writers come to the longer form from the shorter, rather than vice-versa; there is something to be learned about plotting novels from the careful crafting of shorter fiction.

Beagle's rocky personal life has never been reflected in his fiction. Rather than dwelling upon the negatives in his two marriages, or on his fight with a major corporation about royalties, he has always focused on positive personal relationships among his characters. This was evident in his earliest work, with the major mortal characters in *A Fine and Private Place* lovingly based upon his parents, and continued throughout his writing career. In his fiction, at least, Beagle sees the glass as half full rather than half empty; in the worlds he creates love is the only reason for living, and it overcomes all obstacles.

While most noticeable in *The Last Unicorn*, Beagle's almost overwhelming sense of humor permeates all his work. Its many appearances in narrative passages belies any claim that he uses it as a device of characterization only, although it is also quite effective in that arena in, for example, *The Innkeeper's Song*. Wordplay and punning are as much a part of Beagle's character as they are of Schmendrick's, and he would be less likely to produce a piece of fiction without them than he would be to write an effective piece of socialist realism. It's just not in him, fortunately for his readers.

Ursula K. Le Guin, in her 1979 essay "From Elfland to Poughkeepsie," discusses the use of language in high fantasy. She finds it to be the most crucial element, because it creates a sense of place. The misuse of a formal style is a dangerous trap for the fantasy writer because it sounds so prosaic when done wrong. She warns writers away from imitating the styles of Lord Dunsany or E. R. Eddison. Language which is too bland or simplistic creates the impression that the fantasy setting is simply a modern world in disguise. Le Guin prefers what she calls the clear, effective fantasy writing of J. R. R. Tolkien and Evangeline Walton.

What may be said of the language used by Beagle? It is immediately clear from the many excerpts contained in this text that Beagle does not write in the "high fantasy" style admired by Le Guin. Beagle is no Tolkien, nor does he wish to be, even though he wrote the introduction to the paperback version of *The Lord of the Rings* so popular in the United States in the 1960s, and even though he is credited with the screenplay for Ralph Bakshi's aborted animated film. His interests lie elsewhere, and his language leads elsewhere.

Whether we have the omniscient narration of *A Fine and Private Place* and *The Last Unicorn*, the first-person narration of a young girl in *Tamsin*, or the shifting narration of *The Innkeeper's Song*, the voice is that of Beagle. His wit and intelligence shine through the text, and his philosophy and view of life dominate the reader. That he writes "low fantasy" rather than "high fantasy" doesn't matter a whit. He is a consummate storyteller who knows how to entertain an audience. While in *The Lord of the Rings* there is scarcely a joke to be found, in all of Beagle's works, including that arguably closest to "high fantasy," *The Innkeeper's Song*, there are jokes galore. This undeniable fact gives us the most telling insight into Beagle's purposes.

The existence of ghosts and the supernatural in his work begs the question of Beagle's cosmology. Ancient gods make their appearance in more than one novel, and ghosts in at least three. Is there a religious, or at least a spiritual, consistency to the worlds he creates, as there arguably is in the fantasy of J. R. R. Tolkien and as there admittedly is in that of C. S. Lewis? The answer must be a qualified no. There may be a consistency within the world of each novel, for example in the undeniable prayers recited in *The Innkeeper's Song* and the other Lal and Soukyan stories, but there is no overarching cosmology that was imposed or may be discerned from the outside. These are what I would term "metaphysical speculations": a working out of the possibilities if the world were different than it is. As in Le Guin, there is no Christianity, or even Judaism, *per se*; nor even a reliance upon an undifferentiated theism. There is merely a verbally felicitous intelligence inviting the reader to examine these speculations with him. When we do so we come away better men and women, believing in the transforming power of love and laughing at ourselves in the process. No writer could ask for more, or succeed better. There are more things, Beagle would have us believe, in heaven and earth than are dreamt of in prosaic Horatio's philosophy. In his fantasy Peter S. Beagle invites us to explore them with him. I for one enjoy the exploration immensely.

LIST OF WORKS CITED

Aichele, George, Jr. "Two Forms of Metafantasy." *Journal of the Fantastic in the Arts*, 1(3) (1988): 55-68.

Beagle, Peter S. *A Dance for Emilia*. New York: New American Library, 2000. (Also included in *The Line Between*.)

_____. *The Fantasy Worlds of Peter S. Beagle*. 1978. (Contains *A Fine and Private Place*, *The Last Unicorn*, "Come Lady Death", and "Lila the Werewolf.")

_____. *A Fine and Private Place*. 1960; rpt. New York: New American Library, 1992.

_____. *The First Last Unicorn and Other Beginnings*. San Francisco: Tachyon Press, forthcoming April, 2012.

_____. *The Folk of the Air*. New York: Ballantine Books, 1986.

_____. *Four Years, Five Seasons*. San Francisco: Conlan Press Audiobook, 2010.

_____. *Giant Bones*. New York: Penguin Books, 1997. (Contains "Lal and Soukyan.")

_____. *Green-Eyed Boy: Three Schmendrick Stories*. San Francisco: Tachyon Press, forthcoming 2012 (?). ("The Woman Who Married the Man in the Moon" appeared in *Sleight of Hand*.)

_____. *I'm Afraid You've Got Dragons*. San Francisco: Tachyon Press, forthcoming 2012 (?).

_____. *The Innkeeper's Song*. 1993; rpt. New York: New American Library, 1994.

_____. *The Last Unicorn*. 1968; rpt. New York: Ballantyne Books, 1973.

_____. *The Last Unicorn.* San Diego: IDW Publishing, 2011. (Graphic novel originally published in comic book format in six issues; adapted by Peter B. Gillis, and illustrated by Renae De Liz with colors by Ray Dillon.)

_____. *The Last Unicorn: The Lost Version.* Burton, MI: Subterranean Press, 2006.

_____. *The Line Between.* San Francisco: Tachyon Publications, 2006. (Contains "A Dance for Emilia.")

_____. *Mirror Kingdoms: The Best of Peter S. Beagle.* Burton, MI: Subterranean Press, 2010.

_____. *My Stupid Brother Marvin the Witch.* San Francisco: Tachyon Press, forthcoming 2012 (?).

_____. *Return.* Burton, MI: Subterranean Press, 2010.

_____. *The Rhinoceros Who Quoted Nietzsche and Other Odd Acquaintances.* San Francisco: Tachyon Publications, 1997. (Contains "Come Lady Death" and "Lila the Werewolf.")

_____. *Sleight of Hand.* San Francisco: Tachyon Press, 2011.

_____. *Smeagol, Deagol, and Beagle: Essays From the Headwaters of My Voice.* San Francisco: Tachyon Press, forthcoming 2012 (?).

_____. *Strange Roads.* Minneapolis: DreamHaven Books, 2008. (Contains "King Pelles the Sure," "Spook," and "Uncle Chaim and Aunt Rifke and the Angel," all later published in *We Never Talk About My Brother.*)

_____. *Summerlong.* San Francisco: Tachyon Press, forthcoming 2012 (?).

_____. *Sweet Lightning.* San Francisco: Tachyon Press, forthcoming 2012 (?).

_____. *Tamsin.* 1999; rpt. New York: New American Library, 2001.

_____. *Three Faces of the Lady.* San Francisco: Tachyon Press, forthcoming 2012 (?).

_____. *Three Unicorns.* San Francisco: Tachyon Press, forthcoming 2012 (?).

_____. *The Unicorn Sonata.* Atlanta: Turner Publishing, 1996.

_____. *We Never Talk About My Brother.* San Francisco:

Tachyon Publications, 2009.

_____. *Writing Sarek*. San Francisco: Tachyon Press, forthcoming 2012 (?).

Feimer, Joel N. "Alchemy of Love in *A Fine and Private Place*." *Journal of the Fantastic in the Arts*, 1(3) (1988): 69-78.

Foust, R. E. "Fabulous Paradigm: Fantasy, Metafantasy, and Peter S. Beagle's *The Last Unicorn*." *Extrapolation*, 21(1) (Spring 1980): 5-20.

Iser, Wolfgang. *The Act of Reading: A Theory of Aesthetic Response*. Baltimore: Johns Hopkins University Press, 1978.

Jackson, Rosemary. *Fantasy: The Literature of Subversion*. London and New York: Methuen, 1981.

Le Guin, Ursula K. *Cheek by Jowl*. Seattle: Aqueduct Press, 2009.

_____. "From Elfland to Poughkeepsie," in *The Language of the Night: Essays on Fantasy and Science Fiction*. New York: G.P. Putnam's Sons, 1979.

Manlove, C.N. *The Impulse of Fantasy Literature*. London: Macmillan, 1983; Kent, OH: Kent State University Press, 1983.

_____. *Modern Fantasy: Five Studies*. Cambridge: Cambridge University Press, 1975.

Matheson, Sue. "Psychic Transformation and the Regeneration of Language in Peter S. Beagle's *The Last Unicorn*." *The Lion and the Unicorn*, 29(3) (September 2005): 416-26.

Miller, David M. "Mommy Fortuna's Ontological Plenum: The Fantasy of Plenitude," in *Countours of the Fantastic*. Westport, CT: Greenwood Press, 1990.

Norford, D.P. "Reality and Illusion in Peter Beagle's *The Last Unicorn*." *Critique: Studies in Modern Fiction*, 19(2) (1977): 93-104.

Olsen, A. H. "Anti-Consolatio: Boethius and *The Last Unicorn*. *Mosaic*, 13(3/4) (1980): 133-44.

Rabkin, Eric. *The Fantastic in Literature*. Princeton: Princeton University Press, 1976.

Riggs, Don. "Fantastic Tropes in *The Folk of the Air*." *Journal of the Fantastic in the Arts*, 1(3), 79-86 (1988); also in *The Dark Fantastic: Selected Essays from the Ninth International Conference on the Fantastic in the Arts*. Westport, CT: Greenwood Press, 1997.

Roberts, Dave. "Love in the Graveyard: Peter S. Beagle's *A Fine and Private Place*." *Vector*, No. 204 (March/April 1999): 11-12.

Siebers, Tobin. *The Romantic Fantastic*. Ithaca and London: Cornell University Press, 1984.

Sigunick, Phil, and Peter S. Beagle. *Acoustic: The Lost '62 Tape*. San Francisco: Conlan Press. (CD with 11 songs recorded in 1962.)

Soyer, Abraham. *The Adventures of Yemima and Other Stories*. Trans. Rebecca S. Beagle and Rebecca L. Soyer; Foreword by Peter S. Beagle. New York: Viking, 1979, Originally published in Hebrew, Tel Aviv: Shilo Publishing Co.

_____. *Forgotten Worlds*. Trans. Rebecca S. Beagle and Rebecca L. Soyer. Berkeley: Judah L. Magnes Museum, 1991.

Speiler, Maureen K. "Werewolves, Unicorns, Ghosts, and Rhinoceroses: The Worlds of Peter S. Beagle." *Vector*, No. 204 (March/April 1999): 10-11.

Spencer, Kathleen L. "Purity and Danger: *Dracula*, The Urban Gothic, and the Late Victorian Degeneracy Crisis," *ELH*, 59 (1992), 197-225.

_____. "The Urban Gothic in British Fantastic Fiction, 1860-1930." Diss., UCLA, 1987.

Stevens, David. "Incongruity in a World of Illusion: Patterns of Humor in Peter Beagle's *The Last Unicorn*." *Extrapolation* 20(3) (Fall 1979): 230-37.

Suvin, Darko. *Metamorphoses of Science Fiction: On the Poetics and History of a Literary Genre*. New Haven: Yale University Press, 1979.

Tobin, Jean. "Myth, a Memory, a Will-o'-the-Wish: Peter Beagle's Funny Fantasy," in *Reflections on the Fantastic*.

Westport, CT: Greenwood Press, 1986.

_____. "Werewolves and Unicorns: Fabulous Beasts in Peter Beagle's Fiction," in *Forms of the Fantastic*. Westport, CT: Greenwood Press, 1986.

Todorov, Tzvetan. *The Fantastic: A Structural Approach to a Literary Genre*. Trans. Richard Howard. Ithaca: Cornell University Press, 1975. Original French publication, 1970.

Tolkien, J. R. R. "On Fairy Stories," in *Tree and Leaf.* London: Allen & Unwin, 1964; Boston: Houghton Mifflin, 1965.

Tompkins, Jane P. (ed.). *Reader-response Criticism: From Formalism to Post-structuralism*. Baltimore: Johns Hopkins University Press: 1980.

Van Becker, David. "Time, Space and Consciousness in the Fantasy of Peter S. Beagle." *San Jose Studies*, 1 (ii) (February 1975): 52-61.

West, Richard C. "Humankind and Reality: Illusion and Self-Deception in Peter S. Beagle's Fiction." *Journal of the Fantastic in the Arts*, 1(3) (1988): 47-54; also published as "Humankind Cannot Bear Very Much Reality: Illusion and Self-Deception in the Fiction of Peter S. Beagle," in *The Dark Fantastic: Selected Essays From the Ninth International Conference on the Fantastic in the Arts*. Westport, CT: Greenwood Press, 1997.

Zahorski, Kenneth J. *Peter Beagle*. Mercer Island, WA: Starmont, 1988. (Starmont Reader's Guide No. 44).

Zgorzelski, Andrzej. "Is Science Fiction a Genre of Fantastic Literature?" *Science-Fiction Studies* 6 (1979), 296-303.

_____. "Understanding Fantasy." *Zagadienia Rpdzajdw Literackich*, 14 (1972), 103-10.

ABOUT THE AUTHOR

DAVID STEVENS is a retired professor and attorney who has read and written about fantasy and science fiction for many years. His previous book, written in collaboration with Carol D. Stevens, *J. R. R. Tolkien: The Art of the Myth-Maker*, was published by Borgo Press in 1992. He is also the author of a legal memoir, *For Three Weeks I Owned the University of Illinois* (2011); an instructional book for beginning and intermediate bridge players, *Wait-A-Minute Bridge* (2010); and an annotated bibliography, *English Renaissance Theatre History: A Reference Guide* (1982). In addition he has published some twenty-five articles in juried journals ranging from fantasy and science fiction criticism to theatre history to Illinois criminal procedure, as well as over fifty reviews. He resides in Charleston, Illinois.

INDEX

In the following listing, real people are listed last name, first name, as in Bakshi, Ralph, while characters in the novels, novellas, and stories are listed first name last name, such as Joe Farrell. The titles of Beagle's works are listed alphabetically under his name. Other authors are listed by name only, as in Tolkien, J. R. R. Some titles are listed without authors as I have used them in the text, as in *The Way of the World*. I have arbitrarily alphabetized titles beginning with "The" under "T" rather than under the first letter of the second word of the title, as in *The Last Unicorn* rather than *Last Unicorn, The*. One index combines authors, titles, and subjects. I have indexed only the Introduction, Chapters One through Seven, and the Conclusion; neither front matter (Dedication, Table of Contents) nor rear matter (List of Works Cited, About the Author) is included in this Index. Nor is every word indexed, nor every single occurrence of indexed words; I have been perhaps overly selective for some readers, yet too inclusive for others. I pine for the days of WordStar, when an automatic index tool would index every word, and I could choose what to save and what to discard! At the same time, though, indexing has come a long way since the time I used index cards (hence the name!) to prepare the index of my first book by hand.